THE BEST

of US

BY THE SAME AUTHOR

FICTION
Baby Love
To Die For
Where Love Goes
The Usual Rules
The Cloud Chamber
Labor Day
After Her
The Good Daughters
Under the Influence

NONFICTION
Looking Back
Domestic Affairs
At Home in the World
Internal Combustion

THE BEST
of US

A MEMOIR

JOYCE
MAYNARD

BLOOMSBURY

NEW YORK · LONDON · OXFORD · NEW DELHI · SYDNEY

Bloomsbury USA
An imprint of Bloomsbury Publishing Plc

1385 Broadway	50 Bedford Square
New York	London
NY 10018	WC1B 3DP
USA	UK

www.bloomsbury.com

BLOOMSBURY and the Diana logo are trademarks of Bloomsbury Publishing Plc

First published 2017

© Joyce Maynard, 2017

This is a work of nonfiction. However, the author has changed the names and identifying characteristics of certain individuals to protect their privacy and has reconstructed dialogue to the best of her recollection.

Excerpt from Wendell Berry's "The Country of Marriage," copyright © 1971 by Wendell Berry, from New Collected Poems. Reprinted by permission of the author and Counterpoint.

Excerpt from Raymond Carver's "A New Path to the Waterfall," copyright © 1989 by the Estate of Raymond Carver. Used by permission of Grove/Atlantic, Inc. Any third party use of this material, outside of this publication, is prohibited. "Late Fragment" by Raymond Carver originally published in A NEW PATH TO THE WATERFALL, currently collected in ALL OF US: The Collected Poems. Copyright © 1988 by Raymond Carver; 1989, 2000 by Tess Gallagher, used by her permission.

ISBN:	HB:	978-1-63557-034-2
	TPB:	978-1-63557-179-0
	ePub:	978-1-63557-036-6

LIBRARY OF CONGRESS CATALOGING-IN-PUBLICATION DATA IS AVAILABLE.

2 4 6 8 10 9 7 5 3 1

Typeset by Westchester Publishing Services
Printed and bound in the U.S.A. by Berryville Graphics Inc., Berryville, Virginia

To find out more about our authors and books visit www.bloomsbury.com. Here you will find extracts, author interviews, details of forthcoming events and the option to sign up for our newsletters.

Bloomsbury books may be purchased for business or promotional use. For information on bulk purchases please contact Macmillan Corporate and Premium Sales Department at specialmarkets@macmillan.com.

For Jim

What I am learning to give you is my death
to set you free of me, and me from myself
into the dark and the new light. Like the water
of a deep stream, love is always too much. We
did not make it. Though we drink till we burst
we cannot have it all, or want it all.
In its abundance it survives our thirst.

>   —Wendell Berry, "The Country of Marriage"

And did you get what
you wanted from this life, even so?
I did.
And what did you want?
To call myself beloved, to feel myself
beloved on the earth.

>   —Raymond Carver, "Late Fragment," his last poem

Prologue

On the Fourth of July weekend three years ago, at the age of fifty-nine, I married the first true partner I had ever known.

We spoke our vows on a New Hampshire hillside with friends and children gathered, as fireworks exploded over us and a band backed us up for a duet on a John Prine song. That night we talked about the trips we'd take, the olive trees we would plant, the grandchildren we might share. We would know, in our sixties, the love we had yearned for in our youth. Each of us had been divorced almost twenty-five years. How lucky, everyone said, that we had found each other when we did.

Not long after our one-year anniversary, my husband was diagnosed with pancreatic cancer. Nineteen months later, having shared a struggle that consumed both our lives in equal though different measure, I lay beside him in our bed when he took his last breath.

I had once supposed I was done with marriage. A few decades of disappointments and failures had left me reluctant to try again. Then I got married that second time—to Jim—but with the belief still that nothing, and no man—not even one I dearly loved—could alter my course of fierce and resolute independence. I came and went, always happy to see him when he picked me up off a plane, but happy to hop on the next one that would take me away again. I had my life, he had his. Sometimes we'd share them. That was my idea, though never my husband's.

Not until we learned of his illness, and we walked the path of that terrible struggle together, did I understand what it meant to be a couple—to be a true partner and to have one. I learned the full meaning of marriage only as mine was drawing to a close. I discovered what love was as mine departed the world.

This is our story.

PART ONE

Before

1.

Ever since the end of my marriage to my children's father I had wanted to fall in love. But if you had asked me—or if I ever asked myself—what it meant to fall in love, I doubt I could have told you. "Falling in love" was an idea I had picked up from a lot of rock-and-roll songs and movies and the fairy tales that came before them.

My own experience of love had not contained the happy ending, though passion was part of it, as was romance, and certainly drama. (Drama: an addiction of mine, maybe. To look at my history, at least, you would have had to consider that possibility.)

Age had changed me in many ways, but not in this one. Into my fifties, and closing in on the next decade—my children grown and gone, along with so much else I had held on to once and now let go—I still looked for that feeling of my pulse quickening, of holding my breath when a person walked in the door—*my person*. But when I tried to imagine what this falling-in-love thing would look like with the passage of time, my imagination—though it seldom failed me—provided no picture. Mostly what I had known of falling in love was that heartbreak followed soon after.

I had been, at the point our story began, a writer of fiction, and in the writing of fiction, it is well understood that for a story to hold the reader's interest, conflict must exist. I might have told myself otherwise, but for years I think I carried that belief into my life off the page. Where was the drama in happiness? If there was no trouble present, what kept the story alive?

What did I know of love? What had I witnessed? My parents

had started out with a big love affair, filled with extravagant emotion and conflict. The fact that when my mother met him, my father had been twenty years older than she was—and divorced—had not even been their biggest obstacle. He just wasn't Jewish.

He had courted her for ten years—writing her poems, sending her drawings, swearing his devotion, taking a job under a made-up name as a radio host on the prairies of Canada so he could recite romantic poetry to her over the airwaves without her parents knowing it. He was handsome and funny, brilliant and difficult. But romantic—and in the end, irresistible.

Within days of the wedding, our mother told my sister and me later, their love affair was finished, though my parents remained together for twenty-five years—slinging barbs at each other across the dinner table and sleeping in separate bedrooms. This was what I saw of marriage, growing up, balanced only by a decade of situation comedies on television, in which romance between the parents never went beyond that moment when Donna Reed's husband comes back after heading out the door to work, to plant a kiss on her cheek.

At twenty-three I married a man who was as unwise a match for me as I was for him. But he was handsome and talented and interesting, and his silences seemed to suggest mysteries I was ready to spend my life exploring. When I'd tell him a story from my day, he would say, "Cut to the chase."

I was thirty-five when we divorced, and single for the two decades that followed. The phrase I employed to describe myself: "a solo operator." There had been a time when what I wanted most in life was to make a home with a partner and to raise our children together there, but after losing the home of my marriage, and the dream of what is referred to as "an intact family," I had made good homes on my own, and watched my children move back and forth—brown paper bags in hand, containing their possessions—between the worlds of two parents deeply at odds with each other. I grew accustomed to doing things alone and doing them my way, and I discovered, as I did this, the pleasure of my autonomy.

As the years passed, less and less did the idea of marriage play a role in my picture of my future. Divorce, and all the sorrow surrounding it, had left me reluctant to go down that particular road again, and anyway, what I yearned for—big love, big romance— seemed to contradict what I'd known of marriage.

By the time I reached my fifties, I had lived alone—or alone with my children—for longer than I'd lived with a man. It was living with someone that got me into trouble, so why try that again?

Still I kept searching, without knowing what I was looking for. No surprise I did not find it. And then—though it took a while to recognize this—I did.

2.

I met Jim on Match.com. I liked his photograph—a rakish hat over a head of good hair, a smile that seemed to contain genuine delight in whatever it was that had been going on as the camera captured the moment. I liked the things he said about himself in that short profile, but I had learned long before that how a person described himself in a dating profile often bore little resemblance to the real person who had posted it.

I had studied Jim's profile only briefly, anticipating (after years of this stuff) the inevitable red flag. I closed my laptop.

But the man in the photograph had taken note of the fact that I'd looked at his profile, and looked up mine. He wrote to me. "Maybe another time," I wrote back. I looked at his photograph again, and the others he'd posted—one in which he was wearing a tuxedo.

"Probably a Republican," I concluded.

There was another reason why I had been reluctant to find out more about the man whose online moniker (this alone would later indicate how little relationship exists between the man and his profile) was "Jimbunctious." At the time he sent me that first message (sent to me at "Likesred shoes") expressing an interest in meeting me, I had recently started spending time with a different man I'd met online just a few weeks before. And I was having a good time with him.

Jim wrote to me again, suggesting a conversation by phone. Without particular expectation or enthusiasm, I sent him my number. In the twenty-five years since the end of my marriage to my children's father, though no shortage of men entered and left my life, I had never engaged in the practice of exploring a relationship with more than one man at a time. But a special circumstance existed here. Martin, the man I had been spending time with—spending the night with, on occasion—was both a very good man and also a man with whom I knew I had no extended future.

Only recently separated from his one and only wife of twenty-six years, Martin had been called to the Bay Area in his career as a structural engineer to oversee crucial aspects involved in the rebuilding of the San Francisco Bay Bridge following its collapse in the Loma Prieta earthquake. This would be the earthquake of 1989: an event whose date contained an odd significance for me, though I had been living in my home state of New Hampshire, not in San Francisco, when it occurred. The Loma Prieta earthquake took place eleven days after the death of my mother, at age sixty-seven, to a brain tumor, and exactly one week after I had moved out of the home I'd shared for twelve years with my husband Steve, after he'd told me he'd fallen in love with someone else. Two not wholly unrelated events, as it turned out, that served to create the effect of an earthquake within my life as well.

Though he had been put in charge of one of the key aspects of the bridge project, Martin was a modest man, and one who lived pretty simply. He made his home on a sailboat he'd bought after his marriage ended, that he kept docked in Point Richmond. That's where I was spending two or three nights a week. Sometimes, too, Martin and I would go out in the boat and dock it overnight in a bay by Angel Island. Though never a sailor, I liked sleeping on Martin's boat. I loved the feeling I had when I was there that I could leave my life back on shore for a while. At the time, I had a lot of reasons for wanting to do that.

But as much as I enjoyed sleeping in the tiny below-deck

bunk room with Martin and waking up to have my coffee with him on the bay, and as good a man as he might be, I also recognized that the two of us were not suited to be together in any long-term way.

As a person who'd been single at this point for over twenty years—a woman who had supposed, early on after the divorce, that she was ready to make a new relationship, but one for whom it would take a couple of decades to get over all the bitterness and anger that had gotten in the way of that—I also believed that Martin needed to spend a lot more time on his own, and with other women, before he'd begin to know what he really wanted and needed. As enjoyable as it was spending nights on the boat with this good man, the situation could not last.

I'd encouraged Martin to continue going on dates, and he, reluctantly, agreed. The night I got that first e-mail message from Jimbunctious, Martin was in fact out on a Match.com date—at my insistence—and though later, when he got home, he would call me up and tell me again that really, he just wanted to be with me, I knew that our days of sailing in the bay were numbered.

So when Jim wrote to me I'd written back. Some people go right to the coffee-shop phase here—that event, well-known to online daters, where you pull into some Starbucks, scan the room for the person who resembles, however remotely, the one on the profile to which you responded, and unless he is so far from the mark as to suggest that there's not one honest thing coming from this man, you approach the table.

"You must be Bob," you say. (*Sam. Joe. Bill. Ray.*) At which point he looks you up and down with a gaze that conveys interest, disappointment, or nothing, and you order coffee.

I tried to avoid the coffee-shop phase. In the many years I'd spent engaging in some level or other of online dating, I had come to set far less store by the words a man posted on his profile than I did in the sound of his voice. Often I found that someone whose online profile had seemed promising would reveal himself to me within the first sixty seconds at Starbucks or Peet's to be a person as unlikely to inspire my affection as a game show host or a tax auditor. This saved me from a lot of wasted cappuccinos. And probably saved a lot of men the same.

Within minutes of receiving my phone number, Jim called me, and right away, I liked his voice—the timbre of it, and a way of speaking I recognized as having its origins in the Midwest, which it turned out he did, despite having spent all but the first four years of his life in California. Though I would later discover that he was not a talkative man—more inclined to listen than to speak—it was a conversation that lasted four and a half hours.

By this point, I was all too familiar with how this type of conversation generally went. You got the basics out of the way first. How long since the divorce generally came first. It was usually a divorce, though when I met a person who had actually known the experience of a good marriage and lost his wife, I registered a humble awe. He knew something that I didn't, and even though he had also known something else I didn't—the loss of someone he loved more than anything—I still tended to view the widowers as the lucky ones. They had made a good relationship once. Maybe they'd even know how to make one again.

From there, the conversation would go to children—how many, how old—and the new question (here came a measure of just how long I'd been at this stuff): how many grandchildren. Sometimes, though, the person on the other end of the phone could not get past the ex-wife part. He'd be talking about what her lawyer did, how she got the house. Looking back on my own early years after my divorce, I realized I was one of those people myself once. Endlessly reexamining old injuries, picking at the scabs, and because this was so, unable to heal them.

Then came the subject of career and living circumstances. We might tackle politics, favored recreational activities. ("I'm a naturist," a man told me once, before proposing that we meet up at a nudist colony.) Every one always said he worked out five times a week, and rode a mountain bike, and loved to dance. They generally expressed the view that they were equally comfortable in a tuxedo or jeans, and (when in jeans, no doubt) liked walks on the beach.

Jim had not read the rule book concerning Internet-dating conversation. He read books that weren't on the best-seller list. He talked about real things. He told me about things that had been difficult. Starting with his family.

He was born in Cincinnati, he told me—an only child, though he had a beloved grandmother and cousin, and an uncle he adored—all of whom were largely lost to him when his father took a job for Hughes Aircraft when Jim was four and the family left Ohio for Southern California.

That very first night we spoke, he told me about the train ride west, which he still remembered with stunning clarity. It was just Jim and his mother together on the train, his father having gone ahead first, and if there had been nothing else good about that train ride, the fact that his father had not been a part of that trip would have been reason enough to make those four days among the happiest of his life.

But there was more. He remembered the sleeping car, and the porters on the train—all black, in those days—who were so kind to him and turned down the sheets of his small bed each night, and the meals in the dining car, the little soaps in the bathroom, the other passengers, the feeling of going to sleep every night with the rumbling of the wheels on the track beneath him. Most of all he was happy just having his mother there, without the scary part of his father's ever-present and unpredictable rages, generally directed toward him.

His mother had sewed him a train conductor's uniform in mattress ticking fabric, with patches stitched on by hand naming all the different train lines and a cap to match. As an only child he knew how to entertain himself, and he was happy spending the days looking out the window as the landscape of America unfurled before the two of them. If that train ride had lasted a year he wouldn't have minded. He wished it could have gone on forever.

When he and his mother reached L.A., there was his big, scary father, bringing him home to their little ranch house near Venice, where their new life began. A new life filled with the same old bullying and rages, but more so over time.

He missed his family back in Ohio—most particularly his uncle Al. A small, compact man built much like the one his nephew would become, and as comfortable on horseback as he was on a Cincinnati sidewalk, Al could do a headstand and backward flip while galloping, and even into his sixties could perform a hundred one-arm pushups. He was a sharpshooter who, though too old to serve in World War II himself, had trained the troops that landed at Normandy on D-Day.

That night on the phone, Jim spoke of his uncle more than his father. Al took him fishing at his cabin in Minnesota and drove around with him in his convertible talking about cars, a passion Al had instilled in his nephew. He listened. He did not yell.

Later I would come to see how those early experiences had shaped the man Jim became and the way he functioned in the world.

Separated by the Southern California move from the rest of his Ohio family, Jim set out to make friends in his new neighborhood in smoggy Los Angeles. When a black family moved in down the block—the first black family in the whole neighborhood—his father called them a bad word and told him to stay away; but Jim, though he was still just four at this point, had decided he wanted to say hello, so he ventured down the street by himself and knocked at their door. There was a Jewish woman living on the street, too—also a source of his father's displeasure. It turned out she was some kind of editor who had once worked at the *New Yorker* and liked to talk about ideas and art and politics. Well into his teens, Jim continued to pay her visits, where the two of them would sit for hours talking about these things.

He read a lot. This included the encyclopedia. He had a chemistry set, and he loved doing experiments, though sometimes these had to be conducted in secret. Who knew why this got on his father's nerves? Everything did.

There were so many ways to make his father angry, and his anger was a terrible thing. Jim wanted to play in Little League, but his father said no, that it would cut into his responsibilities around the house doing yard work. (That first night we talked, he told me about a time, when he was seven or eight, when he'd found a frog in the yard, and decided to conduct an experiment. Wanting to keep track of this particular frog, he'd wrapped a rubber band around one of its legs, not understanding that this would cut off its circulation. Days later, he found it again, with one leg gone, and wept so bitterly his father chided him for being a baby.)

He joined the Cub Scouts. That was allowed, and he loved Scout gatherings for the friendships they permitted, and because he was happiest outdoors and hiking in nature and, above all, escaping the rages back home. But then his father decided to become his Scout leader. This was a source of deep embarrassment, though Jim stayed with the Scouts into high school.

"Believe it or not I'm an Eagle Scout," he told me. Quietly, without fanfare.

Jim remembered, with a certain ambivalence, the camping trips from his youth. Every year the three of them—just Jim and his parents—would pile into the station wagon and head to a part of the Eastern Sierra known as the Owens Valley, where his father had acquired a strip of utterly barren land—eighty acres in the middle of nowhere, without electricity or running water. There they would put up their tent for the week. Their land lay in the shadow of Mt. Whitney, but they never climbed it or explored the hiking trails of that area. As was the case through much of Jim's childhood, he was left to his own devices mostly, to read or ride his bike over the vast expanse of dusty dirt. But he and his father did engage in one activity together: They brought his rifle and shot at old cans and bottles.

When he was twelve, Jim fell in love with the Beatles, but was forbidden by his father to turn on *The Ed Sullivan Show* that January night in 1964, when every other young person in America—including me—tuned in to watch. Still, he listened to their music in secret. Age thirteen: He bought a guitar with his own money and joined a band, practicing at friends' houses so his parents wouldn't know.

Once his father found out, he made Jim quit the band. Jim grew his hair. His father brought him to the barbershop and ordered it cut—with plenty of skin visible around the ears. "Sidewalls," he called this.

That's how it had been for him growing up. If, he told me, he could have freed himself from the powerful directives of his father—Jim might have loved to become a science teacher or a teacher of history or political science. He would have loved to make a study of music, but his father had refused to pay for any other form of education than the one he deemed right for his son.

So Jim had gone to law school. And it turned out that he deeply believed in the law. He considered the Constitution a beautiful and meaningful document. To him, certain Supreme Court justices— Benjamin Cardozo, William O. Douglas—and U.S. Judge Learned Hand represented what the pastors who preached to him in those days did not, voices of social justice and compassion and clear-eyed wisdom, with a respect for science and history and facts. Maybe the rules of law offered Jim a structure he could accept whereas the structure of the church had come to feel impossibly constraining. There had been no room in the faith of his youth and early marriage, or in the world of the church, for Jim's brand of questioning.

Though his passions lay with social justice and the environment, he had been pragmatic when it came time to practice law— and made a choice that would please his father. For much of his career he had specialized in estate litigation. ("Fights about money," he said. Fights among family members were often the worst.)

The only thing Jim said about himself that first night we spoke that came close to evidencing pride was in the measure used to rate attorneys on their performance, he had a perfect Avvo rating of 10. He was a very good lawyer.

Raised as a fundamentalist Christian, he had married in a branch of the faith. He was a virgin, at the age of twenty-one. In the early days of his marriage, while in law school and then practicing law in San Francisco, he had attempted to shore up his own questioning by immersion in a Bible study group and a rigid set of rules governing moral behavior. Photographs of Jim from those days—I came to study these much later—reveal not only a much younger version of the face I came to know so well, but in another way, a nearly unrecognizable one. In the photographs with his children, I can see traces of the man I knew—with his daughter in a backpack, hiking, or holding a baby. But I see a tight control there too, a man trying to be someone he is not, quietly adhering to the rules of the world he inhabited, much as he'd done in his childhood, while an interior struggle raged.

What was I thinking, hearing this story unfold? Here was a man with a singular willingness to allow himself to be known by me. I had no idea that night what might be possible for the two of us. But one thing I recognized from the first: Here was a good man.

He had three children, two sons and a daughter, as I did, and close in age to my own, though his daughter was still in her twenties, whereas all of mine were older now. In his profile photographs he wore suits and nerdy glasses, but I learned that his politics were extremely progressive. He loved science and philosophy. He still loved rock and roll—and not just the old stuff. On his iPod he had music from Bill Withers and Nine Inch Nails, a group called the Psychedelic Furs, the Cave Singers—also Pat Metheny and Gustav Mahler. He read science fiction and thought about black holes.

He believed in God.

Jim was not a big talker, he told me—though that night on the phone he was. But as much as he told me about himself he also wanted—more—to hear about me, and he listened closely.

Over the course of those four and a half hours on the phone, it came out that my mother had been Jewish, my father the son of fundamentalist Christian missionaries, and that this had resulted in a certain questioning in my own life where God was concerned. I did not really feel Jewish, or Christian. In the world of Match.com, in the place on the questionnaire where they ask about your religion, I could easily have checked the box "Spiritual," but in a deeper way I did not have a real grasp on what I believed in beyond the easy phrases about goodness and kindness and helping one's fellow human beings. When it came to the existence of God, and what God meant, I still wandered in the desert.

It turned out that Jim had wrestled with questions of faith in a big way all his life. He had acquired a fierce distrust of rigid orthodoxy. At the moment we met, he attended no church, but he would call himself an Episcopalian.

Not long after the birth of Jim's third child, the longed-for daughter—and having been unhappy for years, he told me—he had fallen in love with another woman. Bound less by the rules of strict religion than his own moral code, he did not have an affair with her. But he told his wife he needed to leave their marriage.

It was a choice he had to make, he told me, to save his life. Still, leaving nearly killed him. He had marked the event by climbing Mt. Whitney—fourteen thousand feet, up and down, in a single day. He knew his decision would be painful, and felt a kind of obligation to put himself through an experience of great physical challenge. Twenty-five years later, the guilt he felt at having left his marriage—and the consequences in his relationships with his three children—endured.

Coincidentally, Jim's marriage had officially ended, like mine, the month of the Loma Prieta earthquake; unlike me, however, he had maintained a relationship afterward for nineteen years. The woman he'd been with—the same one he'd loved since the day he told his wife he was leaving—had also become his law partner. They'd built a successful two-person practice.

Because Jim's oldest son had so deeply disapproved of his father's new relationship, Jim had never actually lived with his partner, Patrice. What finally did in their relationship after all those years, he told me, was the hostility that existed between her and at least two of his children. In the end, he had found himself in the position of having to choose between loyalty to Patrice and support of his teenage daughter. He had chosen his daughter.

That was just over three years before. Since then, he'd had a lot of first dates and a couple of relationships that lasted less than a year. He was clearly not a player. He was unskilled in small talk. He raised questions of substance. He possessed a strong moral code and registered all the ways he fell short of being the man he wanted to be.

And now came the fact of his history that may have shaped the destiny of Jim's story with his children more than anything else: Two years after Jim left, his ex-wife was diagnosed with MS.

I have no doubt that had this diagnosis occurred while he and his first wife were still together, he would have remained in the marriage, like Ethan Frome, in a bond of commitment that would have been a source of misery for them both. As it was, he had been cast in the role of the man who abandoned the mother of his children; and, for a quarter century, he had inhabited that place. What I observed in Jim that first night we spoke, and all of those that followed, was that at some deep level, whatever his more rational perspective offered up that might have justified his choice, part of him had never stopped believing this himself. He had been a good, though imperfect, father—but a father consumed by guilt and haunted by a sense of failure to his family. He had been thoroughly punished by nobody more than himself.

Typically, a man expresses self-confidence and assurance in an early conversation with a prospective online match. Most women I know are attracted to this quality, and I had fallen for that brand of Alpha male myself plenty of times over the years. So when Jim told me that first night, "I have a lot of self-doubt," and said, "I worry that I'm not a good enough man," I might have turned and run; in fact I felt an impulse to do so. I suppose others would have too, though I am not sure that Jim had shared that level of self-disclosure with many. He could play the game of successful San Francisco attorney, and he looked the part. He just never played it with me.

From the first day we spoke, he told me the truth about himself. I did the same.

3.

The night I met Jim, I had my own failures haunting me. Some of them very recent.

It was June of 2011, two months before I'd met Martin, the bridge engineer. I had taken a trip to Italy as a last-minute replacement to teach writing at a workshop on the Amalfi coast. Ten days before I left for Italy—having just resumed online dating after a hiatus of a few years—I'd found myself on a Match.com date with a man named Doug: divorced, about my age, recently relocated to San Francisco from the East Coast, and working "in finance," which is how a lot of men described a pretty wide range of activities that might have meant anything from hedge fund operator to bank teller.

Looking back now on this episode—one whose only significance is to illuminate how far off course I found myself at this point—I recognize that I was never attracted to Doug. Nothing about him suggested any real possibility for kinship or connection beyond liking the San Francisco Giants (a passion for him, mild interest for me) and Italian food. His most appealing quality on our first date, and the only reason why I agreed to a second (though it was an insufficient justification for that), lay in the degree of his apparent enthusiasm for me.

"Don't ever cut your hair," he told me, as if he expected to be around to caress it, which I felt sure he would not be. Still, there was something compelling in his self-assurance (something singularly lacking in the man I would meet eight weeks later, and come to love). He also paid for dinner. It is not a source of pride, but a sorry truth, that I noted and liked this behavior. It was surprisingly rare.

On our follow-up date, which I had been sure would be our last, I mentioned to Doug that I was heading to Italy the following week.

"Bring me along," he said.

I said OK.

Later I tried to reconstruct how I could have agreed to this, though every single reason serves as a sad commentary on what can happen to a woman when she's fifty-seven years old and she's been single nearly twenty-five years and she's had a lot of disheartening experiences in the dating world—disheartening, or much worse.

In my case, I think I had been left with vastly lowered expectations for my life. My romantic life, anyway. At that particular moment it had seemed to me that perhaps having the company of a reasonably intelligent, reasonably fit, financially solvent man under the age of eighty with no apparent substance abuse issues, and the financial wherewithal to take me out to dinner and buy his own plane ticket to Naples, might be the best I could expect. What I did not yet recognize, though you might have thought the previous twenty-two years would have supplied abundant evidence on this score, was that if that's the best you can get in a companion, you are better off alone.

But I had this picture in my head, of Italy. Italy with a man. As my trip to the workshop approached, I had registered the old familiar sadness: Here came another trip that I'd be sharing with nobody.

A big part of my compensation for my teaching at the workshop involved airfare and a hotel room overlooking the Mediterranean in a little coastal town called Vietri sul Mare, said to be particularly lovely and atmospheric. Once I'd gotten that far, I figured I'd make the most of it.

So I had made the plan that after my teaching responsibilities were over I would take a boat to Positano and from there make my way to a nearby town called Praiano, where two very old friends, a gay couple named Eddie and Tony, made their home. I'd stay with them for a few nights and then travel on to Venice, a city I had never visited before and one that for me seemed to conjure the most romantic picture of an Italian adventure. I saw myself sitting in little outdoor cafés, having meals of fresh pasta with fresh marinara sauce and red wine, wandering the streets, stopping into old buildings and shops, riding a gondola while the gondolier sang something that surely included the word "amore." One thing alone was missing: the man to share it with.

I did not suppose, when Doug suggested that he accompany me to Italy, that we'd be embarking on some extraordinary life-long love affair. I was foolish and unrealistic, but not quite that unrealistic.

What I thought was that I could have a pleasant interlude with this man, with lots of shared meals and wine, a good companion for exploring Italy, a warm and affectionate person to curl up and have sex with at the end of the day, and that the next morning we might sit on the balcony of our beautiful, expense-paid hotel room over-looking the Mediterranean Sea and have our coffee together. If I didn't expect too much more than that, I should be able to achieve it.

The plan was made. Because Doug had some commitments keeping him in San Francisco, I would fly to Naples a day and a half ahead of him. He would join me at the hotel shortly, and then would come the marinara, the wine, moonlight over the ocean. A scooter ride in Capri, maybe.

I e-mailed my friends in Praiano, letting them know I'd be bringing a man along. "How wonderful," they wrote back. "Can't wait to meet him."

I told Doug I'd book us an Airbnb room in Venice; he'd pitch in for his half. The room I found was a tiny fourth-floor walkup, but the great part was its location, just two blocks from San Marco Square.

Under other circumstances, I would have kept my packing light. But now that I was going to Italy with a man—picturing myself having dinner in wonderful restaurants, dancing maybe—I packed three suitcases filled with dresses, accessories, and shoes. No doubt I went overboard: There had been a couple of decades' worth of solo trips in my past. I had waited a long time for one like this.

The town of Vietri sul Mare is an hour's drive from Naples. When I landed, I looked for a car service. Another woman was there, with the same destination in mind.

She was older than me—in her late seventies, I figured, though spry-looking and lively.

"I'm going to a workshop," I said.

Her name was Charlotte. She was headed there too.

On the ride we filled each other in on our stories. Charlotte had been widowed five years before this, though in many ways she'd lost her husband, Jack, years long before that, to Lou Gehrig's disease.

They had met when they were young parents but married to other people. For years they'd had a secret affair, but Jack had broken it off when his wife, the mother of his children, had become seriously ill with cancer. She survived, but Jack and Charlotte had gone their separate ways, though all through her forties and fifties, Charlotte still thought about him every day.

Jack's marriage, though unhappy, had endured. Charlotte's had not. She lived alone for many years, and made a full life for herself, filled with many good things. But she never stopped loving Jack.

Then one day, when she was sixty or so, he called her. His wife had died. He wanted to see her.

After that they were joyfully together. "It was the best thing ever," she told me in the taxi. One look at her face as she said it and you knew this was so.

They had almost ten good years before illness caught up with Jack, and when it did Charlotte remained at his side. She took care of him right up to the end, when he could no longer speak or get up from the bed or even move.

The day we rode that taxi together to the Amalfi coast turned out to be the five-year anniversary of Jack's death. On the way, Charlotte took out a photograph of him to show me. She'd pasted it on the front of the notebook she was bringing to the workshop.

Of course she wanted to hear my story, and I told her about my marriage, my divorce, the many years raising my three children as a single parent and the ones that came after, still on my own. I told her that a man I had recently met would be meeting me the next day and traveling with me in Italy after the workshop.

"How wonderful," she said. "He must be really special for you to have invited him here. I can't wait to meet him."

Doug showed up late the next afternoon, irritated by the long trip from Naples and the fact that his driver had not spoken English. In the days since I had last seen him, I had realized that I couldn't remember clearly what he looked like, and now that I saw him, I was unnerved. He was red-faced and sweaty, in worse shape than I had remembered, with a loud, crude voice and beefy fingers that now plucked at my breast.

Evidently the Giants had played earlier that day. He wanted to check the score. Also, to check the stock market. And to have sex. In that order.

The workshop where I'd been hired to teach was in fact an event whose primary focus was not writing but classical music, and it was for the musical performances that the participants, including my new friend Charlotte, had chosen to attend. Every day there were lectures about aspects of classical music, and at night performances of selections from operas by world-class young musicians. My own role as a teacher of memoir had been offered as an add-on for those who might want to give writing a try.

The morning after Doug's arrival I met Charlotte at breakfast. Doug was sleeping in.

"Your lover arrived," she said happily. "How romantic."

I shook my head. This man was definitely not my lover. I had known that much within sixty seconds of his presence in the room. Now I had two weeks scheduled to spend in the company of a man with whom I recognized I had nothing in common. Worse than that. I didn't even like him.

That night, I put on one of the many dresses I'd packed for my romantic Italian escapade. High heels. Earrings. Lipstick.

"I think I'll pass on the singing fat women," Doug told me, heading to the bar. "I'm not a big opera fan."

That night the music was to be performed in an ancient church high in the hills above the village. I sat next to Charlotte on the bus. All the way there, encouraged by my questions on this topic, she told me stories about her life with Jack. If there were to be romance that week, my best and only shot at finding it would come from the music on the stage and the stories on the bus.

Next day it was the same thing, but worse. While I taught my class, Doug hung out in the bar. After, he accompanied me on a field trip to Pompeii, where his contribution to a tour of the ruins came when we got to what was left of the ancient house of prostitution that had thrived during the years before the volcano buried the town.

Over the lintel of each room in the establishment, our guide pointed out, were carvings of sexual positions. Doug, seeing this, had announced loudly to the group. "Get a load of this, Joyce. Take notes."

That night, before I headed out again for the musical performance Doug had no interest in attending—wearing another of my many dresses—I had mentioned that I'd gotten a note from my friends in Praiano.

This inspired Doug to produce his best imitation of a limp-wristed and lisping gay man. This inspired me to produce my best imitation of a stone.

On Day Three, I discussed the situation with Charlotte. "You have to tell him," she said. "You will never find a truly good man so long as you keep settling for ones like him."

That afternoon I made Doug an offer. Instead of eating in the hotel dining room with the group as we had been doing, I wanted to go into town for dinner at one of the little cafés there. Knowing that Doug had shown reluctance to eat in other places besides our hotel—where everything was free, he pointed out—I told him the meal would be on me.

Over dinner at an outdoor café that would have been lovely with a different partner, I told him the news. I softened my reasons for the sake of his feelings.

"I know you're a great guy," I said, though in fact I did not. "But I can see it's not going to work for the two of us. We need to go our separate ways."

He looked stunned. "What about the hotel? Venice? I spent a lot of money on my plane ticket."

I said I was sorry. I should have known better. Luckily, Italy was a wonderful place to explore. With or without me.

He made a final pitch for staying together through the end of the week—pointing out that I had this great free hotel room anyway—but I stood my ground.

"It's not going to work," I said. "You need to leave."

"When?"

"Tomorrow."

The next day, when I got back from teaching my class, Doug had cleared his things out of the room. It was not until the end of the week that I discovered he'd left me with his bar bill and the charges for his meals.

I set out alone for my visit with my friends Tony and Eddie. When the boat dropped me off in Positano with my three bags full of shoes and dresses, I looked around for someone to help me get them to the spot, high above the beach, where I'd catch my bus. After a few unsuccessful minutes, I started making my way up the hill by myself. With no way to carry all three bags at once, I developed a system: carry two bags a few hundred feet. Leave those sitting and go back for the third. Repeat as many times as necessary. Many times were necessary.

It was hot that day, and I could feel the weight of every pair of earrings, every shoe. At some point, an old man called out to me. I don't speak Italian, but I understood what he was saying.

"*Dove tuo marito?*" Where is your husband?

It was a question I had asked myself plenty of times.

After my visit with my friends—in which I reflected how much nicer it was to spend three days with two wonderful men who were gay than three days with one awful man who happened to be straight—I headed out, again with those three suitcases, this time for Venice.

The cobbled streets of that city and the lack of taxis were a challenge, and even more so the four flights of stairs leading to the walkup I'd rented, with the plan of sharing the bill with Doug. Money was tight now, and I no longer envisioned wonderful meals in outdoor cafés—because those would not be so much fun alone and I didn't have the money anyway. But I made myself the promise to have an extraordinary time in Venice with or without a companion to share it. Better no man, I said, hearing Charlotte's voice in my ear, than the wrong one.

I spent the week walking the streets alone, looking at art, having an occasional glass of wine at some little café, with a simple meal of bread and olives, a piece of cheese. I studied the couples in love, and there were many, or at least, there appeared to be.

On the last night I donned one of the many dresses I'd hauled across Italy with the intention of having a fine time, regardless of my solo status. With stunning ease, I managed to sneak into an outdoor concert in San Marco Square—expensive, and sold out—where Sting was performing with the Venice orchestra. Not in possession of a ticket, I leaned against a pole off to one side.

A woman approached. Someone official, evidently.

"You need to sit down now," she said in Italian, though once again I understood.

Something possessed me to answer her in French. *"Je cherche mon mari."* I am looking for my husband.

How odd, I thought, that I'd be saying this. Not just because I didn't have a husband; more so because the word had come to have an almost alarming connotation: For me, marriage had signified pain, and then trouble. As much as I had wanted a partner over my many years alone, I had never talked about wanting a husband. *Mon mari.* Maybe the prospect seemed less problematic in French than it did in English.

Not unpleasantly, but firm, the woman told me I had to sit down. The show was about to start.

This was when I saw it: a single vacant seat in the sea of those that were occupied. Some person—solo like me—had paid the four hundred dollars for a ticket but failed to show up. Now I had a spot in the third row.

Sting came out to a roar from the crowd, and began to play. "Every Breath You Take." "An Englishman in New York." Behind him, the orchestra. Above me, the moon.

At first I stayed on alert for the true owner of my seat, but after half a dozen songs, I settled in for the extraordinary experience I'd planned on to conclude my week in Venice. I kept my seat all the way through the encore, and then, like Cinderella after the ball, made my way back to my fourth-floor garret to take off my dress, wash the makeup from my face, and go to sleep.

Next morning, I wrangled my three heavy bags down the four flights of stairs, through the streets, to the train that brought me to the airport. Fourteen hours later I was back on American soil.

Though I had succeeded, in the end, in pulling off an Italian adventure—had seen my friends, had taken in the museums of Venice, not to mention the concert—I returned home with a deep sense of sadness, not simply for my continued status as an unattached woman, but for the humbling recognition of how misguided I had been to have thought the company of a man like Doug would have been an improvement over my own.

One last reminder of my terrible selection of a travel companion also awaited me when I got off the plane: a three-page e-mail from Doug, not particularly well-written, expounding on all the reasons why I was a terrible person, a lousy sexual partner, an all-around loser in life. "They should post warnings on Match.com about people like you," he wrote.

I did not write back.

4.

My attempt at an Italian tryst with my Jack Daniels–loving sports fan was followed by a brief stop in New Hampshire to see my daughter. Then as now, Audrey lives in the town where her father and I made our home for the twelve years of our marriage, a town I'd come to some years before that, on my own.

In 1973, when I was nineteen years old and recovering from what I supposed at the time to be the great heartbreak of my life, I had used the money from the sale of my first book to buy a farm in that town—fifty acres at the end of a dead-end dirt road. I believed that I would live on that piece of land forever, and four years later, when I met the man who would become the father of my three children, I believed we'd live together on that farm for the rest of our days.

My ex-husband owned that farm now. At the point where I found myself returning there to see our daughter, on my way home from Venice, Audrey was working as a counselor at a school for troubled boys and renting my old writing cabin from her father. The cabin sat out behind our old house, just down the road from the ` waterfall and the swimming hole where I used to walk every day of every summer, where I used to bring my children to swim, and we'd launch little boats we made and chase them along the banks of the brook. I could not pass that waterfall and that swimming hole without registering a stab over all the history I'd lived there, all that was gone.

When I was twenty-three I'd celebrated my wedding at that farm. All three of my babies were born on the bed there. I'd swum and skated over twelve summers and winters on our pond on that land, and planted a garden, and cooked a few hundred meals, baked a few hundred pies. That farm had represented all of my most hopeful dreams for my life, of marriage and children, family and home. When I left it, at age thirty-five—the year of my own earthquake, when my mother died and my marriage ended—I believed I might never know a true home again. Not one I loved as I had loved that one anyway.

Now when I returned there, it was with the oddest combination of joy at seeing Audrey—in her thirties by this point and living a good, full life on that land in my onetime writing cabin—and regret at how far I'd traveled from the young woman I had been at her age. My daughter and I lived three thousand miles apart and saw each other only two or three times a year now. And so I asked myself: What happened to my dream of family and home?

That visit on my way back from Italy had been brief but good. I stayed with my old friend Danny and regaled him with the tale of the Doug disaster—now transformed into a funny story for the purposes of entertainment. The next day I swam under the waterfall with Audrey and picked blueberries and made a pie that we brought to the home of other friends that night and shared, along with a meal of eggplant parmigiana (the eggplant, basil, and tomatoes from their garden) and several bottles of Chianti on the porch of their cottage overlooking a pond.

It was a little after ten o'clock when the evening wound to a close, and I was feeling lucky and happy at all the good things in my life. I would return my rental car at the airport and fly home to San Francisco in the morning.

Outside the old writing cabin, I said good-bye to my daughter. "Maybe you want to sleep over here," she said. "You could leave early tomorrow."

I said no, better to drive back to Danny's house that night.

Five miles down the road, there it was: the flashing blue light in my rearview mirror.

The policeman wanted to see my license and registration, of course. Then came the question. "How much did you have to drink tonight?"

After the test—"Follow my finger"; "Say the alphabet backward"—he shook his head.

"Since you haven't given me any trouble," he said, "you can wear the handcuffs in front instead of behind your back." He helped me into the back seat of his police car then and brought me to the police station I remembered from long ago, when I'd gone there to report a lost dog.

In the end, I passed the Breathalyzer test. The policeman let me go with only a speeding ticket and brought me back to my rental car, which had been towed to the local auto body shop—another place well-known to me from my years as a young mother in that town, when I'd driven an old wood-paneled station wagon that was always breaking down.

The next day I flew home. Two weeks later, having chosen to disregard Doug's words in his send-off to me—that women of my ilk should be barred from online dating—I met Martin on Match .com and, two dates later, sailed off on the boat with him to dock in the bay by Angel Island. I was just grateful to be in possession of my driver's license, and more grateful still that I was in a safe place with a kind man, even though I knew I wouldn't be having any big romance with him. Comfort was enough.

Three weeks after that, I met Jim.

5.

After our marathon telephone conversation, Jim and I decided to make a date. Not a Starbucks meeting. He chose a restaurant in Marin County called the Lark Creek Inn—closer to my house in Mill Valley than to his in Oakland, because he liked to drive and I did not.

He was already there when I walked in the door, and he looked better than his profile picture. He was a handsome man, with the kind of hair that hairdressers (mine, for instance, when she met him for the first time) would invariably mention with admiration.

He had come from work, so he wore a suit and a very good shirt and a tie. He looked the part of the San Francisco lawyer, all right, but there was something in his smile that suggested another aspect that the Rolex and Brooks Brothers suit failed to conceal. There was barely perceptible pain, and a sense that he had learned (by necessity perhaps) to keep a large part of himself hidden from view. But also visible in him was a large capacity for joy—the joy part plainly evident as I approached the table. He had a wonderful smile.

"I didn't expect you to be such a knockout," he said. To no objective eye would this have been so, but with my fifty-eighth birthday closing in, and so many recent reminders of all the ways I'd failed to make the life I had once envisioned for myself, I liked it that he saw me this way.

It had given me pause, in Jim's profile, when I read that he was five feet eight. This was still two inches taller than me, but I'd had it in my head that I should be with a tall man. Six feet anyway—"tall" representing, for me, some kind of stand-in for "strong." I wanted a partner stronger than I was, and maybe, if he were tall and large, this might be so.

My old and trusted friend Bill had said to me once—after the failure of yet another of my relationships—"You know what you need, Joyce? A burly man." Bill had known me well, and when he said this I took it with sufficient seriousness. Every time I met a prospective partner, his phrase, "a burly man," came back to me.

Jim was definitely not that. He probably weighed under 150 pounds, and had the build of a runner, which he had been for most of his life, until he blew out first one ACL and then the second in two successive skiing accidents. By the time I met him, Jim was mostly a cyclist, but also a hiker, and an all-around active person. Though he didn't run anymore, he still moved fast, the way I did. He could weave through a crowd at triple speed when he needed to—as I could—and though he couldn't cover distances as he had in his days as a long-distance runner, he could break into a run anytime he wanted without evidence of difficulty.

Now though, he stood still as he greeted me. Still, and then silent for a surprisingly long time. For some reason, there was no awkwardness in this. We both just took in the moment.

We had talked so much on the phone by this point that he felt like a friend, and I believe that was true for him also. When he ordered drinks, I explained to him why I would limit myself to one.

"Four weeks ago I was handcuffed in a police car as a suspected drunk driver," I told him. Not the usual first-date information, but already this was not a usual first date. Where, more traditionally, a first date like this one featured mutual recitations of each person's successes, with an eye toward highlighting their most attractive qualities, this one seemed more about revealing to each other all the aspects of ourselves that might be most likely to send the other person running in the opposite direction. Only they didn't. We stayed talking for over three hours. We had met at the bar, and somewhere into hour two, when no indication had been given that he'd contemplated ordering food, I asked Jim, "Don't you ever eat?"

"I'm sorry," he said. "I was just so blown away by you, I forgot."

He didn't focus much on his thirty-five years as an attorney. We talked a lot that night about divorce, and all the damage that comes after. The story of my children and me was not without its hard chapters, but for Jim in particular, the bitterness that had come from ending his marriage to his children's mother seemed, all these years later, far from finished. "I don't think my daughter and my older son have ever forgiven me for leaving their mother," he told me.

It was not the central bond we recognized that night, but it was a real one: the shared sorrow of having failed to raise the three children each of us had brought into the world with their other parent, and the sense left in each of us that our family would always feel broken because of this. For Jim, as for me, raising children had been a central part of life. Being a good father to his sons and daughter— a different kind of father from the one who raised him—had been the chief goal in life. I could see, sitting across from Jim that night, that he carried profound sorrow over his children's assessment of him as a man who had fallen short.

"It appears that I failed at the thing that mattered most," he said to me, though it was difficult to believe, hearing him tell the story, that he hadn't tried desperately hard, and done plenty of things right, too. Of all the single fathers I'd met on Match.com, I'd never met anyone else who had taken three children camping into deep wilderness when the youngest was three years old. When his children's mother moved from the Bay Area to Salt Lake City and put them in a Christian school there, he made the trip to see them on a regular basis, and when his teenage daughter was unhappy in the Christian school, he brought her back to live with him. I had known a few attorneys over the years, and had an idea of what was required of a person to be part of a high-powered law firm. Jim was the only one I ever met who left the office at five to make it home to cook dinner, and no doubt the fact that he had made this choice had cost him in his professional career.

I had my own large failures, I told him. The drunk driving charge, the foolish choice to go to Italy with a man I didn't even like, the double-digit numbers of relationships that had gone nowhere, the hard things my children had said to me over the years, generally concerning my tendency toward highly emotional behavior, the times they'd heard me cry, or rail against their father—all of that was real, but there was a more recent failure that had left me gutted that summer. Then I told him about that one.

6.

There is no easy way to tell this story. But like everything else of substance that came before—the things that made us the two people we were by the time we met that night at the bar of the Lark Creek Inn—the story of my adopted Ethiopian daughters had brought me to this place.

The woman who walked into that restaurant that night to take her seat across the table from the handsome, well-dressed attorney was a person who had recently—just six months earlier—experienced the largest devastation of her life, and one of her own making.

Where to begin? I had given birth to three well-loved children, who were five, seven, and eleven when their father and I parted. And though I believe we went on to make a strong family together, and certainly a loving one, none of us had escaped injury in the divorce, and in different ways each of us bore its scars. My children had seen way too much of my sorrow over the years, way too much of my anger toward their father. Sitting across from Jim that night at the restaurant, hearing the story of a man on the other side of a bitter divorce—a man I deeply liked—whose ex-wife had, like me, moved to another city to raise the children, I could see the other half of the story I'd lived, played out in the life of a truly decent and loving man who had wanted nothing more than to be a good father. Twenty-four years later, he still suffered over his failure to protect his children from the pain of growing up in what much of the world refers to as "a broken home." I carried that regret too, and it was vast.

For all the years my children lived with me, I had held on to the dream that I would somehow have the chance to redo the old dream, but better next time. Later into my forties than any sensible person should, I had maintained the hope that maybe I'd have another child one day with a partner who would be there to share raising him or her, and that somehow through this experience we would all manage to become whole again as a family.

My ex-husband actually accomplished this, becoming the father to a son born when our three children were all grown and he was fifty—a son whom my children considered from the day of his birth not as a half-brother but simply as their deeply loved brother, Taj. It was a beautiful thing to see.

In my own life, the years passed with one failed attempt at a relationship after another, until finally my children had all left home to make their own lives in the world and I had at last accepted that I would never give birth to that fourth child, the magic baby.

I missed being a parent as much as a person crossing the desert misses water. I missed soccer games and family meals and coming in out of the snow after sledding, dancing in the living room, and putting on plays and making Halloween costumes and art projects. I missed the first day of school, and all the other days—driving them to school, listening to all the things my children had to say not only to me but to each other. I missed holding a child and reading to her. All those nights on the bed, with one or another or all three of them pressed up against me, showing them the world one page at a time, starting with the first book, the beginning of everything—those first five words that were, for us, where all the other nights of reading began. *"In the great green room . . ."*

I missed the simple fact of loving someone in a constant, daily way as I had done with my children. With my children, and no one else, ever. I had always seen myself as a person whose first and best gift was the ability to give love. But there was no one around anymore to receive it. And no one around loving me back.

I WAS TRAVELING to Guatemala a lot in those years—having bought a house in a small Mayan village on the shores of a deep volcanic lake. At the point that I started traveling there regularly, Guatemala was still, as it no longer is, a center for international adoption. Every time I landed at the airport in Guatemala City, I'd see the hopeful couples—most of them young, but some not so much younger than me—carrying their empty strollers and diaper bags in anticipation of the child they'd be meeting there and bringing home to be part of their family.

But it was the flights back that got to me. Because surprisingly few Americans travel to Guatemala as tourists—nearly every Caucasian person on the plane (everyone but me) had come with the same purpose: to bring home a baby.

Here's how it would go every time I made the trip to Guatemala in those days: I'd be sitting on the airplane, and all around me were the anxious couples, the beautiful dark-eyed children, around eighteen months old, but sometimes a little older or a little younger. Looking shell-shocked, generally, but seldom crying. Guatemalan children don't do that much.

I read a lot about international adoption in those days. I studied websites. I clicked on links, a few of which actually showed photographs of children for whom homes and parents were needed.

"Here is this child who needs a parent," they said. And who was I? A parent who needed a child. There was a red flag in that line, but I missed it.

I had no partner. But I was accustomed to taking care of things on my own. I knew how to do without a husband. I did not ask whether a child could do without a father.

For a long time I resisted the impulse to pursue an international adoption as a single person out of the recognition that I lacked the financial resources to provide for a child. The other part—about emotional resources, the presence or absence of a strong support system—was one I was too naive or ignorant to explore.

Then a novel of mine was sold for more money than any book I'd ever written, and though I was not rich, I felt I was. One of the first things I did then, after receiving the check for *Labor Day*, was to click on the bookmarks of my adoption websites.

By this point Guatemalan adoption had been shut down. And a new thought came to me: Rather than adopting a baby or a toddler, I saw myself providing a home for an older child who might have a harder time finding one.

I read a book by a woman around my age, Melissa Fay Greene, who had adopted several older Ethiopian children and was raising them very happily, it seemed, along with her birth children, and though, unlike me, she had a partner at her side, Melissa's story inspired me greatly.

But it was a CD-ROM sent to me from an agency dealing with Ethiopian adoptions that convinced me to act. The orphanage had lined up the children there—ranging in age from three or four to eleven or twelve—to introduce themselves in front of the camera. Each one had about fifteen seconds to say his name, his favorite subject in school, his hopes for the future.

I sat on my bed watching the CD, weeping as the face of one hopeful child after another filled the screen, their voices eager to please and so filled with longing you could almost touch it. "I am Abebe. My favorite subject is English. I hope an American family will adopt me. I am clean and neat." "I'm Negasi, and my favorite subject is English." It always was.

It was unnervingly easy, getting approved as an adoptive parent for an Ethiopian child. Nobody seemed to care that I was fifty-five years old, unmarried, living on the undependable earnings of a writer. I had made a lot of money that year, and almost none the year before. Good enough.

A number of close and wise friends attempted to discourage me. My friend Becky, who remembered well how hard I'd struggled all those years as a single parent, shook her head. "You've finally got a little space in your life to take care of yourself for a change," she said to me. "If you take this on, all that is gone." My daughter Audrey, who worked with troubled adolescent boys, knew firsthand how many of them still struggled with issues of adoption. "Please, Mom," she said, "don't."

No one could talk me out of it. In the spring of 2009, I received an e-mail containing two JPEGs, each showing a pair of girls, dark-skinned, bright-eyed, and full of life. Two different pairs of sisters, in which the older looked to be nine or ten and the younger one around five.

I had thought initially that I'd adopt one child. But here were these beautiful sisters, and it seemed to me, studying the pictures, that if a child had to do this terribly hard thing—leaving her country and what was left of her AIDS-ravaged family, giving up her language, even, and coming to an unknown place where every single thing (the food, the religion, the music, the climate, even the alphabet) would be unknown to her—that she should have some-body at her side: somebody known to her, and loved, to support her in the journey.

Something in the gesture of the older sister in one of the two JPEG images—the way she draped her arm around the little one, suggesting not only love but fierce protection, spoke to me. She was not smiling in the picture, though her little sister (who had no doubt been told to do so, as they both had) was.

"I'd like to adopt those two girls," I wrote back. Simple as that.

IN THE SUMMER of 2009, I traveled to Addis Ababa to meet my future daughters. I will speak of them as Layla and Adenach, but those are not their real names.

They were very beautiful, and very thin, no doubt from years of deprivation. Though the particulars of their lives up to that point remained unclear, I knew they had endured more hardship in their few years on the planet than many people do in a lifetime, but they had not lost the capacity for joy. It was only later that I'd learn the other part—the depth of sorrow that a child must navigate when she has endured as much as my girls had.

The moment we laid eyes on each other, in the hard dirt yard outside the orphanage, the younger sister, Adenach, leapt into my arms and pressed her face against my chest. Layla held back, with a tight, slightly worried smile. I had been told their ages were five and nine, and Adenach seemed like a five-year-old all right—just a very small one. But I knew right away that Layla was not the age the agency had told me in their letter. Tiny as she was, there was a kind of wisdom in her eyes. If I were to guess, I would have said she was twelve, though she herself might not have known the answer, it had been so long since anyone was there to keep track.

I took the girls' hands, one on each side, and we headed inside the orphanage—a cinder-block structure filled with cribs and one sparsely furnished room offering a couch, a television set, pictures taped on the walls of Americans who'd come to bring children home, and a few coloring books. The sound of babies crying never let up.

For five nights I slept at the orphanage and shared my meals with the girls—*enjera* and *doro wot*, which we ate with our fingers, gathered around a low little table with the two other older children at the orphanage and the nannies, and sometimes another American, come to bring home a baby. The girls spoke almost no English then, but we found plenty of ways to learn about each other. I had brought crayons and markers and card games and a ball. For Adenach, it was enough just to sit on my lap, her arms around my neck, mine around her. Layla sat a little ways off, watching.

The day before I arrived in Ethiopia, I had learned about the death of Michael Jackson, whose music I had brought with me to entertain them over the course of our visit, knowing we would not share language. After I played them *Thriller*, and all the other Michael Jackson songs on my laptop, all they wanted to do was dance to his music. They were wonderful dancers and they loved his videos. I didn't have the heart to tell them he'd just died.

America, they said, over and over. *Michael Jackson. Hamburgers. Barbie. Mom.*

One night I brought them to a restaurant where a live band would be performing traditional Ethiopian music. When the music started, Adenach rose from her seat like a person in a trance and made her way to the front of the room, right beside the drummer. She began to dance, moving her hips and arms in a way I could not have replicated if I'd practiced all week—a five-year-old with the moves of a grown woman. I should have recognized it then: She had a history and culture that went beyond the orphanage. And I was taking her away from it.

As she always did, Layla hung back. She was a wonderful dancer too, but she was wary in ways her little sister was not. No doubt there were reasons.

This was not the trip in which I'd be bringing the girls home.

I had made this journey so they would know there was someone looking out for them now, ready to be their mother once the paperwork was completed.

On my last day at the orphanage, we lay snuggled close on the bed where I slept—not just Adenach this time, but Layla too. They were braiding my hair. Adenach was begging me not to leave, and crying. She was holding on to me so tightly her fingers left a mark on my arm.

I made them a calendar and told them to cross off the days, one by one. I had an idea—just a guess—of how many days it would take before the documents would be filed and I'd come back for them.

As it turned out, the adoption moved faster than we'd expected. Layla and Adenach were legally my daughters by that November, and in January I returned to Ethiopia to bring them home with me.

There was a party for them at the orphanage the night before I took them away. Their older brothers came. Watching them say good-bye to those brothers, whispering in Amharic words I would never know, dancing in the firelight to beautiful, haunting songs we would not hear again, spinning around the orphanage yard with their friends, the other children still waiting for someone to come for them—I wondered if I was making a terrible mistake taking them away. When the girls said good-bye to their brothers and their friends that night, we spoke of returning one day for a visit, but everyone knew the truth: They might never see each other again.

They entered a different world then. They loved the hotel swimming pool and the elevator, and the breakfast buffet where they piled on so much food that pancakes tumbled onto the carpet. They thought the airport escalator was the plane.

Every single thing was new: the seat belts, the food, the vast landscape out the window as we made our long journey. Home in

Mill Valley, California, after twenty-six hours of travel, I tucked them into their bunk beds and kissed them. They called me Mom. Later, Adenach climbed upstairs to join me in my bed—but because she had almost never encountered stairs before, she took the steps on all fours, like a kitten.

For the first few weeks, they were not yet enrolled in school as they would be soon, so we stayed home a lot, drawing and watching movies that didn't require so much language—Charlie Chaplin, Laurel and Hardy—and dancing. I learned to put berbere spice in every food I prepared. They were ravenous for meat. "I love you I love you I love you," they told me.

This was the honeymoon period, when they recited those words at three-minute intervals—the first words of English they'd been taught at the orphanage.

It was a good and necessary step, when they got beyond this and their truer feelings emerged concerning what they had gone through. These included a lot of grief, and for Layla, a great deal of understandable anger. A depth of pain so vast it seemed to have no end.

The fact that this was so was terrifying to me. From the outside, we seemed to be managing. The girls learned English, learned to read, to swim, and then to ride a bicycle (with me running behind, out of breath, until they got the hang of it—as they swiftly did). They were wonderful athletes who picked up every new challenge as effortlessly as breathing. The first time Adenach saw the monkey bars at school, she climbed to the top and flipped upside down. She swung back and forth, laughing, for an hour, then jumped off and performed a cartwheel.

But later, home again, there was a manic wildness to our nights. Adenach loved everyone, but especially men, and boys (my sons, when they came to visit, or any pizza delivery boy). And Adenach was, from the first, unfailingly affectionate with me.

Not Layla. There seemed to be a stone pressing on her heart. There was nothing more beautiful than her smile, when you got to see it. But you might wait a long time.

I spent my days that year attending soccer games and volunteering at school and bringing the girls to birthday parties—especially Adenach, who was queen of her kindergarten class—and to the houses of friends, whose mothers all looked around the age of my daughter Audrey. I was living the life of a thirty-five-year-old suburban mother, only my children's story was nothing like the stories of those women's children, and my life was nothing like theirs.

One day I listened as a young mother told me about breaking the news to her daughter that her fish had died—an experience that had prompted her to consult a therapist. The daughter I was waiting for, outside her fourth-grade classroom, had sat on the dirt floor of a hut with no running water at age four, watching her mother die of AIDS. She hid bread in her pocket—the tiny portion allotted to her—to give to her baby sister, Adenach.

We struggled daily over the girls' hair. At first I had tried to help them comb it myself, but one day a Haitian woman stopped me on the street and kindly asked (no mystery as to why) if I needed some help with my daughters' hair. All she had to do was look at them to know I did.

After that, I drove to Jasmine's house every Sunday while she worked first on Layla, then Adenach—one knot at a time. The job took so many hours that we got through two movies on DVD every trip, and when Jasmine got to the braiding part, their eyes filled with tears. But they didn't want her to stop.

THEY WANTED TO be American girls, and they wanted me to be their all-American mother. So we went to the Justin Bieber movie twice, and to the mall, and to Oakland, where I spent three hundred dollars at a beauty parlor because there was nothing they desired more than to have their hair straightened, even though one week later it would be back to how it was before—which I thought was more beautiful, if only they could have felt that way too.

For hours every night, I worked with Layla on her reading: She didn't want to read *Hop on Pop*, though that was her level. She wanted to read a real fourth-grade book, *Diary of a Wimpy Kid*. Every night we made it through a paragraph, a process that took hours, and generally involved bitter tears.

It was a big moment when Layla performed in a school talent show to a song picked out for her, and written by, my son Charlie. Her dancing was so good she brought down the house. From my seat in the audience, with tears in my eyes, I watched her radiant smile as the crowd cheered. But at home, dark clouds enveloped us.

All my life, I had counted on my abundance of energy to get me through difficult times, but suddenly I was exhausted all the time. Always before, however bad things might have seemed, I had managed to summon optimism about the future, but now hope abandoned me. All I could see ahead was an endless series of lonely struggles and failures.

I called up my son Willy's best friend from his school days in Mill Valley, Bridget—now completing her studies to become a social worker—and enlisted her help, and as the weeks passed, I relied on Bridget more and more. The girls adored Bridget. The trouble was mostly reserved for times with me.

We started every day, often before sunrise, with battles—over hair, over clothes, over food, but they were never about any of those things, really. One of our battles left Layla and me on the floor together, our arms and legs wrapped around each other in a wrestling match. I wept but she was silent as a stone, her jaw set, her eyes looking through me.

"I love you," I told her, through tears, but what did that mean anymore?

"*I hate you*," she told me.

With an ignorance that staggers me now—ignorance, and some arrogance no doubt—I had believed my love would be there like an eternal flame, and that this love of mine could fix whatever had been broken in my daughters' lives. When it became apparent, as it swiftly did, that they would have miles to go before they trusted me (let alone loved me)—and that I would somehow have to keep going this way, for months and maybe years, with only the barest sign of affection coming back—I was filled with the most profound sense of despair I had ever known.

None of this should have been surprising. The two girls I called my daughters were bright, funny, strong, tenacious, brave. I also saw them as wary and hurt, and wisely defended against future loss, distrustful, and angry. They had not asked for some woman old enough to be their grandmother, who couldn't even provide them with a father, to show up at their orphanage and take them away from their homeland, to Marin County, California, of all places. Why should they love me? And here came the hardest, most shameful and terrifying question I asked myself, alone in the dark: How long could my own love endure?

Visits to a therapist did not help. We'd sit in her office, week after week, as Layla said nothing. Finally the therapist told me there was no point bringing her back. "Just come on your own," she told me. "You could use some help."

I had always believed my stores of energy and devotion to children to be inexhaustible, but as the days wore on I could feel my reserves disappearing. I was sick with a sense of my own inability to be for my daughters the mother they had dreamed of finding in America, the mother I had always believed myself to be.

Six months into our time together I developed pneumonia and it hung on for months. I couldn't work. I could barely climb the stairs. I couldn't work.

I couldn't meet the mortgage payments on our house, and called a Realtor about putting it on the market. I looked at apartments, debated moving back east where life would be cheaper. But moving would not address the real problem. The problem was not the house, but the homeowner.

The first time the therapist suggested that I consider relinquishing the girls, I had put my hands over my ears and told her never to suggest this again. I talked with my other children—the ones I'd given birth to—who had their own grief to deal with over the girls. My sons, who knew them best, had loved them. They just weren't around all that much. My daughter Audrey—the one who'd never believed this was a good idea—sighed deeply and long. "I don't know what to tell you, Mom," she said. Too kind to add, "I told you so."

Then something happened that was, for us, the breaking point.

Layla was a beautiful natural runner, and with her long legs and graceful stride—and her fierce tenacity—she could run forever. For months, I'd brought her to the track in our town to run with her— in my old sweatpants, out of breath, with my knees aching, Layla in a purple tutu she loved, sailing past me on the track, effortless as a gazelle. The fact that I would even try to do this, as a fifty-six-year-old woman who had never been a runner, no doubt served as indication of my desperation.

The idea had come to me that maybe, if I could find someone to run with Layla—if, in the company of a real runner, she could run far enough and hard enough—things might go better for her. English was frustrating to her. The alphabet was frustrating. Reading was frustrating. My presence infuriated her.

But for Layla, running was as natural as breathing, and so I allowed myself to imagine that if she could just keep running, she might actually find a way to gain her footing in America.

I went on Craigslist, not even sure who I was looking for, but the person I found there seemed, briefly, like the answer to my prayers.

Ashley was a distance runner, training for the Olympics on the trails of Mt. Tamalpais and looking for a place to stay rent-free. I called her up and offered her a room in our house if she would run with my daughter every day. Miles, if possible. The faster, the better.

Ashley moved in with us, and every day she took Layla running with her. But it had been a naive and foolish idea on my part to suppose that somehow Layla could run her way out of the place where we found ourselves. Her troubles just followed her onto the trail.

It turned out that Layla hated running with Ashley. One afternoon on the trail, the two of them got in a bad fight. When Layla started screaming, something terrible happened. The muscles in one side of her face suddenly froze. When Ashley brought her home that day—neither one of them speaking—she looked like a stroke victim. This would have been hard for anyone, but for a twelve-year-old girl who already felt out of place at school, it was a disaster.

Every day now—to address her medical condition—we were making visits to doctors, to the emergency room, the acupuncturist, the therapist. Layla hated this, of course, but she hated what had happened to her face even more. And so she visited those doctors, and subjected herself to their tests, her eyes brooding, her jaw set. On the ride home after, she seldom spoke to me.

Whatever else was true of Layla's condition, I knew she was deeply unhappy, and terrified by the idea that her face would look this way forever. I wanted to help her. But I was part of her problem.

The freezing of my Ethiopian daughter's face gradually resolved, but the medical crisis became, for me, a stark message. I needed to find a better home for Layla and Adenach with two parents who could give them what I had failed to provide.

One night a couple of weeks after the running incident—with Ashley gone now, and Layla's running shoes put away—I suggested to the girls that the three of us get in the hot tub and talk. It was a kind of conversation no parent I'd ever known could imagine having with her children, and one I would once have viewed as unthinkable. Now, though, we sat together in the bubbling water under the night sky, and I began, slowly, to speak the words.

"Before we left Ethiopia, to bring you home with me," I told them, "I made a promise to everyone who loved you there that I would make sure you have a good life in America." Silence then. The girls studied my face. The water swirled around us. "And you will have a good life here," I said. "The best way for you to get that is for me to find you the right family."

They needed a different mother, I said. They needed a father.

Of the many people I would encounter who would later judge me harshly for the decision I made to relinquish the girls—both strangers and those who knew me well, or supposed they did—there were two people at least who did understand, at least some ways, or did on that night anyway, my choice to relinquish my daughters. Those two were Layla and Adenach.

They sat very still in the hot tub as I talked to them that night, but for once there was no argument. They asked if they could bring their bicycles and their American Girl dolls to their new home. They asked if, in their new family, there would be other kids. "That would be a good idea," I said.

There was no website to go consult to locate a new family for Layla and Adenach. The agency that had been so ready to accept my checks two and a half years before had nothing to tell me now beyond the suggestion that if I broke the girls up, and made them available separately to different families, they were more likely to be re-adoptable.

"The little one in particular should be easy," a woman at the agency said over the phone. "She's so cute."

"The girls stay together," I told her. "There can be no question about that."

On that first trip I'd made to Addis Ababa a year and a half before, I'd met a woman named Rachel, much younger than I—around the age of my daughter, in fact—who had come from Missouri to bring home a baby. She and her husband, Henry, had three birth children and were also raising a foster child, but they had made the decision to adopt an Ethiopian baby. Rachel had made the first visit to meet him at the orphanage. Later, Henry would be making the trip to bring him home.

These people were not even close to wealthy. In so many ways—religion, politics—we differed. But their decency and commitment was never in doubt, and neither was their strength. It had been clear to me, meeting Rachel, that for them a big, diverse tribe of a family was the most natural and right thing, not only for them but for the children.

Back before the girls came to live with me, when I used to get reports from the orphanage telling me how they were doing, the director had written to me about something that had happened after the visit of Henry, Rachel's husband, when he'd come to bring home their infant son. After Layla had met Henry, she came to the orphanage director with a suggestion. Not having understood that Henry was married to Rachel, and taking a great liking to Henry, as anyone meeting him would, Layla suggested that I should marry Henry. That way we could all be together as a regular family with a mother and father.

Maybe I saw even then, in the innocent fantasy of a twelve-year-old, an underlying wisdom. Though I had the heart in me for loving two more children, I did not possess the rest: I had no husband, no father to offer them, and at least for these particular girls, with their particular stories, that was crucial. More than this, I lacked the stability within my own life that would have allowed me to help them build stability in theirs.

In February of 2011, just thirteen months after the bright, hope-filled day I'd brought my two girls home to begin our life together in Mill Valley, I wrote an e-mail to Rachel and Henry to ask whether they would consider becoming parents to Layla and Adenach.

Within hours, they wrote me back. They had never stopped thinking about the girls, they told me. They had loved Adenach and Layla the minute they had met them so long ago back at the orphanage, even though they had traveled all those miles to adopt a different child.

Their house was small, but they had room in their lives. Their other children would love having two more sisters, and I knew my girls would feel good about the idea of living in a home bursting at the seams with children and grandparents—with a mother and father who seemed born for this.

Over the days that followed, Henry and Rachel and I spent hours talking over what it would mean for the girls to leave the home where they had lived with me and come to theirs, and to become their legal daughters.

At the time, I held out hope that we might carve out a way I could continue to know the girls; but we all knew better. If they were to make a life with their new family in Missouri, they would need to separate totally from me. Once I said good-bye to them, we would not see each other again or communicate. Not for a long time anyway.

I'd met Rachel in Addis, but I wanted to meet Henry. I told him that I'd recently taken a speaking engagement in Aspen, to which I was bringing the girls. It was a job I signed on for specifically because it would allow Layla and Adenach to spend three nights at a condo on the mountain there and see snow, which they loved. Because my sons, as well as my daughter's boyfriend, Tod, were snowboarders, they wanted to be snowboarders too.

It was a fourteen-hour drive all the way to Aspen from the Missouri town where Henry and Rachel and their family lived, but Henry said he would come—not to check the girls out, but to give them a chance to see him again and make sure they felt good about what we proposed. He would bring along his two sons. If anyone was on trial that day, it would be Henry's family, not the girls.

By the time Layla and Adenach and I made the trip to Aspen in early March, the situation at our house had become almost unbearable for us all. Though that night in the hot tub they had seemed to accept the reasons for my choice for us, by this point the girls had pulled away from me to the point where, when I spoke to them, they often didn't answer. They did not look at me. It was simply too hard, I think, for them to hold two different families in their hearts at one time. They had to let go of someone. That person was me.

"I feel as though I'm suffering from a terminal illness," I told my friend Becky. "The girls and I have no future together, and we know it. How do you go through the days when you know you're about to say good-bye forever?"

The trip to Aspen made for a good distraction. The girls loved snowboarding. I had told them about Henry and his sons coming to meet us there. They may have pretended as though this was no big deal, but we all knew it was.

I was with the girls at the top of a ski run at the moment Henry and his two sons arrived after their fourteen-hour drive. Even from high above the base and the lodge, I could make out the three of them. Something in the way they stood there—three solid-looking figures in brown work jackets, nothing like the brilliantly colored ski ensembles of everyone else on the mountain that day—made me know that they were not skiers or snowboarders on vacation, out for an afternoon's recreation. This was a father of five who worked as a plumber, who had set out in his truck before dawn on his day off with his eleven- and fourteen-year-old sons to meet his future daughters, their future sisters.

After two days with me in Aspen, the girls were much more skillful on a snowboard than I was on my skis. Now, having caught sight of the man who would be their father, I watched them tear down the mountain ahead of me, snow flying behind their boards, headed for the three waiting figures—one big, two smaller—who represented their new family.

When they got to the foot of the slope, Adenach did not even stop. She plowed right up to Henry on her board, flung it aside and leapt into his arms. Layla hung back a little more, but the boys took care of that. From where I watched as I made my way down the mountain, snowplowing most of the way, I could see the brothers in their puffy jackets, encircling Layla. She was a girl who had left three brothers back in Ethiopia she might never see again, had fallen in love with two brothers in Mill Valley who were never around as much as she and her sister longed for them to be. And here she was, meeting the two who would be brothers to her now.

Because Henry had to be home for work the next day, the visit back at our ski condo lasted no more than two hours, just long enough for everyone but me to get in the hot tub while I ordered pizza. Already, Adenach was settled into Henry's lap. Layla was playing with her future brothers and laughing in a way I had not seen her do in months.

I might have been invisible. If I had any doubt, it was clear to me then that they weren't my daughters anymore. There was relief in this, and a world of sorrow.

Three weeks later, heading to the airport with their possessions packed up and shipped to Missouri ahead of them, my Ethiopian daughters walked out the door of our house for the last time. They did not look back.

My younger son, Willy, flew to the airport in Kansas City to make the three-hour drive with us to the girls' new home and to say good-bye. The girls spotted him all the way down the long airport corridor and went running toward him—their handsome, funny brother who had played soccer with them and swung them in the air. Adenach pulled Willy's hat off his head and stuck it on her own, laughing. Layla just smiled, but that was a lot.

We had a long drive ahead of us. Somewhere along the highway we stopped at a restaurant and ordered hamburgers for everyone. Just as the girls started to eat—all of us still laughing over something Willy had done—a man stopped by our table on the way to his own.

"I just had to tell you," he said to me. "What a beautiful family you've got there."

I made no effort to correct him. In his way, he was right.

Just before dinnertime, we reached the town where Rachel and

Henry and their cheerful, boisterous family lived. Rachel had a big pot of chili on the stove, the table set with places for seventeen; the relatives were coming. Many times over the course of the meal, from my seat at the far end of the big table, I watched the girls laughing and smiling and reaching for seconds. Watching them, you might have thought that they'd lived here their entire lives.

Willy and I had planned to come back the next morning for one last visit, but that night I knew there was no point in staying longer. When we set out for the hotel after dinner was over, I told Henry and Rachel that come morning we'd be heading straight to the airport. "I'm going to say good-bye now," I told the girls. My daughters. But not anymore.

My son got down on his knees to hug both girls, one at a time. His sisters, he called them still. They stayed that way, with their arms around each other, for a long time.

Then it was my turn, but I knew it would be different for me, and it was. Their bodies, which had melted into mine all those months before at the orphanage in Addis, were stiff now, arms limp at their sides. I placed my hand on Layla's hair, that I had spent so many hours trying to tame, and then Adenach's, and told them I would always love them. Then I walked out the door.

After, in the parking lot of our hotel, my son sat in the car for an hour with his head on the steering wheel, weeping. The next morning we got up and made the long drive in silence back to the airport. Willy got on his plane back to Los Angeles. I boarded mine. Of all the losses I'd known, this had been the worst.

After I left the girls that day, and said good-bye to my son at the airport, I flew home. Once I landed in San Francisco I made my way back from the airport, alone as usual. I walked back in the door of my empty house and turned on the lights. No more Justin Bieber music blasting, no more scattered Barbie shoes or the smell of berbere spice. Nobody there but me.

And who was I? Those fourteen months had shaken me to my core, to the point where I no longer knew anything for sure except that parents should not look to their children to meet their needs. You don't adopt a child because you need more love in your life. You had better have the love part figured out already. As I did not.

7.

This was the other story I told Jim that night we met. After the part about the bad trip to Italy and the Breathalyzer and the handcuffs—stories that seemed meaningless in comparison to this one.

"The woman you are sitting across from," I told him, "relinquished two adopted children who'd already lost one mother. Many people have concluded that makes me a terrible person."

"That's not how I see it," Jim said.

After it was over, I told him, I lost faith in myself. I had always believed that if there was one thing I could do well, it was loving someone, a child in particular. After I said good-bye to the girls— and it had been good-bye all right; there had been no further word from them or their adoptive parents (nor would there be, I now believed, and I understood this)—I wasn't sure anymore what kind of a person I was. I no longer trusted the steadiness of my own heart.

"You're very hard on yourself," Jim said. Later, when we left the restaurant, we stood together in the parking lot. It turned out that when I had arrived all those hours before, I had pulled my car into the spot next to his. His, a silver Porsche Boxster with the top down. Mine, a 1995 Honda Civic I'd bought a dozen years before when I first came to California, for $1,500.

"I'm not a very good driver," I told him.

"But I am," he said.

8.

The next morning I rose at six to find an e-mail already waiting from Jim. "That was one of the best times ever," he wrote.

That night I was back on the sailboat with Martin. Not because I was in love with Martin. I wasn't sure I should try love anymore.

Still, I invited Jim to dinner at my house—the place I'd chosen for my children and me when I moved to California fifteen years earlier, which looked out at Mt. Tamalpais. He studied everything closely—the art on my walls (paintings by my father mostly, gone from my life longer than he'd been in it, but a daily presence through the paintings he left me). He studied the CDs and books on my shelves, the bedroom I'd fixed up for the girls, empty now, though there was a Disney princess sticker on the window still. Jim didn't say a whole lot, but I could feel how intently he was taking everything in. He particularly loved my father's artwork, he said. Then he told about the huge new addition to the San Francisco Museum of Modern Art just getting under way. "It won't be open for years," he told me, "but I'm going to be there when it is."

What kind of man got excited about an art museum still under construction? This one.

He kept me company in the kitchen while I cooked. I set our plates kitty-corner on the table, not across from each other. I liked being close to him.

Though I would not normally have done this with a man I'd just met, I took his hand before we started to eat and closed my eyes—the grace I liked to say, in my head mostly, before the start of a meal. As I picked up my fork, he reached over for my arm and brought my elbow to his lips.

"You have a little food here," he said.

He licked it off.

"I am a very messy person," I told him. "I don't know how it happens but I'm always getting food on myself."

"I don't mind," he said. I still hadn't kissed him.

The next night I headed to the sailboat again. My son Charlie was in town, and Martin had invited the two of us to come out in the bay to sail under the Golden Gate Bridge. I sat on the prow of the boat, thinking how lucky I was—to have gotten all this way from New Hampshire, to find myself and my son on a beautiful boat on a perfect late-summer day sailing under the vast span of this great red bridge.

Later, I would say good-bye to Charlie and spend the night on the boat with Martin. I realized I missed Jim.

That weekend Jim came to see me at my house in Mill Valley again. We had made the plan to go hiking in Point Reyes, one of my favorite places, and a favorite of his too.

He showed up in the Boxster—top up this time, on account of the weather. The day had turned out to be foggy and cold, but we went ahead with our plan anyway.

In the seat next to him I studied his fine profile and the easy, assured way he shifted around the sharp curves of Highway One. Even before I learned how much he loved James Bond movies, I recognized the James Bond quality in Jim, and not only because he was a bold, self-assured driver. He wore a beautiful jacket that day— casual but perfectly fitted, immaculate. This too I didn't know yet, but all his clothes were like that: good shirts, silk ties, soft leather shoes, a Rolex watch. When he dressed as he did that day for a casual afternoon of hiking, he was equally well turned out, whereas my own outfit had come, as they nearly always did, from a Mill Valley thrift shop, the castoffs of some woman who (more like Jim) probably replaced everything every year or so at the first sign of wear.

But I knew by now that the Eddie Bauer jacket and the Patagonia hat and the expensive sunglasses were not the truest measure of Jim. He had interesting music on his iPod that day—Curtis Mayfield, Bill Evans, Nine Inch Nails, Chet Baker, and a band I'd never heard of called Camper Van Beethoven, and the sound system in the Boxster was great, thanks to a subwoofer in the trunk.

He turned the music off. "I'd rather listen to you," he told me.

It was too cold for hiking. This didn't matter. I was happy to be sitting next to him in the car.

For the many years I'd lived on my own, except for when some man or other took me out, I had been the one at the wheel, though I was never a natural driver. I used to say when people asked me why I'd left New Hampshire for California that if I'd stayed there one more winter I would probably have died on the road, I'd had so many accidents driving in winter. California presented no issues with snow and ice, but I still clutched the wheel tightly and felt anxious on the highway, especially at night, though I was more careful now about wine, and no longer drove if I'd had anything to drink.

Jim loved to drive, and I loved being his passenger, with my feet on the dashboard, the position I'd assume every time we got in the car together from that day on. With Jim at the wheel—music playing, some that I knew and a lot of it unknown to me, but singing along anyway—I was no longer in charge, and I knew I was safe with the person who was. I could have stayed in that spot forever.

We drove out to Chimney Rock to see the elephant seals, and stood together on the cliffs, looking down at the crashing surf, listening to them playing in the water and calling out to each other with their strange, deep, guttural cries. A cormorant swooped overhead. How much richer it was, I reflected, to experience the world with a partner than, as I so often had, on my own.

Jim had brought his camera along that day. I learned that Jim always brought his camera, or a couple of them. Ever since boyhood— film cameras only in those days, of course, no digital—he had loved photography, and made a study of it. He knew light and lenses and composition, and because he was a lover of the outdoors and hiking, his passion found an easy expression there. But I think Jim's feeling about photography was about something more too. For Jim, an introvert, the camera provided a way to be in the world of people without necessarily having to say too much. When he sat at a table with friends, he listened closely, and he would always have interesting observations to contribute, though he was generally quieter than most. But he might also take out the camera, as I would see him do hundreds of times over the years. Once he did, he entered the world through that lens. After he'd captured his images he could disappear again at his laptop, deep into the editing.

That day, the fog made it a lousy day for shooting, but neither of us cared. We made our way to the town of Point Reyes Station and got oysters and wine. Two dozen, not the half dozen I might more economically have opted for.

That night I was scheduled to be part of a literary event at a little theater in Mill Valley. I hadn't planned on this, but on the way home I asked Jim if he'd like to come with me, so we went back to my house where I could change—he, unnecessarily concerned that he might not be well-dressed enough for the event—and headed to the theater together.

In the marriage of my youth, it seemed, I took up too much space, a phenomenon I'd been aware of all my life. I talked too much—and what I said was a little too direct for some tastes. I cooked messily, I laughed too boisterously, and when I danced, I occupied more room on the dance floor than some. I never intended to do this—in fact, I tried consciously to do otherwise—but it always happened, and when it did it was probably an irritation to some.

That night at the theater could have been one of those times, but it wasn't. I had worn a gold dress and heels that made me taller than Jim, a fact I registered briefly as I put them on, and then dismissed. If this man couldn't take it that I might look a little taller than he was, better to learn that now.

But he had reveled in the evening. He loved seeing me up on the stage, he told me. Driving us home from the theater and up the road to the mountain, he looked over at me in the seat next to him. "I was so proud to be with you," he said.

It was late, and he lived almost an hour's drive away in Oakland. (An hour if I were driving. Thirty-five minutes for Jim.)

Still, he came in and we sat on the couch together, close. We had spent more than fourteen hours in each other's company by this point and neither one of us had been bored.

"I need to tell you something," I said. "I've been seeing another man. I've been sleeping on his boat with him."

Everything stopped. Jim's arm, which had been around my shoulders, pulled back. For a surprising amount of time he said nothing.

"I'd better go home now," he said.

I told him I wanted to know him better, and that I had no intention, in telling him what I had, of saying good-bye. I just liked him way too much to deceive or mislead him.

"You are not the kind of person I'd have a fling with," I said.

"With you, it would be serious. I don't know if I can do that anymore. I would never want to hurt you."

I had done that in the past with people I'd loved.

Jim still sat there, head in his hands in a way that made it impossible to see his face. "I don't know what to say," he told me. A minute later, he was out the door and gone. I could hear the sound of the Boxster heading down the mountain.

The next morning there was an e-mail waiting for me again when I woke up, despite how early I got up. It was from Jim.

He couldn't see me again. He had begun to fall in love with me, he said. Had probably done that already. He could not risk having his heart broken. How he'd felt, driving home, had been bad enough.

He left the door open, but just barely. If I was ever truly free, he wrote, I should let him know. Maybe he would be free at that point too. (Though I knew this: He was a man who would find someone. Possibly not the right person, possibly not a person who would love him for the same reasons I might come to love him and did, but he would not be alone long.)

"You're a wonderful woman," he wrote. And then, "Goodbye."

I had no doubt then what to do. I picked up the phone.

"You're not making a good choice," I said. "And you're being unfair too."

I was fifty-seven years old, I reminded him. Almost fifty-eight. I'd known a lot of big losses. Was it such a surprising and unforgivable thing that after three dates—granted, long ones, very good ones—I should not yet feel ready to dive into the kind of relationship he wanted to have with me? And if I had done so—if I had been so quick to sign on—what might that have indicated about my capacity for constancy?

I could be with Martin, I told him, because being with Martin represented a far less complicated choice than being with Jim.

I did not say, in this conversation, that I was now ready to make the kind of commitment Jim wanted from me. I did not even say that I would cease spending time with Martin. What I said was that I believed he needed to give us more of a chance. I also told him that even if he did feel the need to end our relationship at this point, he should tell me face to face, not in the text of an e-mail.

We made a plan to get together the following Sunday. He would bring me to the de Young Museum, where he had a membership.

When we got there we heard music. It turned out there was a weekly swing dance gathering on Sundays just outside the museum.

Most of the dancers were clearly regulars. Many even wore special swing dance outfits and dancing shoes. When I suggested to Jim that we give it a try—we who knew none of the moves—he looked uneasy.

But that only lasted a second. He set down his backpack. We danced. Not well, but gamely, and with joyful abandon. And as with so much of what followed, I can see now in the story of those early days the evidence of who Jim was, and who he would be to me. Also who I would be to him: Jim, my cautious, steady partner, seldom the initiator of the big bold move, but invariably ready to come along when I suggested one, as I always did.

He spun me, and we even dipped. We danced only a couple of dances, but told each other we'd come back here another Sunday and learn to do this well. We had potential in the dancing department.

We did not end up going to the museum that afternoon. We took a walk through the park instead.

"I was supposed to have dinner with Martin on the boat tonight," I told Jim. (Martin, who had heard about Jim, same as Jim had heard about Martin. Martin, who had not seemed as troubled by Jim's presence in my life as Jim had appeared to be by Martin's.)

"I'm going to cancel the plan." I said. "I just want to spend my time with you now."

Nobody had a better smile than Jim, when he was deeply, purely happy. I saw it now.

"I want to tell you something else," I said to him. "I will not be having sex with you for thirty days."

The smile disappeared.

"What I'm suggesting is actually good news," I told him. "It means I'm taking this seriously."

What I hoped I might have with Jim would bear no resemblance to what had gone on with Doug—an unpleasant man—or with Martin—a good man. Or any of the others, some good and loving men, some not, with whom I'd spent my time over the more-than-twenty years I'd been on my own.

"I don't know what might be possible," I told him. "But I want to do this right for once."

We got in the Boxster then and headed for North Beach. Driving along the streets of San Francisco, Jim looked at me in the passenger seat again, with the worried expression his face bore too often.

"I'd better tell you," he said. "I'm not one of those rich San Francisco lawyers."

The Porsche was old. The watch, a gift from his former lover, Patrice. The Brooks Brothers suits, a necessity of his profession. Maybe he'd been that person once, for a time anyway—the kind of man he referred to as a swinging-dick attorney. But who he was, really, was a quiet man who played Led Zeppelin loud and liked to sleep under the stars of the Eastern Sierra. He could spend a whole day on a trail with his camera, or at his desk, editing photographs.

He had ridden on the Bacchus float in New Orleans in a blood-spattered George W. Bush "Mission Accomplished" costume. He read every book Richard Feynman ever wrote, and if he could, he'd quit estate litigation and work for some nonprofit doing environmental law. His days of big-money cases were behind him.

"Well, that's a relief," I told him. "That means you'll have more time for me."

9.

We spent most of those first thirty nights sleeping on an air mattress—arms wrapped around each other, but no more than that—outside on the deck of my house in Mill Valley, under the stars, with the fog over the mountain when we woke. After the thirty nights were over we moved inside to my bedroom. We slept naked. I liked to rest my palm on his stomach. My head on his shoulder.

Now and then Jim went back to Oakland, mostly to get clothes or legal papers, but almost every night from then on he was there on my doorstep by six thirty, setting down his briefcase to put his arms around me, always looking, as he stepped in, as though there were no place on earth he'd rather be. Sometimes he brought flowers; other times olives or cheese, and always wine. It always felt like a big event when I heard the sound of his Boxster coming up the hill.

For forty years I'd worked at home, in blue jeans mostly, or yoga pants. Now Jim was spending every night at my house on Mt. Tamalpais, and every afternoon before he was due to show up from work, I liked dressing up as if a great event were taking place, which for me it was. I put on velvet some nights, silk on others, and Jim never failed to notice when I did this. I loved making good dinners for the two of us, and we lit the candles and put music on and held each other's hand before we began the meal—a prayer with no words.

After, we'd clean up together and sometimes dance in the kitchen. We went to bed early, but first he had a ritual.

A beam spanned the length of the ceiling over my bed. Wearing nothing but his underwear, and sometimes nothing at all, Jim would stand on the bed and reach to grab hold of the beam to do pull-ups. Ten in the beginning. Later many more. I lay back on the pillows counting, sometimes in English, sometimes Spanish or French. Then he'd drop down onto the mattress. *My man*, I said. An unfamiliar concept.

We were sitting on my deck one late afternoon that fall. This was early still in our time together. I was growing deeply attached to Jim, but I was cautious too. This was not the burly lover I had imagined for myself, a fact I had explained to him. "You might be too short for me," I'd told him.

It was Fleet Week in San Francisco. This meant the Blue Angels flyers were in town, the amazing team of Navy fighter pilots who for three days leading up to the big event could be seen and heard flying at top speed in precision formation throughout the Bay Area. At this particular moment, the Blue Angels were roaring in a perfect V directly over Mt. Tamalpais.

"There's something so sexy about them," I told Jim.

For a moment Jim said nothing. Then he set down his cigar.

"Did you know one of the first qualifications for becoming a Blue Angel?" he said, looking at me with particular intensity.

I did not.

"They have to be five foot eight or under. They're tough as nails but they're little guys."

My five-foot-eight-inch tall lover did not say more or need to.

10.

An event I loved took place every October in San Francisco—always the first weekend of that month. An exceedingly rich and generous man by the name of Warren Hellman—a billionaire financier who also happened to be a banjo player and a lover of folk and roots music—had started a free three-day music festival in Golden Gate Park called Hardly Strictly Bluegrass. In fact, the festival featured much more than bluegrass music; I'd heard Elvis Costello perform there, and Patti Smith. Emmylou Harris, always.

Jim and I had just passed the one-month anniversary of our meeting when the festival weekend took place. Though he was more of a rock-and-roll man than a folk type, there was no question we were going to this together.

I never missed that festival. Over the years, as the crowds grew and the number of acts increased, I had developed an elaborate strategy for taking in those three days in a way that allowed me to hear as much music as possible. I'd pack a picnic basket for the day and arrive a few hours before the music got under way. I left picnic blankets at three or four different stages, with a folding chair positioned in at least a couple of the spots, to hold my place. By early afternoon the crowds were huge, but I was one to push through firmly, no matter how tight the space. After—when I'd gotten to my spot, sometimes with friends, sometimes alone—I'd take out the wine and cheese. Sometimes I'd get up and dance on the grass. Then, as the music ended, I'd grab my backpack and hightail it to the next stage, pushing through the crowd once again. I moved fast through the crowd, with no one slowing me down.

That first October I went to Hardly Strictly Bluegrass with Jim, who knew nothing of the festival before. A distance runner, always sturdy and agile, Jim was never the type to push through a crowd as I did, and I worried he might not be able to keep up with me. As I wove through the wall of bodies—leading the way, less by virtue of muscle than resolve—I looked back now and then for the sign of his hat. He was always there, a few steps behind. He never lost sight of me.

I think it was seeing how gamely Jim made his way through the crowds to keep up with me that weekend, how ready he always was to come along with me on whatever adventure I cooked up—that made me realize I loved him. In all my years, I'd never known the experience of looking back over my shoulder to see a man there, bringing up the rear. Or in the seat next to me driving us safely home. I never fully understood the phrase "he has my back" until I met Jim.

"I'm your guard dog," he told me. I'd never had one of those before, either.

That fall was the honeymoon time for us. Every day we woke up in each other's arms and told each other how lucky we were. We'd waited a long time to find each other.

MONTHS BEFORE MEETING Jim, my French publisher had purchased the rights to bring out a translation of my memoir, *At Home in the World*. (*Et Devant Moi, Le Monde*, the title in French.) It turned out that my books had become surprisingly popular in France. Now I was invited to spend a full week at a hotel in Paris to promote the book.

The trip was scheduled for mid-October. Though my last attempt at inviting a man to accompany me to Europe had been a disaster, I invited Jim to come with me.

It had been twenty years since I'd been to France—with my daughter Audrey, when she was a teenage exchange student. This would be a different kind of trip. Interviews were lined up almost round the clock, though there would be time in the evening for Jim and me to go out for dinner and walk through the streets.

It was a setup for big romance, of course. We stayed at a lovely little hotel in St. Germain featuring a sunroom where we started every morning with a basket of croissants and fresh-squeezed orange juice and very good coffee.

In my old days I would have been out the door to explore the city by eight A.M. if not earlier. It was a new experience for me to linger over our coffee as we did. Jim was an early riser like me, and like me possessed no shortage of energy. But he had a capacity to relax that I had never acquired. With Jim, I could slow down at last.

Still, we got around the city that week. Jim had his camera, as he always did, and though he loved Paris too, he made me his chief subject. He took a few hundred pictures—at the Café Deux Magots, in front of the giant clock at the Musée D'Orsay, the garden of the Rodin Museum, the walkways along the Seine and in the subway, mugging in front of a poster of three monkeys (see no evil, hear no evil, speak no evil). My favorite of these photographs Jim took of me was made in the Tuileries, just after we'd emerged from a show of photographs by Diane Arbus, which had inspired me to affect the dark and troubled look of an Arbus subject, or possibly Diane Arbus herself. Long past the age when I would have served as anybody else's fashion model, I was that for Jim, sucking in my cheeks, slouching moodily for the camera, tousling my hair—the same thing I liked to do with his. In the most romantic city in the world, perhaps, we were a pair of late middle-aged lovers giving ourselves permission to behave as if we were very young. But the wisdom acquired through age allowed us to recognize, as the young might not, how precious it all was. We had gotten our order in just as the bartender announced the last call.

After Paris, we rented a car and drove to Provence. We drank a bottle of wine every night, and sometimes a glass at lunch. We bought runny cheese in the market and figs and good pastries that we shared in the car, driving from one gorgeous village to the next, with the top down on our rented convertible. We were Albert Finney and Audrey Hepburn in *Two for the Road*. The sun shone every day.

Two weeks after Paris, we celebrated my fifty-eighth birthday. Jim took me out for dinner in San Francisco. Driving across the Golden Gate Bridge in his silver Porsche past the palace of the Legion of Honor, the gold dome of City Hall, the Opera, I saw our life before us like the glittering waters of San Francisco Bay, dotted with sailboats. Here was the life I had dreamed I might know one day—the picture I'd constructed over my many years alone of what a perfect relationship would look like. Music and dancing, good meals and a drive home with the top down, to climb into bed. We were tourists in the country of love.

11.

It wasn't perfect, of course. But even our difficulties, or what I thought of then as difficulties, were the kind you have to be lucky to experience. I wanted Jim to talk more and spend less time on his laptop. I wanted him to take more time off from work, and to go to the beach with me instead of sitting at his desk studying legal briefs.

Sometimes we argued, and when we did, I discovered what a low tolerance he had for anything that felt to him like criticism or—as he perceived it—an attack. What in my mind constituted lively, constructive discussion felt to Jim—the son of a man who had cut him down relentlessly throughout his childhood—like a threat.

One night, in the middle of one such exchange (a discussion, in my eyes; in his, a fight) he had gotten up from the table, picked up his briefcase and moved toward the door. "I'm going home now," he said.

Home being the house that had been sitting mostly empty in the Oakland hills. It was eleven o'clock at night.

But he didn't leave. He stayed to talk things out. Years of failure for each of us in our past relationships—times we'd let anger or pride or stubbornness obscure what mattered most—had taught us plenty, and as much as I sometimes found myself wishing I'd met Jim when I was thirty-five, or forty-five, or fifty, even, I doubt that my younger self would have possessed the wisdom or humility to get past all the ways our flesh-and-blood relationship fell short of my dreams and do the work of making it stronger. The concepts of compromise, adaptation, and acceptance were new to me. But Jim was a peacemaker—a man who sought to locate the common ground, or the meeting place, anyway, that would keep his clients out of court. Now at home, he practiced this skill. Slowly, I got better at it.

I had lived on my own for many years and worked alone writing my books, in a house where—once my children left—nobody was around to get in the way. Some years back, on a visit west from a very good and loving man, David, with whom I had tried to make a long-distance relationship, I had exploded at him once for his request that before I head to my desk to work in the early morning hours, I tell him "Good morning."

"I might not want to say 'Good morning,'" I snapped. "It might break my concentration."

In the end I said the words he'd wanted to hear from me, then sat at my laptop, irritated, fuming, for a full half hour—accomplishing nothing—reflecting on how demanding David had been, and how impossible the relationship was.

Now there was a man living with me, not merely paying occasional visits. I wanted him there, but on my terms. As a woman whose only designer-label clothing made its way to my wardrobe through the auspices of some thrift shop, I had come up short on closet space even before Jim entered my life. Once he had, I'd given him a box to store his pants and shirts—his shoes, even—and a couple of hooks for his ties. One or two suits made it onto the rack. No more than that.

Every morning when he got dressed for work, and not without a certain wry amusement (amusement, not complaint), Jim had examined the contents of his box and taken from it, uncomplaining, whatever he needed to wear into San Francisco that day.

At the time, this was my idea of how to have a man in my life. I'd wrap my legs around him all night long, but all the stuff of his life (shoes, shirts, underwear, socks) would remain in the corner, so as not to disturb the life I'd made for myself.

I got the closet. He got the box.

It was because of this, I think, that he sometimes made the round trip to Oakland and back, all on a Saturday morning, just to pick up a particular fleece or a suit. And then I gave him a hard time about wasting so much time driving. You could have called me insufferable, but he never did.

He liked the drive. He probably needed that time alone in the Boxster, playing Social Distortion at top volume. I loved him, but I never let up on him. My demands were many. My expectations high. He hardly ever complained.

I also know I was blaming Jim at this point for a problem that had nothing to do with him. For a long time I'd been having difficulty writing, having been unable to work much for nearly the entire time the girls lived with me. Now that Jim was in my life—happily so, mostly, but distractingly too—I was dangerously behind in my work.

In mid-November I placed a call to an artists' retreat center in Virginia I'd gone to in the past, to ask if they might fit me in. They called me back to say there was an unexpected three-week opening, starting the following Saturday.

Ten minutes later I'd bought my plane ticket.

That night I told Jim I'd be going away to write. He didn't question my choice or the fact that I had not consulted him. He even told me he was happy for me that I'd gotten this opportunity. It's only now that I can look back and realize the disappointment he must have felt at my leaving. Not at my desire to work, or my making work a priority. It must have made him sad, that I still saw my life as divided in this way. There was my time with him, and my time with my work, and I could not yet envision a truly integrated life, where the work might have been accomplished without my having to go someplace else to do it.

Between November of 2011 and the following May, I left many times. I went to Virginia and to New York and Guatemala and New Hampshire, and Virginia again. I rented a cabin in Guerneville once—the kind of place a couple might go for a romantic getaway. I went alone.

I loved Jim. But I had never had a man in my life before who was so totally committed to being with me, and I didn't know what to do with it. I loved it that he was part of my life now. I loved it that when my plane landed in Oakland, or San Francisco, he was always there in the Boxster, or if I had a lot of luggage, the Prius, waiting in the cell phone parking lot for my call. Then he'd speed over to whatever airline door I'd be standing at on the sidewalk, and leap out to pick up my bag. Never without wrapping his arms around me first.

If he'd gotten a haircut in my absence, I gave him a hard time about that. I always wanted him to grow his hair longer, and to let it be a little less tidily groomed. I'd reach across the seat and tousle it up, then kiss him again.

But there was this other part of me that felt a need to run away, be alone, with nobody's needs but my own to consider. I'd love him like crazy when I was around. I'd take off on some plane or other when it suited me, happy in the knowledge that when I returned, Jim would be there waiting for me.

12.

At the point when I met Jim, in the fall of 2011, he was practicing estate and trust litigation—his field of specialty for
most of the thirty-five years of his career up to that point—at a firm
in San Francisco. He was good at that, but he was restless too.

Although from a young age he'd been passionate about politics
and social justice, he'd made the choice early on in his career to go
into a field that would ensure a good living for his family, and he
did that—first in corporate law and later in a series of smaller firms.
It was in the course of his practice that he met Patrice.

At the point Jim and Patrice met, he and his wife had been
married for sixteen years; they had three young children. He had
been raised to believe that a man stayed with the woman he married,
no matter what; but he was deeply unhappy and lonely in that
marriage, and alienated, too, from the church that had brought him
and his wife together—a church whose rigid and punitive struc-
tures he had tried to embrace but no longer could.

Jim had told me the story. Like him, Patrice was an attorney,
about Jim's age. She was beautiful, and very smart, and crazy about
Jim. The two of them never ran out of things to talk about—ideas,
politics, the law. Jim's sharp, wry humor was an important aspect of
who he was, but in the years of his marriage, he had come to keep
that part under wraps.

"That was one of the things I loved about her," Jim said, of
Patrice. "She got my jokes. I could always make her laugh."

They were just friends, he told himself. But he fell in love
with her.

They did not have an affair. Not that he didn't think about this. He just couldn't allow himself to act on it. He was a man who still attended Bible study every Tuesday evening, raised to believe that divorce was a total failure of character.

He told his wife he had to leave, gave her the house, and moved into a little apartment, where his children came on weekends.

He and Patrice got together. The two of them started a law firm, and it turned out they were perfectly matched as law partners. They earned a reputation for winning, and they made a lot of money. They had some great times spending it, traveling to glamorous, romantic places all over the world together, then flying home to take on the next case.

Back when Jim had left his marriage, his older son—age eight at the time—had told Jim that if he ever saw his father with another woman besides his mother he'd never speak to him again, and Jim honored this edict, he told me, over the entire nineteen years that constituted his romantic relationship with Patrice. Sometimes they talked about getting married, but they maintained separate homes, and never lived together. In the end, Jim explained to me, it was Patrice's difficulties with his children, and theirs with her, that had ended the relationship.

Even before the breakup of their personal relationship, however, their law partnership had ended. (*Imploded* was the word Jim used.) He had joined a more conventional firm specializing in estate law, and though he did well enough and made a reasonable income, he never again experienced anything like the success of those days with Patrice.

Once, walking near Jackson Square in San Francisco, Jim had pointed to a bronze medallion set into the sidewalk. On closer examination I saw the names cast into the bronze: Jim's and that of Patrice, memorialized on the streets of San Francisco. Whatever it cost to buy that medallion was probably nothing for the two of them in those days.

The firm where Jim worked after he and Patrice dissolved their relationship—though not free from stress—was no doubt a calmer work environment than Jim's two-person firm. He had colleagues there he liked and respected. But it held little of the old excitement. The great days of six-figure settlements were behind him.

It was during this time that Jim embarked on a project about which he told almost nobody. He went back to law school, nights, at Golden Gate University. Over the course of a few years of night classes, he earned a degree in environmental law. He had a dream of one day leaving the world of estate law and its bitter fights over money and applying his skills instead toward protecting land, water, air.

There wasn't much money in this—at least, not for an attorney wanting to work on the public interest side. And the jobs for a newly minted sixty-year-old environmental attorney were few.

The spring after we met, Jim made the decision to pull out of the estate law firm in the city and set up a solo practice in San Francisco. He rented an office space and printed cards. And waited for the clients to call.

Jim was never a schmoozer or a marketer. Though he had many friends in the legal community of San Francisco, the task of setting up a firm, solo—without benefit of a legal assistant or secretary or a team of colleagues—proved more daunting than he had anticipated. Though I would have said there was no subject we didn't talk about, he told me very little about this. I just saw it on his face. Worried about money and clients, he did his own filing now, but the papers piled up on his desk. He set up a website and made sure his ranking as a Super Lawyer was up to date, and he let old friends know he was out on his own now. But Jim wasn't a rainmaker. The glory days and big money he'd known in his practice with Patrice appeared to be over.

13.

One day the phone rang. Jim told me the story over dinner that night.

A young medical student by the name of Samuel Nwanu had contacted him—referred by another attorney who'd turned down his case, as several already had. By the time he got Jim's name, he was running out of options.

Samuel Nwanu had recently been kicked out of medical school one semester shy of graduating with his medical degree. He believed he had grounds for a lawsuit. Short of this, he wanted to fight for reinstatement.

Samuel had grown up in Nigeria—not in the capital of Lagos, but in the bush, where he lived without electricity or running water and attended a school that had no books or paper. Raised chiefly by his grandmother, he'd been schooled since he was very small in the properties of the many medicinal herbs that grew around his small village. The memories of walking through the bush with her as she pointed these out remained a powerful influence.

An ambitious student, Samuel managed to get to Lagos, where he gained entrance to a good school. His country was filled with young people who had struggled to get an education, only to find they had no way to put their schooling to use once they received their diploma.

"Why do you think you get all those scam letters from Nigeria?" he had told Jim. "Those people don't have anything better to do."

But Samuel set his sights on the United States. When he was eighteen a friend entered his name in a lottery whose prize was a

U.S. visa, and he won. To help Samuel come up with the ticket, every farmer and shepherd in his village contributed whatever meager sum they could. His father rode the bus from their village to the capital carrying this money in his lap—a giant sack of coins that he set on the counter at a travel agency to purchase Samuel's one-way ticket to San Francisco, where the family knew of a young Nigerian man who was attending college in nearby San Jose.

Samuel arrived speaking no English, though he taught himself fast. He got a job, and as soon as his English was good enough, gained entrance to San Jose State. Over the next four years he earned an engineering degree and got a good job in Silicon Valley. He was well paid. He sent money home regularly.

But on a flight to New York City, he found himself sitting next to a young pediatrician. He talked with her the whole five hours, and by the time he landed he was convinced—despite having just spent four years earning his engineering degree—that he should go to medical school.

Back he went to San Jose State for more science classes in preparation for the medical boards. When his scores on those proved low, he took another year of classes and tried again.

Now came the surprising part of the story. Out of all the medical schools to which Samuel had applied—including several that accepted him—one had displayed sufficient enthusiasm to offer him a big scholarship and actively encourage him to attend. This was one of the top medical schools in the country.

Samuel did not feel confident that he was equipped to attend such a competitive school, particularly after meeting a young Harvard graduate who'd been turned down there with scores vastly surpassing his own.

The admissions team assured him they'd help him with the first year of his studies, which were bound to be unusually rough for a person of his background.

As he expected, he did poorly that first term, but his advisors told him not to worry. They'd help him get through this.

Samuel may have been operating at a significant disadvantage compared to his fellow students, but no one could have been more determined. Only then another challenge presented itself: a series of alarming symptoms that compromised his eyesight and his ability to walk. Diagnosed initially with severe stress, he took a leave of absence. It was months later that Samuel finally received the correct diagnosis for his problem: a rare form of MS.

He was put on medications—astronomically expensive, though paid for as a result of his student status. This got his medical condition largely under control. He was a third-year student now. Struggling, but getting by, he told us, though there was one administrator at the school who made it clear she wanted to get rid of him.

It was the fourth year—the last—that did him in. This was the stage in a student's medical training when he was placed on actual hospital rotations and given the responsibility to work with patients, though always overseen by interns and residents and med school faculty.

Here, Samuel's record was hard to understand. A few of his superiors spoke glowingly of his compassion and gentleness with patients, and on a couple of occasions it appeared he had actually identified a significant factor in a case that others had overlooked.

But other reports of Samuel's performance on rotation—particularly those of a couple of prominent faculty members who had been critical of Samuel since his early days at med school—now spoke of him as an individual who should never hold a medical degree. One superior spoke of Samuel's curious inability to make eye contact with patients. (A behavior, Samuel later explained to me, that had to do with customs in Nigeria, where to look a person in the eye would be considered disrespectful.)

Another evaluation in Samuel's file referred to an attending physician's difficulty in understanding what he was saying due to Samuel's strong accent. Mention was made too of Samuel's having referred in his medical practice to highly nontraditional methods of treatment employed in Nigeria—like herbal medicine. Most damning of all was an account, by one superior, of an interaction in which Samuel spoke with the family of a terminal patient in a manner suggesting that death was a natural part of the life cycle, a view easily accepted in the culture in which Samuel was raised but frowned upon on the wards of the hospital where he'd been on rotation.

The result of all this was crushing. Not only would Samuel be denied the dream of receiving his med school diploma that June (an event for which his entire family and village stood ready to celebrate back in Nigeria, unaware of any difficulty), but worse yet, the institution would place in his file the irrevocable opinion that he was not suitable for admission in any other medical program in the country. From his many years' pursuit of his dream to become a doctor, he would emerge with nothing but a gigantic medical school debt. That, and a diagnosis of MS, the medication for which he could no longer afford now that he was no longer enrolled at the medical school.

Without this medication, his doctor had suggested, Samuel was likely to become seriously ill within a handful of years.

Jim related this story to me over our nightly candlelight dinner, and by the time he finished I was begging him to take the case of Samuel Nwanu.

"You don't understand," Jim said. "It's not just that the guy has no money. This is an unwinnable case. It won't even be fought in a regular court of law. The lawyer here would have to argue his case before the med school oversight committee, and there is no way they're going to rule against their own highest-ranking people. Not to mention, this isn't even my field of expertise."

"If you don't help this young man, who will?" I asked. But I knew the answer.

"I can't afford to take this on," Jim told me. "I haven't got a single paying client right now. Everything's contingency. And not much on the table, at best."

"I'll help you," I said. "I'll work as your assistant on this one."

Two days later, I drove into San Francisco, headed to Jim's office. In the elevator heading up with me was a very handsome black man, dressed in a beautiful white shirt, perfectly pressed. This was Samuel Nwanu. Every time I met with him, he was wearing that same one shirt. He must have washed it every night and hung it out to dry for morning.

In the weeks that followed, Jim and I spent dozens of hours on the case. I served as the investigator, sitting with Samuel in coffee shops, taking notes on his story. Jim worked on the legal part and followed up on potential witnesses willing to testify on Samuel's behalf and researched precedents.

Over the course of this period, I set my work aside for our case. For Jim's part, with few other clients, he had all too much time for Samuel, but even so, he was getting up at four in the morning now—three, sometimes—to prepare.

As costly as it was to me—not to mention to Jim—part of me loved this. Sitting with Samuel over those long hours, taking down the details of his long struggle, I felt an old familiar but too-long-dormant fire that came from doing something I believed might truly matter for an individual in dire need. Most of all, I loved being part of a team with Jim, who—despite my complete lack of legal education—listened to every one of my ideas with interest and respect.

My hours in the company of Samuel Nwanu persuaded me that a grave injustice had been done. From a distance of years, many of the particulars now escape me, but I remember passages from the letters and e-mails Jim procured from Samuel's medical school records making reference to Samuel's allegedly inferior intelligence, and calling into question whether a person with his unsophisticated background belonged at a school of this caliber in the first place. In one letter his acknowledged tenacity and work ethic were cited as an example of what a person like Samuel must have trained himself to do, as compensation for a lack of intellectual skills—the virtue of his work ethic transformed into proof of a liability.

The morning Samuel's case was to be heard by the medical school board, Jim and I were out of bed even earlier than usual to pack up his files and drive into the city together. I had picked out for myself a rare example of a conservative suit. Jim already owned plenty of those.

"Don't have any illusions about this, sweetheart," he told me grimly, as we crossed the street to the building where Jim would be arguing Samuel's case. "This is a kamikaze mission. We're going down. The best we can do here is give Samuel a chance to be heard." Jim deeply believed in that right.

However, once in that windowless room where the group hearing the case would assemble, everything changed in Jim's demeanor. He became the attorney he must have been in all those cases with Patrice in which millions of dollars of estate proceeds were at stake. He opened his briefcase, set out his yellow pad and pens and the file he'd assembled that was by now over a foot thick. He had introduced me, in as low key a manner as possible, as his legal assistant, in attendance to offer materials and notes as needed. He had told me already that if I had anything to contribute, I should write it on my pad and pass it to him.

Samuel was late. The presiding administrator checked her watch again.

"My client will be here any minute," Jim said, his voice level, but I knew he was worried.

"We'll give him three more minutes," the administrator said. "After that, this case will be dismissed."

Jim sent me out into the hall to make a call to Samuel. Two minutes later he showed up—in the beautiful white shirt as always, and looking as cool as he might if he were attending a lecture on suture techniques or performing a tracheotomy.

The presentations began. The issue: Samuel's dismissal—without honor, or the opportunity to receive credit for his schooling. Jim's motion: to reinstate him, but with the fallback position that while the school might be unwilling to rescind its dismissal, it would not get in the way of his applying to other medical programs.

Looking back now on Jim's presentation of Samuel Nwanu's case—a period that lasted less than three hours, start to finish, though weeks of preparation had gone into this—it is a source of some amazement to me that this was the one time, ever, that I got to actually hear Jim argue a case. The fact that it should have happened there, at a table of stone-faced medical administrators who gave all indication of having made up their minds about Samuel's future long before they entered the room, is a source of both regret but also pride in Jim.

He had prepared for this case no differently from how he might have prepared—and in times past, how he *had* prepared—for more seemingly important clients, with large amounts of money at stake. His arguments and presentation of the evidence, when he began to speak, were delivered with all the same gravitas and sober, finely articulated grace and knowledge of the law. To me that day, he was like those soldiers at the Battle of the Somme, crouched in his trench, awaiting certainty barrage of German gunfire and certain death, but holding his ground.

At every point in the morning, however, it seemed to me that the medical school administrators displayed an attitude of boredom, condescension, and dismissiveness. None more so than the presiding officer—a woman whose reports on the subject of Samuel's short-comings as a medical student had formed the cornerstone of the case against him. As she launched into her speech about his total unpreparedness for the medical profession—having made the sugges-tion earlier that he consider massage therapy, or chiropractic—an odd smile came over her face.

When it was Jim's turn to respond, I handed him a series of one-line suggestions based on my familiarity with Samuel's file— testimony that contradicted the administrator's, or called certain aspects of it into question anyway, and contradictory testimony from other physicians with a higher opinion of Samuel.

The presiding medical officer brushed these aside, looking at her watch. "We're going to need to wrap this up," she said.

"You know what this is?" I wrote on the note I handed next to Jim. "*A mind fuck.*"

In all my years, I had never employed that phrase. The fact that I did now spoke to my utter frustration and a sense of wild injus-tice, as well as futility. Beside me in his Brooks Brothers suit, Jim's eyes scanned my note.

"You know what this is?" he said to the assembled group. "A mind fuck."

Everyone in the room froze. So did Jim. In his thirty-five years of practicing law, he had never spoken that word in any legal proceeding, or anywhere else for that matter. He might as well have pulled down his pants and mooned the assembled gathering. The effect would have been no more shocking. To nobody more than himself.

The hearing ended soon after this. No need for time to deliberate. The vote on the future of Samuel Nwanu took all of one minute, and with the exception of a single low-level administrator, it was unanimous. Samuel would not be receiving credit for his three and a half years of grueling study at medical school. The recommendation that no other medical school should accept him would remain a part of his file.

After it was over, the three of us sat in a coffee shop and talked of Samuel's plans for the future. He would go to Guatemala, he said (not far from my house there, as it turned out), to study Spanish, with the hope of attending medical school in Cuba once he had the new language down. Or possibly he'd go to Mexico. First, though, he would need to deliver the news to his family, and all the other villagers back in Nigeria awaiting the news of his imminent graduation from medical school, that he would not be returning home, triumphant, with his medical degree.

Before we parted, Samuel thanked us both for all we had done for him and paid for our coffee. We hugged each other and set out on our way.

A few weeks later, Jim received a formal letter from some board of legal oversight or other with the news that he had been formally reported for inappropriate language at a medical school proceeding where he had been acting as counsel. Mention was made of some form of censure, but none occurred.

But this came later. That night when we were back home at the end of the day, and we'd taken off our suits and gotten back into our blue jeans, and we were sitting at the table again sharing our pasta and salad—the candles lit, the music playing, the wine poured—I asked Jim what had got into him, that he had actually uttered the words I'd scrawled on my legal pad.

"I guess I have such a high regard for you," he said, "that I just picked up the paper and read the words out loud. If you wrote it, that was enough for me.

"We were going to lose anyway," he said. "At least we went down in flames."

14.

We traveled to France again, for another book tour. Times we were home, Jim kept working on setting up his new solo law practice, but he made time for another trip to New Hampshire with me. He brought me to the ballet. I brought him to see the Alvin Ailey company. We made meals together for friends and rode our bikes. Sometimes Jim brought his bass to the house of his friend Jerry in Sausalito to play music with his friends there. We drank wine and ate oysters and sometimes, on rainy afternoons, with a fire in the fireplace and a big bowl of popcorn between us, we watched three episodes in a row of *Breaking Bad*.

I looked at pictures of rescue dogs online. Jim researched environmental law positions. We climbed Mt. Tamalpais and hiked in Point Reyes and came upon the herd of tule elk that wandered there. Wherever we went, he took pictures. "How lucky can two people get?" we said to each other.

15.

That spring I got some very good news. The long-delayed film adaptation of my novel, *Labor Day*—a project whose future had been uncertain for a while—was set to begin filming in June. This meant that I'd be getting a big check, and could feel a lot less anxious about my finances. Not to mention the excitement I felt at seeing the story I wrote adapted as a movie, with Josh Brolin and Kate Winslet as the stars and Jason Reitman the director.

Nobody celebrated this news more than Jim, and as he did I reflected that in all the years, nobody—not even my parents—had celebrated my successes the way he did.

Long ago, when I was married the first time and raising small children on our old farm, I'd been invited to fly to Portland, Oregon, to give a speech, and when I got there I'd discovered that over a thousand people had shown up to hear me. When I called home that night to tell my husband, he said to me, "Just don't come back with a swelled head."

Jim, learning about the movie, had demonstrated more pride than he might have for any victory of his own in the courtroom.

At moments like this one, he always looked out for me too—studying the contracts that I had only skimmed over, keeping careful files of them all, whereas in my old days I'd never been able to lay a hand on any paperwork.

"You have a guard dog now," he said. His frequent refrain.

That May, Jim bought a motorcycle. It was a Triumph Bonneville, a classic design recently brought back into production.

He signed up for motorcycle school, and it turned out, not

surprisingly, given his affinity for driving cars, that he was a very good student.

"What if we rode across country on the Triumph?" he said one morning. He had earned his motorcycle license just weeks before.

We bought a set of saddlebags and begin plotting a route, but in the end common sense overtook us, and we both concluded that trip would be too much for a new rider—even Jim—and too much for a new passenger. Left to his own devices he might well have pursued the trip, but he would not have put me at any risk. So we came up with a different plan.

In nearly forty years he had seldom if ever taken more than a week off for a vacation. But we decided to ship the motorcycle to the East Coast and ride it there. I could introduce him to the part of the country I came from and the part I still loved best, New England, and to my friends there. We would swim in lakes, ponds, and the Atlantic; we would climb Mt. Monadnock. I would bring him to the waterfall down the road from the farm where my children were born.

Before we left home on this trip, I had called a *New York Times* editor for whom I sometimes wrote with the suggestion of a story for the magazine. Suppose I wrote about our summer-long New England road trip, I told him. My boyfriend—*boyfriend*, an odd term for Jim—could take the pictures.

My editor seemed interested but cautious. Plenty of people said their partner took great pictures, but that didn't necessarily mean their work would be publishable in the *New York Times*.

I sent him examples of Jim's work. (As he always did, when dealing with an issue involving his photography, Jim took extraordinary, sometimes maddening care with his images before he could share them. The day I asked him to put together a few of his photographs to show the magazine, he'd ended up spending the whole weekend choosing them and then another few hours of editing to make them better.)

We got the assignment. I'd write the story of our adventure. Jim would take the pictures. I doubt any legal case Jim ever took on gave him more joy than that assignment did.

Amazingly, too, Jim was up for taking off not just a few weeks or a month, but the whole summer to do this. Once he made that commitment, I expanded our plan. We would visit my daughter, Audrey, of course, and the movie set in Shelburne, Massachusetts, where *Labor Day* was being filmed. I had heard about a photography school in mid-coast Maine and showed Jim the online catalogue of their courses. He spent hours studying it before choosing two: environmental photography and (with the thought that one day he might actually manage to shoot the photographs for stories I'd write) travel photography. Altogether, he'd take two full weeks of classes in the little town of Rockport, Maine.

I rented a house there for the duration of photography school that July, and for August, a cabin on the shores of a place I knew well and loved in New Hampshire, Silver Lake—a place with wood-paneled walls and blueberry bushes and a screen porch and a dock where we could sit together and read or talk or play cards. No Internet, and no need for it. If we had to get a message out we'd head down the road to the general store in town.

As much as I loved riding on the back of Jim's motorcycle, we decided we also needed a car that summer. On the Maine Craigslist I found a listing for a 1992 Chrysler LeBaron convertible—cherry red—for $1,800. Sight unseen, we bought it. The LeBaron was a far cry from the sleek Boxster, but we didn't mind. We were always happy heading out on a road together, preferably a two-lane.

Over the course of that summer Jim took hundreds of photographs for our *New York Times* assignment. Many times a day we'd pull over by the side of the road to capture an image—a giant, weathered road sign featuring a Maine lobsterman, under which I posed myself. A lighthouse, a stretch of rocky shore, the boathouse at the wonderful Silver Lake cabin and the dock there, where he'd sit with his cigar and we'd listen to the loons.

It was on that dock one night that summer—having dinner with my daughter and her boyfriend, the sun just setting over the trees, a perfect night—that the topic of our old farm had come up. The one that used to be mine, that belonged to my ex-husband now.

"You should have a place in New Hampshire again, Mom," Audrey said. "You love it here so much. Maybe this is where you really belong."

Sometimes I felt the same. I mentioned a place I'd looked at. A little cabin on a half-acre of land. In her opinion, Audrey said, the neighbors there were a little close for comfort. Not to mention the place was a dump.

An old bitterness flared to the surface then. "Maybe I can't afford a farmhouse with a pond and fifty acres on my own road like what some people have"—I was speaking of her father—"where they get to name the road after themselves and start their own yoga studio," I said to her.

I could feel it happening: my old downward spiral of anger over my divorce. Here came the bitterness that had eaten me up for a couple of decades, that I had hoped I was done with by now. It overtook me like a sudden, virulent fever.

I could feel Jim's hand on mine then, his other arm circling my shoulders. *Careful. Careful.* Easy now.

In the past, when this kind of moment occurred—and they had—I might have gone the other direction: might have wept, or delivered some big speech, poured myself a glass of wine or poured it over my head, maybe. This time I stopped myself.

This was new for me. Though I was not completely safe yet. I could still feel my heart beating too fast. Then slowing down. My breath returning to normal.

I stood up. Though I was wearing nothing underneath it, I pulled my dress over my head. "Namaste," I said. And dove into the lake.

Jim stood on the dock with the others, watching me swim around the point. Until I returned, I knew, he'd have his eyes on the water.

Sometimes I was actually impatient with how cautious he was, how protective—the way he made sure I buckled my seat belt, examined the tread on my tires. I had never had a man at my side as I did now. I never knew a man so fierce in his constancy, or steadfast in his love.

16.

ore miles. A lot of them. We drove to Cape Cod and took a ferry to Martha's Vineyard, where we rented a Jeep and drove to the far end of the island to watch the sunset and share a basket of clams. We drove to the White Mountains, and to Rhode Island, and to Vermont, where we attended a drive-in, seated in the LeBaron with the top down, the stars offering a better show than what was up on the screen.

Sometimes that summer, we drove the LeBaron. Sometimes the Triumph. I loved the bike for how it felt whipping down some road or other with my arms wrapped tight around Jim's chest. He may have been a new rider but I always felt safe with him there.

But I loved the LeBaron for the long conversations we got to have as we covered the miles together. Somewhere in southwestern New Hampshire one day, I had started talking with him in the voice of a woman named Wanda, discussing with her husband—this would be Jim—her desire to acquire a pet ferret. Unprompted by me, Jim took on the persona of Buddy, her long-suffering spouse. Crossing over into Vermont that night, we were still Wanda and Buddy, and at odd moments over the weeks the two characters continued to drop in, or their voices did. Or we were British rockers, or Dumpster-diving hobos, or New York social-register types, debating which variety of oyster we favored. Jim never thought up the games, but he knew how to play them.

In Vermont we swam in a quarry and stopped for diner pie and shopped for souvenirs at a prison craft store and made our way through a corn maze, where I briefly got lost until Jim rescued me.

We went to a contra dance in Nelson, New Hampshire, and ate lobster rolls in Kittery, Maine, and more lobster in Damariscotta, and Brunswick, and Portland. Wherever we went, Jim took out his Nikon. Every night before bed, he did his pushups while I counted them out.

Jim had one of his best times ever at the photography school, so much so that it was hard for me to get him away from the computer sometimes, because he was consumed with editing his images. But we made day trips on the weekends too—to the town in Maine that had inspired my favorite picture book (after *Goodnight Moon*), *Blueberries for Sal*, and to the White Mountains, and to a place near Mt. Katahdin called Gulf Hagas known as the Grand Canyon of Maine. Wherever we went we met up with friends, and when we did, they always said the same thing:

What a wonderful man you found. How lucky you are.

After the photography school ended we rode to Acadia National Park. On our third day, walking along the northern Atlantic coastline, Jim fell on the slick rocks. He knew from the pain that he'd broken a rib—a couple of them, probably—but he was the only one of us who could ride the Triumph, so he drove the hundred miles to my old friend Becky's cottage on Mousam Lake, with me following behind in the LeBaron.

Becky gave Jim whiskey for the pain—one shot, then three more. Then we sat on the screen porch with her son and daughter and her son-in-law, eating fresh-picked corn and, after, strawberry shortcake with strawberries she'd picked that afternoon, and biscuits baked in her old cast-iron stove. Jim was a little drunk from the whiskey, and still in pain, but it didn't stop him from taking pictures of the sun setting over the lake that night, and the six of us playing Taboo around the table and laughing. When darkness fell, I jumped into the lake—no suit required. Jim followed after me, never mind the broken ribs.

It was one of those nights where you could see every star. From where we lay on our backs in the water, Jim pointed out lesser-known constellations, and the faint red glow that was Jupiter. "Can you believe it? I'm in the lake with my boyfriend," I called out to Becky. Always before, when I swam at night, I swam alone.

My visit to Mousam Lake was a tradition I'd held for years but never shared with anyone. Jim—though he had never been to Maine before, or swum naked in a lake, or slept on a screen porch—was game for everything.

"Finally, you've found the right man," Becky said as we were washing the dishes. "It's about time."

Next morning we took off again, though we left the motor-cycle at that point to ship it home. I took the wheel of the LeBaron for a change because Jim had three more shots of whiskey in him for the pain. Since meeting Jim, I had not taken the driver's seat.

Near the end of the summer, we headed to Shelburne Falls, Massachusetts, for the last day of filming of the *Labor Day* movie. This was my second visit to the movie set. I'd come there at the start of filming to instruct one of the stars, Josh Brolin, how to make pie as his character would do in the film. But this time Jim was with me. "Josh Brolin had better not have any ideas about you," he said. In Jim's eyes, every man—of whatever age, and never mind if he might be a movie star—was bound to find me irresistible.

For the visit to the film location, we brought Audrey along, and her brother Taj, age eleven, my ex-husband's son from his current partner.

Taj was a bass player like Jim, and the two of them discussed bass players they loved. Listening to the quiet, respectful way Jim spoke with Taj, I imagined Jim as a grandfather someday, and how good it would be when the two of us could share that, as we had not been able to share being parents. *Family.* I had this now.

17.

We spent our last night of our road trip in Portsmouth, New Hampshire. Mostly we'd stayed with friends on this trip, or places we'd rented on Airbnb, but for that one time, we'd checked into a Hilton.

By now we'd shipped the Triumph back west, but we had not yet figured out what to do about the LeBaron. We'd put four thousand miles on that car over the course of the summer, and by this point it was burning so much oil we kept a few quarts in the trunk at all times. But when the valet parking attendant pulled up in front of the hotel in our red convertible as we were leaving, he gave Jim a look of complete respect and awe as he handed him the keys.

"That is the coolest car I ever drove," he told Jim. (The attendant had evidently never driven a Porsche. He was also very young.)

"Would you like to have it?" I asked the parking attendant. His name was Billy.

"Are you kidding?" he said. "I could never afford a car like this."

"It's yours," I told him. No need to consult Jim on this. I knew he'd be up for the gift.

We made the plan to leave the LeBaron at Becky's house nearby for Billy to pick up later, after we'd left for the airport. Registration and keys in the glovebox.

"It's burning oil," I told him, as Becky pulled up to bring us to the airport bus. "But if you know something about cars, maybe you can work on it."

"I can't believe this," Billy told us.

Taking off on the bus that afternoon, headed for the airport, I reached for Jim's hand, or maybe he took mine first. There was no need to say anything. It had been the best summer of our lives.

18.

From the first time they met him, my children liked Jim. Their initial reason was simple: They saw how happy he made me.

Later they loved him not just for who he was to me but for who he was.

We were way past the stage by now where any man with whom I got together was going to be much of a father figure for my daughter and my sons. They had a father they loved, and anyway, they were off leading their own lives by now and had been for a while. But they could no doubt see from that first visit with Jim that his interest in them was real—real but not overbearing or intrusive, and that he made no attempt to impress them or ingratiate himself. They cared about many of the same things—music for one, and the state of the world, the environment, struggles going on in other parts of the globe as well as at home. They recognized his wit and his kindness, but most of all, how much he loved me.

They called him *Jimbeau*. My beau Jim. And the fact that I had chosen him—after all my years of questionable or terrible romantic choices—probably improved my own stock with my daughter and sons.

For Jim's three children our becoming a couple appeared more problematic.

When we had first gotten together, Jim and I made my home in Mill Valley our base. But later that year we had made the decision that I'd rent out the Mill Valley house and move to his house in Oakland. Up until this point, Jim's younger son, Kenny, had been living in the downstairs of that house, but now he had moved out to live with his girlfriend. He was an easy-going and accepting person most of the time, and seemed to recognize his father's need to have the house back for the two of us. Though weeks might go by in which we didn't see him, there was no doubt he loved his father.

Jim's older son, Jonathan, a computer programmer, had made a life for himself in Germany and kept his distance, as had been true for many years. Mostly the method the two of them seemed to have arrived at for connecting took the form of sending each other eBooks from Amazon, usually science fiction. I had sent a note to Jonathan once—something about a vacation visit—but afterward Jim told me that Jonathan had written to say that he did not appreciate receiving e-mails from me, so I didn't try again.

In many ways, the hardest story was Jim's with his daughter, Jane, who lived in Brooklyn and worked as a teacher to disadvantaged students. He was deeply proud of her, and loved it that when he paid her a visit in New York, the two of them had ridden bikes across the Brooklyn Bridge together. He came home from that trip as happy as I'd ever seen him.

But she had often been critical of him too, and it seemed to me, in my limited time observing the two of them together, that Jane could be painfully harsh. If at first she displayed no interest in meeting me or coming for dinner to the house we now shared, Jim said, this was not about me. Just more of a story he had grieved for years before he and I met, a chasm that had formed long ago.

Eventually, Jane came to visit. By this time I had rented out my Mill Valley house and moved in with Jim at his house in Oakland, the place where he'd lived with his children over the last few years they'd been home.

I could tell how badly he wanted things to go well with his daughter. All day he'd prepared for this—buying organic groceries she'd like, vacuuming—but after he'd picked her up at the airport and she walked in the door, she had scanned the room with a look of displeasure. "What happened to the family pictures?" she said.

Next morning, he set them out again—photographs of her and her brothers when they were little, back when Jim was married to their mother—but it was too late. I had never seen Jim as sad as he was when he returned from taking his daughter to the airport for her flight home.

"Sometimes I think she actually hates me," he said. "And there's nothing I can do to change it."

I should have, but I could not seal myself off from Jim's sorrow over his relationship with his children. I wanted him to be that fighter pilot hero swooping through the sky—my Blue Angel—and when it was just the two of us, he could be that person. But when he reported that Jane had criticized him, all the strength seemed to abandon him. He went silent, or retreated—turned on his laptop and found an online Scrabble game—and when we went to bed that night, it was on opposite sides, and my hand, which usually rested on his amazingly flat, firm belly, stayed at my side.

It would get better, I said. Once his children got used to me. Our children were all grown now, and making their own lives, finding their own partners. Fair enough then that we had found ours.

19.

Some years back—2001—I had traveled on my own to Lake Atitlan, in Guatemala. I'd first visited there in 1973, when I was twenty, and I had not returned in twenty-eight years, but when I did I fell in love with the place all over again.

It was the first year of my adult life in which I had no children at home—my son Charlie having gone to college in New York City, while Audrey was taking a year off from college to do social work in the Dominican Republic. Willy, though only seventeen, had set off on his own for Africa with his savings from waiting tables in Mill Valley.

At this point I was forty-two years old and I had never felt more alone. That winter, for three hundred dollars a month, I rented a house in a small village called San Marcos La Laguna, a place where traditional Mayan indigenous culture overlapped peacefully with a small community of expatriate Americans and Europeans, South Americans and Israelis. I stayed in that village for over six months, and discovered over that time that I had never been happier.

In the end, I bought a little house in that village on the shores of Lake Atitlan, and over the course of the years that followed I built gardens and a guest house there, and another guest house, and a sauna, and a pizza oven, and planted fruit trees and flowers of all kinds, made a waterfall, and then another one. I started a writing workshop there, bringing sixteen or so American writers to the lake every winter to work with me on the craft of memoir. I made friends. I hired local men to build stone walls and a dock and to care for my garden. I made a good life in that village, though as usual, a solitary one. I might have been surrounded with friends there, and often I was, but when the day drew to a close, I swam alone in that lake.

I wanted to bring Jim to Guatemala. For all the traveling he'd undertaken in his years with Patrice, he'd never been someplace like this, but I knew him well enough that I wasn't worried about his ability to adapt to life in an underdeveloped country. Over and over in the months since we'd met, Jim had demonstrated his openness to experiences beyond what he'd known before. He was far better at adapting than I was at that point. For me, that only came later.

He brought his camera, of course, and he took hundreds of pictures, not only of the scenery but—with a form of respect and restraint often absent in Americans photographing the Mayan community—of the people. He climbed the volcano and took Spanish lessons, filling notebooks with verb conjugations. He walked into town with me every day, carrying the basket we'd fill with vegetables from the market for that night's dinner. We ate every meal on the patio overlooking the lake and, after, he watched while I stripped off my clothes and dove in for one last swim before bed.

One day, we set out on an adventure. There was a spot I'd visited once before, in the northern jungle region of Guatemala, called Semuc Champey, that I'd remembered as possibly the most beautiful place I'd ever seen. Semuc Champey consisted of a series of natural turquoise pools, one flowing into the other, surrounded by a pristine Eden of plant and bird life and waterfalls, bordered by a vast underground river a person could swim through, if she were brave enough, filled with stalactites and stalagmites. We'd tackle it, naturally.

Getting to Semuc Champey was challenging, and most people chose to make the trip in a tourist bus, but Jim was up for driving, and we rented a Jeep. To add to the adventure, I suggested a different route from the one favored by the tourist vans.

Ten hours into our journey—with the sun long gone and

Semuc Champey still sixty kilometers beyond us—we found ourselves on a road so filled with potholes we had to slow our vehicle to walking speed. Suddenly, off to one side, we saw a wildfire, with flames approaching. Then, like something in a scene from *Indiana Jones*, a giant bolder tumbled down onto the road, landing directly in front of our vehicle. At the wheel, Jim held steady. "You sure know how to show a man a good time, baby," he told me, and kept on driving.

We arrived safely, early the next morning. And had an unforgettable time. Later, back at the lake, we imagined how life might be if we just stayed here.

"You know, we could always chuck it all and come live here on the lake," I told Jim. "Forget about money worries and all the rest of it. You could take pictures and I'd grow vegetables and write. When life got boring, we'd head back to Semuc Champey, or someplace else."

The truth was, as much as Jim loved our days at the lake, he loved being a lawyer. He loved the law part, and he loved putting on a good suit and driving into San Francisco in his Boxster, going out for lunch with his old friends from the Guardsmen club at the Tadich Grill or Sam's. Life on the shores of Lake Atitlan held little of the stress of home, but neither one of us was ready for retirement.

Still, that first winter we went to Lake Atitlan together felt like a stretch in Eden. We were both sad when the boat came to take us away—to the car that would bring us to the airport in Guatemala City and from there, back home. But I knew we'd be coming back the next winter, and every winter. Summers on the motorcycle in New Hampshire, winter trips to the lake, and in between, I thought, an endless succession of good meals and good music, long drives, small pleasures, and the immeasurable comfort of each other's company. The future seemed to stretch out before us farther than the eye could see.

It was past midnight when we got back to Jim's house in Oakland. We knew the minute we reached the door that something had happened. The door was bashed in. When we opened it: chaos.

So often, people who had never traveled to Guatemala, hearing I went there regularly, expressed the view that it sounded like a very dangerous place. But here we were, just home from that allegedly dangerous place, and the great violation had occurred right in Jim's Bay Area home.

The living room looked reasonably intact, though some stereo equipment was gone. The television had also been stolen. Amazingly, none of Jim's guitars and cameras—some of them valuable, like his Fender Jazz Bass—had been touched. But every drawer had been pulled out, the contents strewn on the floor. A couple of expensive watches were gone. Also, money.

It was two in the morning before we got into bed, but neither one of us had an easy time getting to sleep. At three A.M., Jim thought he heard sounds upstairs, and the realization came to him: There was no longer any lock on the door. Maybe the thieves had come back for more.

Naked, he jumped out of bed. He reached for a baseball bat he kept leaned against the wall and raced up the stairs, ready to confront whoever might be up there.

It was only raccoons, rooting around for garbage. Jim returned to bed, and we fell asleep then in each other's arms as we always did. The next day we put a new lock on the door. Nothing could get us now.

20.

Though we took many trips together, it was being at home with Jim that I loved best. I never got over that moment at the end of the day when he would walk in the door, home from work in the city, like some character out of the situation comedies of my childhood—the hardworking husband setting down his briefcase to plant a kiss on the mouth of the woman he loved.

It was a life I'd never lived before. More often than not, one of us would have brought home some interesting food to share—a piece of good cheese or the makings of bruschetta—and we'd take that outside with a glass of wine and tell each other about our day. During the months we'd lived together at my house in Mill Valley we had done this out on my deck overlooking Mt. Tamalpais, but now that we lived in Oakland, we took in a different though equally spectacular view. From outside Jim's living room we could see three bridges and the Oakland skyline, and on a clear day, the San Francisco skyline beyond it, along with the planes landing at the Oakland airport. We were so high up that even the hawks circled below us.

One night in late March, Jim came home earlier than usual, carrying roses and two dozen shucked oysters that he arranged on a platter and carried out onto the deck with a couple of martinis for us. He had put on an album of Chet Baker. He seemed preoccupied and uncharacteristically nervous.

"I think you should try that one first," he said, pointing to a lone oyster that stuck up higher than the others from its shell.

I knew then what was coming. If I hadn't guessed already, the intense and slightly anxious look on Jim's face would have given him away. Under that oyster, of course: a ring.

The setting was simple, the diamond huge.

I wasn't a diamond person. I wasn't even much of a ring person. For my one and only marriage, in 1977, I'd bought my own gold band for twelve dollars at a pawnshop in New York City. Somewhere along the line I must have taken it off and gotten confused about where it belonged, because on the cover of a book I published in 1984, featuring stories about my young marriage, I am pictured with my three children and that wedding ring clearly visible, but on the wrong hand.

That ring had disappeared long before this, and though there had been no shortage of suitors of various levels of seriousness in the years since my divorce, nobody had ever asked me to marry him this way, certainly not with the kind of seriousness and intention Jim displayed now.

"It's such a big diamond," I said. "It must have cost so much money."

A look came over him then—that anxious look he got when he was worried he'd done something wrong, particularly something that might displease me. It was a look that probably had its origins in that Southern California ranch house where Jim grew up, where the prospect of displeasing his father was a daily certainty, with large and frightening consequences.

"It's beautiful," I told him. "I'm just not used to something like this."

"So what do you think?" he asked me.

We were married on Fourth of July weekend in New Hampshire, at a place called Cobb Hill in the little town of Harrisville, a few miles down the road from the cabin at Silver Lake that we'd rented and loved the summer before. Because the wedding would take place so far away, we didn't expect friends from California to attend, but a surprising number did. My friend Charlotte— the woman I'd met two summers back, in the taxi on the way to the workshop on the Amalfi coast where I conducted my brief, disastrous Italian affair—had made the trip from Washington, D.C.

And there were old friends too: Becky, from Maine; Laurie, from down the road in New Hampshire; and some of Jim's old San Francisco friends from his days in the Guardsmen, a service organization in which for years he had put on an elf suit every December, selling Christmas trees to raise money to send underprivileged children to summer camp.

There was also a stringer for the *New York Times* in attendance, and a photographer, come to take pictures for the "Vows" column, for which we were to be the featured couple the following week. Knowing the column would find an audience with many people our age—long divorced, like us—it made me happy to think that our story might serve as a source of hope for others who might have supposed it was too late to find a partner.

"I feel like I'm really there for this relationship," Jim told the *New York Times* reporter. "I'm not putting a priority on my golf game. I don't have one, actually."

"It has been the quest of my life to create a happy family," I told her. It had taken a lot longer than I'd hoped, but that day it seemed clear I had it at last.

All three of my children were there with their partners, and though there had initially been some uncertainty about this, all three of Jim's. He'd bought a ticket for his son Kenny and his girlfriend to come from Oakland, and his son Jonathan and his girlfriend from Germany. This was the first time I'd met Jonathan, and besides saying the word "hello" he did not speak to me, but Jim told me it was often that way. No need to take it personally. His daughter, Jane, rode up with a friend from Brooklyn.

The wedding took place on a hilltop, with fields and woods all around. My two sons, Charlie and Will, in seersucker suits, walked with me through tall grass filled with wildflowers to the spot where Jim stood waiting for me—each of them looking so much like their father, the man I had once loved and with whom I had fought so bitterly for so long. Jim's daughter and mine stood side by side, holding flowers. I had not worried that Audrey would register joy over our marriage, but to see Jane smiling made me happy—above all else, for Jim, who never stopped hoping for the approval of his older son and daughter.

We had chosen to write our own vows, but the morning of the wedding, Jim had still not gotten anything on paper, while my own vows had been ready for days. Two hours before the ceremony was due to begin, still in his boxer shorts, he had disappeared into the cabin where we were staying. He emerged forty-five minutes later in his tuxedo and red silk bow tie holding a yellow legal pad.

"I love how you love me," he said. "You know me better than anyone ever has."

For my vows, I wanted to name every single thing I loved about Jim, so the vows went on for quite a few minutes. Among other reasons for this, I knew from my own long experience as a single parent that when your fellow parent is not there to say good things about you, or is disinclined to do so, your children are unlikely to have heard them articulated, and I wanted Jim's children to take in, from a woman who deeply loved their father, all the reasons why.

The minister who officiated—an old friend from California— read a Wendell Berry poem called "The Country of Marriage," and my longtime assistant, Melissa, and a folksinger friend from

Maine, Travis, performed a duet of a song called "We Come Up Shining," about a couple who sometimes encounter difficulties but, when they do, work them out. Jim got down on his knees and removed the high-heeled shoes I'd been wearing up until then, replacing them with my favorite pair of cowboy boots with roses on them.

That day, something seemed to change in Jane's attitude toward my getting together with her father. At the dinner after the ceremony, she toasted the two of us. Kenny sang a funny song he'd made up. My son Willy stood up to speak.

"My mom has had a lot of boyfriends . . ." he began. "I mean, *really* a lot." For a moment I was afraid he might actually go over the list. "And I'm here to say, Jim is the best.

"My chief emotion today . . ." he said, "is relief. Let's face it. These two are not spring chickens. Not to mention what good news it is, to those of us who've been her passengers on the road, that my mom won't be doing that much driving from now on."

There was a band led by a friend who'd driven all the way from Virginia, and my three children, singing a cappella a Townes Van Zandt song I loved, "If I Needed You." Jim and I stepped up to the microphone too, for a duet of the John Prine song "In Spite of Ourselves," with lyrics we had adapted for the occasion.

First it was my turn:

"He plays online Scrabble and he loves his Boxster,
Give him a bass and he's a rock star.
His suits are out of fashion and his shorts are pretty old
Studies those contracts like a centerfold.
But he's my sweetheart,
That's his great art
Never gonna let him go."

Then came Jim:

"She don't know her east from west.
How'd she ever pass her driving test?
Her writing though is among the best
Gets us invited to some big film fests.
Keeps on typin'
Thinks like lightning
Never gonna let her go."

21.

One event at our wedding cast a shadow. That weekend represented Jim's first visit with his older son, Jonathan, in over a year, and there was a palpable lack of ease between them. When Jonathan arrived, he'd disappeared into the bedroom we'd set up for him in the house we'd rented for our families, and the next morning he went out to breakfast with his girlfriend. He had barely spoken with Jim since his arrival, and to me not at all.

Then came the wedding ceremony and the reception after. Just as the band had started playing, Jonathan approached Jim to say that he'd like to talk with him.

I'd been looking forward to this moment—the dancing part—ever since we'd started planning the wedding. Jim and I had actually taken dance lessons to get a few moves down for this. But now—recognizing the rarity of Jonathan's making an overture toward him—Jim had stepped away from the tent and disappeared with his son.

They were gone for close to an hour.

So I danced with my sons and daughter and my friends. I had a good time visiting with friends. But I kept looking for Jim, hoping he'd come back before the band finished their set. As one song after another finished without Jim's return, a knot formed in my stomach. I'd picked out every one of those songs with him in mind.

The band we'd hired specialized in covers of George Jones songs. I had requested that they learn one in particular—"He Stopped Loving Her Today."

There was a particular reason why I had asked for this song. It told the story of a man so devoted to the woman he loves—long after she's left him—that he remains faithful to her for what would appear to be decades. It's about a kind of crazy, over-the-top love and loyalty, and though I had no intention of abandoning Jim as the woman in the song had done to the man in the song, the particular brand of true blue devotion George Jones sang about always made me think of Jim. Only in the final verse of the song do we discover why it is that the man in the song has stopped loving the woman, at last: He died.

That would be Jim, I told the band, only partly joking.

Now though, as the musicians launched into the song, my husband was nowhere around to hear it and dance with me.

Something took hold of me then, and I got up anyway. I started dancing by myself, reenacting the story told in the song—of a man so crazed with love he keeps reading his old love letters, and waiting for the woman he loves to come back to the moment he takes his last breath. It was a kind of dancing I typically reserved for the privacy of our kitchen or bedroom—my wild interpretive dances, performed with abandon for an audience of one, as Jim cleaned up the last of our dinner dishes or sat back in his chair to take in the spectacle. Only now I was performing it for all of our assembled guests.

We were down to the final lines of the song—the part about placing the wreath on the man's door, the reason the man in the song had stopped loving the woman after all these years. I was so wrapped up in my dance that I'd gotten down on the floor by this point, enacting with considerable melodrama the picture of the dead man being carried out, when, from my spot on the ground, a pair of black shoes came into my range of sight.

Jim was back. Just in time to pick me up off the ground and wrap his arms around me. We finished the song together and stayed that way the rest of the night. And later, as we were all dancing with my son Charlie as DJ, fireworks started going off, first from one town below us on the hill, then a different one. It was the Fourth of July weekend, of course. But it felt as if they were for us.

"WHAT DID HE want to talk about?" I asked Jim later. We were back in our little cabin on the hillside now, with all but the youngest and most energetic of our guests retreated to their hotel rooms. Here I was in the arms of the man who was now my husband, though it still felt strange to me, saying the word.

"Jonathan, I mean. When he wanted to go off with you. "

"It was nothing much," Jim said. "Science fiction novels. Computer stuff."

In the years that followed, the story of Jim's disappearance from the dance floor that night was one I brought up way too often. I knew the reason why he'd allowed this to happen—his longing to connect with his son. But I had a hard time letting go of my disappointment.

STILL IT WAS a wonderful wedding. The best ever, many of our guests told us later. The *New York Times* story about that day, the editor told me, had been one of the most shared online of any "Vows" column the paper had ever run.

One friend who'd been there told me later how he'd expressed a certain good-natured concern to Jim over the possibility that living with me might prove a little taxing. Jim had shaken his head. "I know I've got a tiger by the tail," he said. "But I'm up for it."

"We could have thirty more years together if we're lucky," Jim said to me that night, as we headed to bed.

22.

We marked the start of our marriage with a four-day hike along the Presidential Range in the White Mountains of New Hampshire, lapsing into our Wanda and Buddy routine on occasion, and totally silent when we needed to be—touching down in a different Appalachian Mountain Club hut every night for a good dinner and a good night's sleep, rising at five in the bitter cold to head out on the trail to the next summit. Every night they gave us two bunk beds but all we ever used was one.

It was a rugged hike—particularly the last day on Mt. Adams, when we watched hikers thirty years younger than we were turn around and go back down.

"What we lack in strength we will make up for with tenacity," I said, as we marked our arrival at the summit. Reaching those peaks—reaching any peak—had always felt symbolic to us. If we could do this, we could do anything.

THE *LABOR DAY* movie came out, and I was invited to attend the Telluride Film Festival that September for its first public showing. Jim and I made the trip together, watching two or three movies a day and having drinks in the bar at the New Sheridan Hotel on Main Street. I got to wear my cowboy boots. He wore his hat.

After that, there was a flurry of publicity around the movie. We went to Denver for another premiere, and to Austin for a book festival, posing in front of the wall on Congress Avenue beside graffiti that said "I Love You So Much," with both of us adopting the demeanor of a couple in the midst of a standoff. We flew to Toronto and walked the red carpet there—I, with a borrowed necklace of Swarovski crystals, Jim in his tux, waving while cameras snapped our pictures and the people lining the walkway tried to figure out who we were. I allowed myself to fantasize that maybe the next spring we'd attend the Oscars together.

The summer before, at a vintage shop in Portland, Maine, I'd found a great dress—a very simple 1960s sheath with a label from Paris, encrusted in bright blue sequins. The dress fit me almost perfectly—almost, because as good as it looked once I'd gotten it on, zipping up the back always required five minutes of Jim's wrangling effort with the zipper first.

Now, at the age of sixty, I was experiencing this unlikely little dose of glamour, Midwestern style: movie screenings in Chicago and St. Louis and Minneapolis and Kansas City, for which the studio always provided a makeup artist and stylist and a very good hotel room. Every night, with assistance from the makeup artist in whatever city I'd touched down in that day, I'd put on my blue dress and my four-inch blue silk heels and step out onto the stage to introduce the movie.

Jim had to stay home for that trip; he was still trying to get his new law practice off the ground. But I ended every night with a call to him, and when I finally got back home he was there at the cell phone lot ready to swoop me up in the Boxster.

The movie flopped, but after I got home, I hung the blue dress in our bedroom as a reminder of my little moment of glory, and settled into my new life. Or tried to. That concept—that two people might know a single, joined life, did not come easy.

I had been very good at throwing a wedding—I, a former high

school prom chairman, the host of a hundred parties and fundraisers. But building a marriage required more than the skills of an event planner.

At the point Jim and I got together, I had been single for twenty-four years. Just putting that ring on my finger had felt odd—almost embarrassing, as later it would be difficult to say "my husband" or to refer to myself as Jim's wife. To me, marriage had meant trouble, failure, pain. Why would a person in her right mind sign up for more of that, once the fun part—the celebration and the music, the dancing and the friends—was over?

For more than two decades I had lived as the most independent of women. Once Jim and I were married, I still operated as if I were one. I made my own decisions about where I'd go, and when, and if Jim had a different idea from mine, I might go along with it, but with the recognition that I was compromising in ways that felt almost like a betrayal of my true self.

Sometime not long after the wedding, we had gone to New York, a city I loved and knew surprisingly well, considering that I'd lived there only briefly, thirty-five years earlier. In the past, I'd traveled to that city on my own, mostly. I moved quickly, and stopped only where I wanted to. I made accommodations to nobody but fellow passengers pressed up against me on the subway.

Jim did not know the city well, and he took it in slowly. He liked to stop and take pictures or sit on park benches taking in the skyline. He wanted to read about each exhibit at the American Museum of Natural History. He thought it would be nice to sit down and get a sandwich, whereas I would have marched on and grabbed a handful of nuts to keep me going.

On a particular block downtown, we had passed the Benjamin Cardozo School of Law, where Jim told me an old friend now taught. Maybe he should call his friend, he said to me. See if he was free for coffee.

"It doesn't work like that in New York," I said to him—irritation in my voice, no doubt, or something even worse, condescension.

"New Yorkers plan their lunch dates weeks in advance. Nobody just calls up and says 'I'm outside your building now.'"

And there was more. In our early days we had so happily prepared meals together. Less than two months after we met, we'd spent hours in my Mill Valley kitchen preparing a traditional mole sauce from scratch for a Day of the Dead party. At the time, I had noted with affection the slow, deliberate way he worked alongside my own hurricane-style of food preparation, and the tender manner in which he'd reach over and clean food from wherever it landed on me, as it so often did.

But now when I cooked, I sometimes pushed Jim aside or invented some task that would take him out of my path and leave me free to work at my own accelerated pace in the kitchen.

"Here's some garlic to chop," I'd tell him—suggesting that he perform the task off in a corner, out of the way, though even then he chopped with maddening precision that left me impatient.

"I can't leave pie dough sitting for so long once I've rolled it out," I said to him when he was too slow chopping the apples. He was a man who measured the cinnamon, whereas I simply flung it.

What did it matter, in the end, if the pie crust was a little stiffer, or the fruit cut into pieces smaller than I would have chosen? At the time, these things seemed so important. Later, not at all.

I believe I felt, at those moments, like a ballerina who had suddenly found herself hauling a chain around her foot. I had grown accustomed to a certain way of living that had not required me to slow down or adapt to anybody else's needs. I'd done that when my children were young, but those years were far behind me at this point. Since my children left home—with the exception of those fourteen months I'd lived with my adopted daughters—I set my own pace and kept to it.

It was an odd irony that though I had a partner at last, it seemed that I couldn't dance the way I used to. I could not see that there might be a whole new set of steps to learn, as intricate and beautiful as an Argentine tango. *He goes forward, you go back. He leans in, you lean out. His hand on your back, yours on his shoulder.* You are no longer two people out there on the floor, but a couple, moving as one. For all my talk of dance lessons, I knew nothing about those kinds of steps.

And there were other worries. After our glorious New England road trip, Jim had returned home to the harsh reality that at least for the first few years, being in a solo practice was a much harder way for an attorney to earn a living than being in a law firm as he had been for so long. He, who had always been free with money, became anxious about how much was going out and how much less came in. I could hear him on the phone sometimes with a prospective client— patient and professional, but the sound of frustration apparent if only to me. These prospective clients never seemed to have any money to actually pay a retainer. Everyone wanted him to work on contingency, and the cases that sounded winnable were few and far between. When he got off the phone, he'd shake his head.

"We'll be OK," I told him. I had always been able to earn my living, and if we were careful that would be enough. But, of course, the idea that I would once again be the breadwinner had not been his vision for our marriage, or mine. He wanted to be my fighter pilot, my protector. I wanted him to be those things too, actually. My burly man. My guard dog.

23.

The year before, Jim had joined a men's social club called The Family, a group of successful professional men who met for dinners in the city on Tuesday nights, and sometimes during the good weather at an encampment south of the city in Woodside, where they drank whiskey and put on skits and played music and ate chili and smoked cigars. With rare exceptions, women were not allowed at the club.

When Jim had first been invited to join and described it to me, I had been quick to make fun of all this, starting with the very name of the group. *The Family.* What did that mean anyway? I knew what constituted a family. This was not it.

There was a tradition at The Family that all the members—no matter what their age, and some were over eighty—were called "the children." The leader was the Father. In their e-mails, when they signed off, they used the letters "K.Y." for "Keep Young." This all sounded pretty silly to me. One of the few tense moments of our summer together in New England had occurred, in fact, when I had questioned Jim why he would even want to be in such a group.

"You are actually going to pay money to go off and put on plays in the woods and sleep in a cabin full of snoring men?" I said.

Evidently the all-important skit for Jim's group of new recruits— "The Babies," they were called—was to be performed during a week when we were to be in New Hampshire, and he was weighing the possibility of flying back to San Francisco for a couple of nights to be part of the show. He would actually fly across the country—leaving our wonderful cabin on Silver Lake, and me—to be in this skit.

"Are you kidding?" I said.

In the face of my merciless derision, Jim decided he would withdraw from the club. If he joined The Family, he concluded, he was only going to let his fellow members down by being absent, or else disappoint me, which for Jim was the worst.

"I can't afford it anyway," he said quietly. "I should never have said yes in the first place."

He sat at his laptop for a good hour and a half then, composing and then deleting his letter of resignation from the group, then starting again. Now came the saving grace, an ability I'd acquired in my sixth decade of life, that I had been unable to pull off before: the capacity for understanding, and the realization that when you love someone, it may be more important to support him than to get your way.

It took me a while, but I figured this out. Witnessing Jim's struggle over withdrawing from the club, I recognized my own severe failure of understanding.

"You're having a hard time pulling out of the club because you don't really want to do that," I said. "And I'm sorry I ever made fun of it. I had no business doing that."

Here was the good thing about the bad parts of our relationship: We still failed regularly, but we were learning to admit to our failures and we were more ready to repair the damage than we would have been when we were younger. Humility about my mistakes was new for me. So was being open-minded to the idea that there might be other valid choices besides my own.

24.

With my encouragement, Jim remained in The Family. He didn't attend every single Tuesday night dinner, but over the months that followed, he drove into the city as many Tuesdays as he could for a rock-and-roll jam session of musicians in the group known as Storkzilla. For my part, I managed to keep my opinion to myself that this was a stupid name for a rock group. Stupid name, worthwhile activity.

More than worthwhile, in fact. That band represented, for Jim, the resolution of a fifty-year-old sorrow.

From the first time he ever heard it, Jim had loved rock and roll, the Beatles in particular. He got his first bass with his own money at age fourteen. But because it was forbidden at his house, he had to listen to his music in secret—not only the Beatles but also Led Zeppelin and Cream, the Rolling Stones, the Kinks.

Jim taught himself to play, and was good enough to be sought out by a couple of bands at his school that had included some seriously good players. Other than Jim, they had been the bad boys mostly, or at least they weren't Boy Scouts.

He kept his bass at his friends' houses, where he practiced. He played at dances, and the fact that he was good no doubt raised his stock with girls. There were several he liked a lot, but he didn't feel confident enough to ask them out.

On one of our long car drives Jim told me a story. With his own money, earned from working weekends at a department store, Jim bought a shirt with a wide collar and a mod print. When his father saw the shirt, he told him to return it to the store.

"Something got into me," Jim told me. "I stood in front of my father with that shirt in my hands and I ripped it down the middle." For a while after that, Jim had kept playing the forbidden music. And then his father found out about the band and made him quit. His friends found another bass player. He missed the band, but said nothing.

There was a nationally known group of young people performing at the time—clean cut, patriotic in the tradition of Barry Goldwater and Richard Nixon, and religious in the style of Billy Graham—called Up With People. They sometimes performed on television in the sixties and early seventies as a kind of antidote for conservative types made uneasy by rock music who wanted some alternative for their children, a concept that only confirmed their cluelessness concerning rock and roll.

In the household where I grew up, three thousand miles away from Los Angeles, with parents who had not felt truly enthusiastic about a presidential candidate since Adlai Stevenson ran for office, Up With People was a family joke. After we had seen them on television once—*The Ed Sullivan Show*, the same place I'd discovered the Beatles—they had become a source of ruthless satire at our house. "Up, up, up with people," my mother sang, laughing raucously as she quoted the lyrics of one of their trademark songs. "You meet 'em wherever you go."

But in the family where Jim was raised, Up With People represented the only acceptable alternative for a young man who wanted to play bass. If Jim wanted so badly to be part of a band, his father told him, he could join Up With People.

And he did.

Of all the stories he told me, this one might have been the hardest for him to reveal, the most painful. After he told it to me, I had sent away for an Up With People album I found on eBay. I thought he'd find this funny, but one look at his face when he opened the package told me otherwise. He had no desire to ever hear those songs again, or be reminded of the time in his life they represented. Or the man.

In the winter of 2012, fifty years after he'd been forced to quit the rock band of his youth, Jim started playing with Storkzilla. The band met up on Tuesday nights at The Family clubhouse in the city and sometimes at the Family camp in the country on weekends to play all the old songs. One of the first songs Jim played with them was "Sympathy for the Devil."

And because I loved Jim, I no longer scoffed when he would go off to an encampment—packing his bass and his amps in the trunk of the Boxster, with a handful of the Cuban cigars I brought home for him from Guatemala to share with his friends.

He seldom stayed beyond Sunday morning. He missed me too much, he said. But invariably, he'd come home with stories of great conversations he'd had—with a physics professor at Berkeley or a former Navy fighter pilot, or a classical violinist. If he would have stayed up till three in the morning making music.

25.

nless I'd made a mess in his car, Jim just about never criti-cized me, but I criticized him plenty in those days. Often the topic concerned how wasteful he could be with money: the gym membership he'd stopped using when we met, for which he continued to pay a hundred dollars a month for close to a year; the drawers full of expensive sunglasses; identical hats, shoes, cufflinks; cigar trimmers and leather cases to hold the cigars. For his part, Jim never once ques-tioned my odd choices—the time I came home with a windmill, for example, or the time I bought a gypsy caravan in New Hamp-shire and hired a trucker to drive it across the Rocky Mountains to California for me.

It was my money. My dreams. He never got in the way of those.

My other refrain had to do with Jim's failure to take initiative. Every trip we took, I pointed out, and every concert we attended, every dinner party we hosted, was the result of a plan that came from me.

One time I read that Bob Dylan would be performing in Oakland, and I mentioned to Jim that I wanted to go. He said he'd buy tickets.

A few days later, I asked if he'd bought the tickets. "I'll get them today," he said. But he forgot, as he often did.

Finally I went online myself, but by this time the concert was sold out. I held onto that grievance a long time—holding on to old injuries being a bad habit of mine, left over from my first marriage. All Jim wanted was to please me, and there I was reminding him of all the times he fell short.

"Why am I always the one implementing all the plans?"

"I'm just not as good at coming up with ideas as you are, baby," he told me. "Unless they have to do with estate law."

I was never short on ideas. His quiet gift—easier to miss, or fail to appreciate—was for being my tireless supporter and sidekick for whatever adventure I proposed. "A tiger by the tail" was an apt phrase for the dynamic between us. I mentioned a plan. He got on board and held on for dear life.

Sometimes I complained about this to my friend Becky. "But let's be honest," she said. "How well would you have handled it if Jim had been more inclined to take the lead?

"Consider the story of your wedding ring," she pointed out. "His decision to buy that diamond might have been one of the only times Jim ever did something involving the two of you entirely on his own. And then you complained about his choice.

"The thing about Jim," she said, "is how he's always up for going on whatever wild ride you suggest."

And, he did the driving.

26.

After all those years on my own, and despite the times when it cramped my style, I also reveled in being part of a couple. For so long, I had been the odd person at every dinner party I attended (though single people were invited less to dinner parties, as I came to realize when I ceased to be one).

For years I had been the one who drove home alone. Now I loved those times when Jim and I went to dinner with another couple, and afterward, in the car, when we got to talk everything over—Jim at the wheel, me in the passenger seat with my feet on the dash. As mundane as that experience might have been to people who'd been married for most of their adult lives, it was not the kind of thing I'd experienced much before. *Ordinary life*, I called it, but for me it never ceased to feel exotic and wonderful.

Sometimes friends came over to the house we shared, or one of my children might be in town, and I'd make a good meal and a pie, though (here I'd go again) it remained a source of frustration to me that on those occasions Jim would feel compelled to spend the afternoon cleaning the house. Vacuuming, in particular. Some old demons from his childhood days, I think, had left him with the idea that our house had to be perfect before guests came over, while for me what mattered was to make them feel welcome, and that the pie taste good.

"People don't care about a little dust," I said. "They'd rather come to a home where the hosts feel relaxed, not worn out from housework."

We spent Christmas at my house in Guatemala, and all three of my children came with their partners, along with Jim's younger son and his girlfriend. We played cards and swam and went for hikes and had long meals together out on the patio. We made pizza in the pizza oven, and before sunrise one morning, climbed to a spot overlooking the lake called Indian's Nose, where we could see five volcanoes and the Pacific Ocean at once. If it wasn't the blended family of my dreams, it was good enough.

Best was this: We ended every night wrapped around each other in the bed, my hand on Jim's belly, his around my waist, my face pressed into his hair that I loved to reach out and stroke in the night. Many evenings still, we danced in the kitchen—to John Prine singing "Glory of True Love," always reminding each other that we were going to take lessons one of these days and get some real moves.

I loved how he loved me—that he was unshakeable, and unfailingly ardent, and I loved his protectiveness of me. (The way he read every line and footnote of every contract I ever signed, where for years I had scrawled my signature, reading none of the small print or the large. The outrage he felt, if he read a mean-spirited review of something I'd written, or observed anyone treating me poorly.) Once, when one particularly hostile person began posting comments on my Facebook page, he created a whole new Facebook persona— "Epicurious George"—whose sole function was to offer devastating rebuttals of every mean comment from her that came my way.

I could not walk down a street with Jim or head down a trail without holding his hand, and in the car, I'd reach across the seat to put my arm on his leg or around his shoulders. Touching Jim was as automatic as breathing.

Here it was at long last, what love looked like: We disagreed about plenty, and sometimes my old habit of judging a man harshly crept in. But I was better now at recognizing the pointlessness of so much that irritated me. What I valued most was that when we hit trouble, as we did, we knew enough to talk it out.

Not one day ever passed in which I doubted Jim's wild appreciation, loyalty, pride, devotion, and—maybe this is the rarest of all—the utter acceptance he gave me, which included an acceptance of my least lovable and most difficult qualities. Every time I walked in the door after being away, whether for a week or an hour, I would know: He was happy to see me. Possibly overjoyed.

"Remember that scene in *King Kong*," Becky said one time. "Where King Kong is wandering through the streets of New York, desperately searching for Jessica Lange? And from a distance he spots a blonde woman inside an elevated subway car?"

I knew that part of the movie. King Kong lumbers over to the train. He reaches one enormous fist up to grab it and brings the car with the blonde woman inside up to his face. He sniffs the train car. That's when he realizes the woman inside isn't Jessica Lange after all, and he tosses the train car on the ground. Without her, he has no further interest.

"That's how Jim is about you," Becky told me. "You're the only woman in the train car. "

27.

A documentary film producer named Sarah Gross wrote me a letter. She was making a film about international adoption and she had heard about my story, though without knowing the particulars. Of all the things that had happened in my life that I'd chosen to write about, the story of my Ethiopian daughters may have been the only one on which I had remained silent.

But three years had passed since I'd said good-bye to the girls in Missouri. They were older now, and launched in their new lives.

Though I had not published anything about the experience, it was known in adoption circles—known and condemned. Over these three years, I'd received letters from a few hundred parents of older children adopted from other countries. Sometimes the adoption had gone well. Sometimes not. Among these letters were some from people who wrote to tell me what a terrible person I was to have abandoned my daughters as they supposed I had done, and there was no shortage of voices online—bloggers mostly—giving voice to a similar point of view. I felt no need to respond to those. But I also received letters—stacks of them, in fact—from people struggling as I had with trying to help a child who had experienced terrible loss and, in some cases (unlike my own two girls, whose prospects for happiness in their new family, I believed, were good) might never overcome the wounds of their young lives.

For these parents and so many others who had not written to me, but were out there somewhere, it seemed important that there be a voice acknowledging that they were not alone in their painful struggle, and neither were their children. Some of these parents had relinquished children as I had—and lived with the belief that doing so had been the most shameful and unforgivable act of their lives. Others remained the custodial parents of children with whom, despite years of heartfelt effort, they had never succeeded in forming a bond. At the time these people entered into their international adoptions, they had no idea, any more than I did at the time, of how often such an adoption fails—not only for the adopting parent, but most devastatingly of all, for the child.

When I read Sarah's letter about the project she was engaged in—and later, when we spoke—it seemed to me that it could be valuable that I share my story. But I also knew my primary responsibility lay with the girls who had been my daughters once. Some parts of our story—many—were not mine to tell.

I spent a long time talking with Sarah, laying out the ground rules for an interview, if one was to take place. Finally, that summer, the date was set. The interviewer would be Dan Rather, long retired from CBS News but still actively working as a journalist.

I spent six hours in a room with him, face to face under the lights and with the cameras going, talking about what I felt able to convey about our experience. He asked tough questions, as I had known he would. There would have been no point in this exercise if he hadn't.

When it was over, we shook hands, and I drove home to Jim, who had been worried about this, and anxious that Dan Rather might come down on me mercilessly. I wasn't trying to absolve myself of responsibility on this one, I told him, or deny my shortcomings and failure, only to offer support and the comfort I might bring to other families who supposed they were alone.

"Some people are going to hate you when they hear that interview," Jim told me.

If they did I'd live with it.

"You know who I am," I told him. "And you love me anyway."

There might have been nothing that mattered more than this. That he knew me. Same as I knew him.

With all our failings, we accepted each other.

28.

For nine years, my daughter Audrey had been renting my writing cabin at our old farm from her father, who lived there now with his second wife, Kristen, and their son, Taj. It had been a wonderful writing space for me, long ago, but the cabin was heated with wood and uninsulated, with single-pane windows and an outhouse some distance away. Trips to the outhouse in spring, summer, and fall were fine. But even for Audrey—a country girl, born at home on that very property—winters were rough.

By this point, she had earned a graduate degree as a counselor and had a good job at a residential treatment facility for troubled adolescent boys in the town where she and her boyfriend lived. She loved her work, and the town where she'd lived all her life—the swimming hole and waterfall down the road, the way when she went to the store or the town dump she could greet nearly everyone she met by name.

But I knew she wanted a home of her own, and that though she and Tod could manage a mortgage, the prospect of ever coming up with money for a down payment seemed remote if not impossible.

Then the *Labor Day* movie came out, and I got my big check, and there was nothing I'd wanted more to do with it than to help my daughter and her partner get a home of their own.

So I lent them money with the instruction that they keep an eye out for a good piece of property. For over a year, she and Tod had been on the lookout, but though they found a few places they liked, the ones in their price range were pretty dismal. A couple of times they put a bid on a place, but they lost out every time.

Then a great prospect appeared. A wonderful old house on the same road as her father's place—on the other side of the waterfall and swimming hole—went into foreclosure. The first day the sign went up announcing it would be sold soon, Audrey contacted the bank.

The place was in rough shape, but its potential was vast: This was a two-hundred-year-old cape set in a sweet, sunny spot at the end of a long dirt driveway, much like the old farm I'd bought all those years back that belonged to her father now. It sat on forty-one acres, the boundaries of which were formed by a brook wide enough in places for swimming.

For a while it was unclear how the property would be sold, but Audrey monitored the situation closely. She contacted the Realtor for the bank, researched the title to make sure it was clear. She wanted to be ready to make an offer the moment the place came on the market. The price was $104,000.

"Offer full price," I said. Once she got a mortgage, she and Tod could pay me back a little at a time.

She prepared to make her offer that day. All cash, no contingencies. She made an appointment to meet the Realtor with check in hand.

Then something odd happened. Twenty minutes before they were due to meet, the Realtor who had listed the property canceled her meeting with Audrey. The next day, when Audrey called her again to find out what happened, the Realtor told her the place had been sold.

Someone else had put in a higher offer, the woman said. But something in the deal—and the timing of events—felt odd. To me and, most significantly, to Jim.

Although he was not a real estate attorney, and not licensed to practice in the state of New Hampshire, Jim got to work researching the situation.

He wrote a tough-sounding lawyer letter—one of the things he was best at. We made sure it was on the desk of the head of the realty company that afternoon. Two days later, Audrey signed the papers that allowed her to buy the property.

"You may not have earned the big bucks on this one, Jimmy," I told him, "but there might be no case you took on all year that brought about a more important change in anybody's life than this one."

My daughter and her boyfriend got their home.

29.

Spring of 2014, I was still having trouble writing. At Jim's house in Oakland, where we lived now, there was no good place for me to work.

My friend Karen offered a solution. She owned a little cottage in the town of Lafayette, a fifteen-minute drive from where we were living. She told me I was welcome to work there if I wanted.

I started driving to Lafayette every morning with my laptop and spending my days at Karen's little red house. By the third day I had a novel in the works. Nobody was happier about this than Jim.

One day on a break from work, something inspired me to go online and see what houses cost in Lafayette. Jim and I had no plan to buy a new home at that point; we each owned a house, though each had a big mortgage attached.

A property had just come on the market that day. The moment I saw the pictures I knew I wanted to live there with Jim.

It was not one house, in fact, but two of them on seven acres of land—an unimaginably large piece of property to find at an affordable price so close to San Francisco and Oakland. The house was located in a place called Hunsaker Canyon, a few miles out of town. This place had not been on the market since 1979.

The original house on the property had been built in the forties, but when the current owners had purchased it back in the seventies they had made the plan to design and build a new house there while living in the old one. Now there were two houses, not far apart from each other, with a stone patio and a pergola connecting them—the original house functioning as a place for guests or work, the new place (not so new anymore) a wonderful, almost magical living space.

The two houses were shingled, with all kinds of interesting architectural features: a huge arched window in the living room salvaged from an old school and another in the bedroom, a cozy nook by the fireplace enclosed by a couple of wooden columns that we would later learn had also been salvaged from the old Black Panther house in Berkeley. I could picture sitting there with Jim—he'd be playing his guitar, maybe; I'd have a book—with a fire going.

The kitchen wasn't huge, but I could tell it would be a great place to prepare meals with enough room that I wouldn't find myself pushing Jim aside as I did now in his small Oakland kitchen. I loved how the room opened up to the rest of the ground floor in a way that would allow the person making the food—or both of them—to talk easily with her guests, or her husband, as she did.

There were skylights and a propane stove to take the chill off on a winter morning, and built-in shelves. The floors were tile with radiant heat. There was an outdoor shower opening out onto a brook. Nobody to see you there but the deer.

The newer of the two houses had only one bedroom, but that room filled the entire upstairs, with a bathroom to the side that had a big, deep, old-fashioned tub and a balcony off to one side where I pictured Jim and me sitting at night, taking in the night sky. This was a spot where the stars would be undimmed by ambient light.

I loved the house, but it was the piece of land that got to me the most. It was situated at the end of a long driveway with no neighbors in sight—meaning we'd have to push our garbage cans all the way out to the road on trash day, not that we cared. Huge old oak trees, the largest of which stood at the entrance, surrounded the property. There was a big sunny lawn, and beyond that a hill rising steeply above the house, full of more live oaks. In another direction, there was a barn with three bays, and a large garage with a big studio above it that would be perfect for writing. A hot tub under the largest of the oaks. We could bring our coffee out in the morning and watch the sun coming up.

I called Jim right away. "The amazing thing is, this place is unconventional enough that it actually costs less than the ranch houses down the road," I told him. "We could afford this. And if we sold our two houses, we'd end up with lower taxes and less debt."

Jim was working at home that day. He said he'd be right over.

Twenty minutes later he showed up on his motorcycle at my friend Karen's little writing house with my helmet strapped to the seat behind him. I hopped on the back and we rode over to Hunsaker Canyon together.

We had no appointment to view the property and we knew we shouldn't disturb the owners. So we just stood a ways off, admiring the property from a distance and picturing the two of us living there together.

Even before the day, a week later, when the Realtor took us inside—the earliest appointment possible—we knew we wanted to buy that house. I had studied the pictures online so closely I knew every room and where we'd put our furniture. But we also recognized this would require a huge amount of effort and no small amount of ingenuity.

My Mill Valley house was rented out at the time, so there was no way to put it on the market yet. But we got to work right away preparing to sell Jim's. I also listed, for sale, the little shack of a cabin on a pond in New Hampshire that I'd bought—without consulting Jim, as usual—a couple of years earlier.

We made an offer in record time, contingent on the sale of Jim's house. For the next three weeks we worked long hours getting that house ready to go on the market, with workmen coming over every day and laboring into the night to get Jim's place in shape to sell. This meant boxing up our possessions, painting every room, refinishing the front entrance, updating the bathrooms.

It was a high-wire act, this plan of ours. To get the house in Hunsaker Canyon, we had to put down a lot of money, but if Jim's house didn't sell—or if the sale fell through at the last minute—we could lose our deposit. Jim worried about the possibility of things going wrong. This was his lawyer's training combined with his own more cautious nature.

One night I woke to see Jim lying awake next to me. A kind of panic had set in of a sort I'd never seen in him before.

"This is a terrible mistake," he said. "If I can't sell my house fast enough we're ruined."

We lay side by side on the bed for a long time, talking. Once we sold both our houses, I pointed out, we'd actually be carrying less mortgage debt than we had before, with a lower monthly payment. We just had to get through this rough stretch, I said, and I knew we would. I, always the voice of wild optimism; Jim, the catastrophizer. Somewhere in the middle lay the truth.

For two weekends of open houses, no bid came in for Jim's house. At the eleventh hour, a couple put in an offer and I found a buyer to purchase my New Hampshire cabin—at a loss, but at that point I barely cared. We were getting the Hunsaker Canyon house.

I was sixty years old at this point. I had bought four houses in my life. Every one of them purchased alone. This was the first time I had a partner at my side to sign the papers with me. A partner at my side, period.

The day we'd first seen the Hunsaker Canyon house—in April—the wisteria had been in bloom and the air was full of sweet-smelling jasmine and bees. The grass had been green and the sun came through the trees like the dream sequence in some movie.

It was July when we signed the papers and moved in. That first night we lay in our new bedroom with the high arched window and the balcony off to one side that looked out over the trees, in awe at our good fortune. "I'm never leaving this place," I said.

Forty-one years had passed since I bought my old farm in New Hampshire when I was nineteen, twenty-five years since I'd loaded the U-Haul and driven away the last time. For all those years after that, I never felt truly at home again as I had in that place; but now with Jim at the house in Hunsaker Canyon, I did.

We got an outdoor ping-pong table, and a table for eating meals outside under the wisteria. "We'll plant Arbequina olive trees on the hill behind the barn," he said. "I'll hang my guitars on the wall."

We talked then about the parties we'd host out on the lawn, with music and long tables lined with friends. I pictured grand-children there, never mind whether the offspring of his children or mine. They'd be ours together.

I'd plant tomatoes. Jim would make an office in the second house, and there'd be room left over for visiting friends and chil-dren. I'd put my desk in the studio over the garage in front of the giant window that faced the largest of the live oak trees.

In only five years, we said, we'd be harvesting olives.

30.

Buying the Hunsaker Canyon house presented a new challenge. Or what looked like a challenge back then.

Each of us had brought to the place a few decades' worth of possessions—far more from me than by Jim, a minimalist. But Jim loved the simple lines of midcentury modern furniture and owned some pieces that mattered greatly to him: a couple of black leather Le Corbusier chairs, and a Breuer chair, and an Italian armoire. The pride of his collection was a stainless-steel-and-glass table—with molded plastic chairs, about which he was so protective that just setting a casserole down on it made me uneasy. I was always afraid I'd break it.

I hated that table. It was cold and hard, I said. Unwelcoming. To Jim, it was an artwork.

I remember the day—this was when we still lived in Jim's Oakland house—my daughter Audrey came to visit from New Hampshire. She'd brought along a gift, an old hand-crocheted tablecloth she'd bought at a yard sale, with me in mind.

"Oh good," Audrey said, when she'd spotted Jim's glass table. "It's the perfect size."

Jim loved Audrey. But I could see him concealing a look of pain. That glass table was his pride and joy. I put the tablecloth away, but in truth, my view was similar to my daughter's. I thought the crocheted cloth was great.

Back then I didn't mind serving meals on the glass table, because it was temporary; I never considered Jim's Oakland house my true home. But when we moved to Hunsaker Canyon, the problem arose: Whose table? Whose chairs? What to do about a living room couch, knowing Jim liked sleek, sharp lines—his dream, an Eames chair—while I favored overstuffed thrift-shop sofas covered with pillows?

For the first days in that house, I worried that we'd never resolve the problem. I implied that Jim's taste was predictable, conventional. He said nothing of equal harshness to me, but I knew he hated my big red wing chair and my flower-upholstered couch.

"Just give my stuff a chance," he said. Up until then, the two matching Le Corbusier chairs had been exiled to the outside patio, awaiting resolution of our dispute.

He set them on either side of the room, across from a sofa we'd bought that we had actually managed to agree on.

"You might even find this comfortable," he said, indicating one of the two leather chairs.

I had never tried sitting in it, but now I did.

I look back now on that day as one of the moments I discovered a small but significant truth about marriage: that it is in the act of surrendering the old, familiar patterns and all the things a person believes to be immutable that she may discover a new kind of beauty. Something better even than her old way.

This was true for us of our odd, unlikely mix of possessions— my Guatemalan masks, his abstract dot painting—as it was true of all the other differences between how I'd spent the first fifty some years of my life and the way he had, and all the things (not just possessions but ideas) we'd picked up along the way. Even then, before the discovery of how little any of this was going to matter in the end, I had actually managed to ask myself, "Which is more important, that I love this man's chairs, or that I love this man?"

31.

In September I traveled to France again to promote another translation of a book of mine. This time, though I knew he hated missing the trip, Jim stayed home to work. He joined me just for the last two days in Paris, where we stayed as we always did on these trips in our wonderful little hotel with the sunroom and the croissants. We returned to the Musée D'Orsay, and the Rodin museum, and the little bar on Rue Cassette where we shared a glass of wine and walked the streets as we always did, holding hands.

After, we flew to Budapest as the guests of my Hungarian publisher, who was just now bringing out a translation of *Labor Day*. My Hungarian editor picked us up at the airport, and for three days we managed to combine my book events with explorations of that city—the museums, the baths, the bridges, life in the street.

Though Hungary was no longer under Communist control, you could still feel, walking down the streets of Budapest, how recently and how painfully the people here had struggled. When I appeared at a book signing, readers came up to tell me they were saving up to buy my book. Earlier that day, at a cooking school there, I had put on for the Hungarian press a demonstration of how to make an American pie—a skill demonstrated by one of the main characters in the novel, the escaped convict played in the movie by Josh Brolin. Well over a dozen journalists and photographers had shown up for this event—along with Jim, of course, who set up his own camera as he always did, snapping pictures of me; the ever-present documentarian of our adventures.

After, my editor and publisher took us out to dinner at a tiny and beautiful restaurant no tourist who did not have a Hungarian friend would ever manage to locate, for one of the most extraordinary meals in my life or Jim's. The courses went on forever, each accompanied by a different great Hungarian wine. The food was so rich we staggered away from the table, vowing to eat not one more bite for the next two days to make up for it.

Our strange Eastern European hotel room had a mirror over the bed. As we lay there naked in the aftermath of our gluttonous debauchery, I took out my iPhone.

"When will we have a better opportunity for this?" I said to Jim.

I am studying these pictures now. There we are, our naked bodies wrapped around each other and in the tangle of sheets, with the phone in my hand pointed up to the ceiling, my hair fanned out over the pillow, Jim's shoes flung on the floor, along with a single sock, my dress, a copy of *Labor Day* in Hungarian. Two aging lovers in Budapest, sleeping it off. Two people drunk on love.

32.

Later, when I considered the arrival of the rat into our little paradise, it seemed like a harbinger of trouble to come. At the time, he was only an annoyance.

We first became aware of the rat a few weeks after we moved into the house in Hunsaker Canyon. We hadn't seen him yet, but every night in bed now we could hear him outside, running back and forth on the beams of the pergola, and sometimes even closer too—out on the balcony just beyond our bedroom, or skittering across the roof, his sharp little claws scraping against the metal, making his way across the balcony beams and sometimes gnawing at the wood supporting the wisteria, the telltale droppings providing evidence, next morning, of his route. From the sound of him, we could tell this was a very large rat.

We tried the usual methods for rat extermination: a conventional trap, and then an electronic trap, and a glue trap, but the rat only seemed to become more brazen. Jim went online to study methods of rat extermination and rigged up a device he read about that called for taking an old drywall bucket, filling it with water, and placing across the top an empty coke bottle with a dowel through the middle, slathered with peanut butter.

The idea was that the rat, lured by the peanut butter, would venture onto the Coke bottle, lose his footing, and fall into the water, where he would drown. But the morning after Jim set out his contraption, the coke bottle had been licked clean and there was no rat to be found.

This was when we knew we had a super-rat on our hands—large

enough that his body could span a drywall bucket without falling in and smart enough that he was onto whatever tricks we might employ to catch him.

By this point we had read up on rats, and the particular variety we believed to have taken up residence at our little paradise home among the wisteria vines. This would be a Norway rat, we believed. A single male, we learned, was capable of fathering—with a harem of female rats—as many as eighty offspring within a season.

That fall, rats—rats and the upcoming midterm election— became Jim's obsession. Every day he set out for the hardware store in search of some new device to get rid of rats, or materials to create his own rat-exterminating setup. Because my son Willy sometimes visited with his dog, we couldn't put out poison, which cut down on our options. There was a device that emitted a high-frequency sound that rats supposedly hated, but ours seemed indifferent to it. One night, Jim set up his bass amp at the loudest volume and attached his guitar. The sound that came out—like a heavy metal band gone mad—was awful, but we let it go on all night. The rat remained.

One day Jim came home from the hardware store with twenty glue traps—enough to stretch the full length of the beams of the pergola where our rat made his nightly forays. The glue trap investment came to a couple hundred dollars, but we were desperate. This was no longer simply about rats either. It felt as if Jim and I had fallen victim to a curse, and our beautiful, perfect oasis was under siege.

Jim set out the glue traps end to end, so even the cleverest rat would have no choice but to step into the glue. "I think I've got him now," Jim told me as he finished his nightly pushups and we climbed into bed.

We were awakened by the sound of flailing. Jim went out on the balcony to investigate.

It appeared that our rat had gotten affixed to the glue, all right.

He had fought so hard to get unstuck that he'd flung himself—himself, and the trap—down onto the ground below the second-floor beam.

Jim grabbed a flashlight and went out into the night. On the ground he found the rat, face up on the trap, staring up at him with his beady eyes and sharp little teeth.

Here, Jim faltered. He knew he should kill the rat then and there, but it was three in the morning and he was tired. The idea of clubbing the rat to death or going for his knife and slitting its throat there in the darkness felt like too much. He figured he'd take care of this in a few hours, with the hope that maybe the rat would have expired on his own by morning.

In the meantime, he placed the drywall bucket over the glue trap with the rat on it. On top of this he placed a large cement garden sculpture of a rabbit. Then he went back to bed.

We were up at five thirty, as always. Jim headed out to dispatch the rat. When he came back in the house he was shaking his head. The rat was gone, having burrowed out from under the bucket. Nothing left on the glue trap but an astonishingly long whisker.

33.

October had been a difficult month for us. There was an election coming up, and though this was the first time Jim and I had gone through one of those together, I'd learned by now that nothing got Jim more upset than hearing certain right-wing candidates holding forth. Reading what was going on in the news—the latest comment from John Boehner or Paul Ryan—was almost physically painful for him.

For me, that fall had signaled breakthroughs in my work. I'd just signed a book contract for two more novels, and after a couple of years of feeling unrooted—living in Mill Valley for a while, then Jim's house in Oakland; setting up a temporary work space in Karen's little red farmhouse—I finally had my own desk again in my own writing studio. My new novel was almost ready to deliver now. I was making good money, for once.

But Jim seemed distracted, absent, and though in the past the one thing I had never doubted for a minute was his delight in me, and his joy in our life together, even that seemed to have faded. I still put on my fancy thrift-shop getups most nights for our dinners together, but he seemed distracted, absent. I still researched recipes and cooked good meals for us every night—lighting the candles, holding his hand to say grace before we'd pick up our forks—but he had little to say. If he spoke, it would often be a rant about some candidate.

"You don't need to convince me about the Republicans," I told him—sharper than intended. "I'm with you there."

One of the things I had loved about Jim—loved about the two

of us together—was how, with him, I had become a kinder, better version of myself. I had been a critical person in the past, particularly with men. With Jim, it had felt easy to be loving, and to be generous.

"I want to shower you with every good thing," I used to say to him, and for a long time I had done that. But now I heard the old familiar habit of criticism creeping into my voice. I felt impatient. Disappointed. Where had my hero gone? My guard dog.

My birthday was coming up the first week in November, and I had learned that as much as he loved me, Jim was not adept at thinking up ways to mark November 5. The year before, he had bought me a gift certificate for an expensive massage and spa day—a good present for somebody, but probably not me. The year before he presented me with a necklace I never wore.

Why did it matter? Was there any doubt of Jim's love? But for me at the time, Jim's inability to choose a good birthday present served as indication of some larger failure to know and see me.

He did see me, in fact. He did know me, as well as anybody ever did, and he revealed his love to me daily. He just didn't always know how to express that knowledge with material gifts, or to mark the day with the kind of big, romantic gesture that once seemed important.

That year, as my birthday approached—with Jim in his disconcertingly tuned-out state—I wondered if my husband had even remembered that the day was coming up. Nothing he said or did suggested he had.

I mentioned this to Becky, who had been my friend first, but now loved Jim too. *Don Diego*, she called him.

"I think he forgot all about it," I said. No doubt there was bitterness in my voice that day. "If so, I won't remind him."

My friend pointed out that this was an unkind test. I had a good and unfailingly devoted man for my husband. Did I really want to set him up for failure?

"Jim is just so oblivious lately," I said. "He doesn't seem to be all there anymore."

"Maybe there's something wrong with him," Becky offered. "Suppose you found out Don Diego had a brain tumor. Think how terrible you'd feel."

It turned out that Jim remembered my birthday. The day before I turned sixty-one, an enormous box was delivered to our house from the Gibson guitar company. The shape made its contents unmistakable.

The birthday box had contained a two-thousand-dollar acoustic guitar—an extravagant and loving present. Just not one that made any sense at this moment in my life, I pointed out, when I told Jim to return it. I didn't know how to play the guitar, and though I had often mentioned my regret about this, it seemed a little late to learn.

In the end, he went to the music store and came home with a very beautiful ukulele. "I'll get you lessons," he told me.

The idea of learning to play the ukulele was more realistic. But I continued to feel irritation over Jim's increasingly distracted manner. Maybe because I'd lived through so much more trouble in relationships than good over the years, I was ready to believe that we were hitting the wall.

Jim hardly ever wanted to go on our walks anymore. He spent more and more time in his office, though what he was doing there was unclear. He talked about broadening his practice to include estate planning—something he'd done when he was a young lawyer—or maybe offering his services to firms in the city when they needed outside help. But it seemed to me he couldn't focus. He was always making lists of things to do without checking anything off. Packages would arrive with some new four-hundred-page volume by some political scientist or science fiction novel from Amazon that he'd pick up briefly, then set aside. Sometimes, hearing him rail against the Republican Congress and the upcoming election, his level of ire ran so deep and bitter that even though I agreed with him, I had to leave the room.

THE WEEKEND AFTER the election, I'd been invited to participate in a performance in the town of Grass Valley, a few hours north. A folk singer from Berkeley had put together a show combining songs she'd written with excerpts from letters home written by soldiers over the past couple hundred years. She'd asked me to be one of the readers—the other, Ramblin' Jack Elliot—and I'd been happy to say yes.

I had hoped the weekend might signal a return to our romantic days. We took the Boxster with the plan to make a weekend of it, stopping along the way at interesting spots in the Gold Country, and went out to dinner together before the show.

But once again it felt as if Jim wasn't fully there. Sometime after the show, as we were settling in to our hotel room, he told me he was having back pain—something he'd complained about intermittently, and noteworthy because he was never a complainer. The next morning his back was worse, and there was something else: His urine had turned amber colored. His skin had a yellowish tint. His mouth was set in an unfamiliar grimace that told me he was experiencing more pain than he was telling me about.

He had still insisted on taking the wheel of the Boxster as we headed home from Nevada City. But I could see tension in the muscles in his neck. We did not talk, on the drive, about our upcoming plan to go to Guatemala with my children, or blast rock and roll, or engage in any of our old banter in our bad British or West Indian accents, or our Wanda and Buddy routine. Though we had talked earlier of stopping at some interesting little diner in the Gold Country, Jim had no appetite, and seeing him this way, neither did I.

When we reached Hunsaker Canyon Jim went straight to bed. No pushups. No kisses. Just the incessant scratching of that rat.

PART TWO

After

34.

Late that night, I got out of bed and Googled Jim's symptoms. We had the idea he might have gallstones, and the thought that this could be so—that he would need an operation—seemed, at the time, like an awful prospect. He had just gotten our mountain bikes tuned up, with the idea that we'd start riding together, training for that bike trip we kept talking about, to someplace like Italy.

At the hospital in Walnut Creek, they gave him blood tests and told us to come back the next day for a scan, and I noted an odd look on the face of the nurse. As we sat in the doctor's office that second day awaiting the scan result, a feeling of dread came over me. When the doctor entered the room I knew it was bad.

"We can't confirm this until we perform the endoscopy," he told Jim, "but it's pretty clear what's going on here. There's a tumor in your pancreas."

35.

How does a person describe the moment her world ends?

I felt it in my heart, a blow as real as a knifepoint going in. I thought I might throw up.

Ten minutes earlier, I had been discussing the need to get my car registered (this being my birthday month) and the question of what color to stain the shingles on our house. Now the room was closing in on me.

I looked at Jim's hands, his shoulders—stiffening—his beautiful thick hair, his dear, lined face. He still looked like himself, but everything was different now, life as we'd known it gone in the space it took for a man we'd never met to deliver that one sentence.

Now this man was putting his hand on Jim's shoulder. Jim's expression remained surprisingly unchanged but the doctor looked as if he might cry.

"I'm so sorry," he said. "My father died of this." Emphasis on the word "father" with the implication clear: *and you will too.*

There was more, though I could only take in part of it, words coming in and out like bad radio reception. The tumor appeared to be 2.5 centimeters in diameter. The good news, if you could call anything good now, was that the cancer appeared to be what is known as "locally advanced," meaning that it had not spread to other organs. Not yet.

The bad news—the bad news on top of the worse news—was that this tumor had wrapped itself around a crucial vein in Jim's pancreas, in addition to being pressed up against an artery. The term for this stage of cancer was "borderline resectable." This meant that the prospects for surgically removing the tumor would be slim. Without surgery, Jim was likely to die within a matter of months. A year at most, probably.

I looked again at my husband. *My husband,* the word I'd had a hard time uttering since our wedding day, but not now. All issues with the election, birthday presents, the appearance of obliviousness, car trouble, money trouble, children trouble, were swept away, but with them, our dearest hopes for our life together. Any doubt on the issue of my commitment to this man vanished in an instant. What was happening to him was happening to me too. The diagnosis was not only Jim's but also mine.

His face conveyed little. I touched his shoulder, drew in my breath.

"And what happens if Jim gets this surgery?" I asked. "If that is possible after all?" (Because it had to be. There was no other acceptable option.)

The doctor laid it out for us. The surgery a person needed in a situation like Jim's—the only route to surviving cancer of the pancreas—was known as the Whipple procedure. One of the most involved of all surgeries, it called for the removal of part of the pancreas, part of the small intestine, the gall bladder, the duodenum, as well as every lymph node the surgeon could get his scalpel on, and a complete rerouting of the digestive system. This was an enormously difficult and painful, life-altering procedure. Only a small percentage of those diagnosed with pancreatic cancer would qualify to undergo the Whipple. And even for those able to undergo the Whipple, the number still alive five years after surgery was somewhere between 20 and 25 percent.

Never mind the part about recurrence. I took just one thing

away from those fifteen minutes in the doctor's office. We had to receive that Whipple procedure. Beyond this, I saw nothing. All focus went to the surgery. Getting that tumor out of Jim.

I do not remember leaving the doctor's office, or how we got down the hall to the elevator, and from there to the parking garage, though I know Jim drove us home.

When we got back to Hunsaker Canyon—late afternoon by now, the hour that on another day we would have sat outside to share a glass of wine and reflect on our day—I took Jim's hand and led him to our bed. I had collected my laptop along the way, and now as we lay down together I opened it.

"Let's read each other our wedding vows," I said. "I'll go first."

36.

This was not the first time in my life I'd received bad news. There was the call from my stepfather in Canada on Mother's Day of 1989 to tell me that my sixty-six-year-old mother had an inoperable brain tumor. The late-night call from a hospital in Victoria, eight years before that: "Your father is in an oxygen tent. He won't live through the night."

There was a night in the summer of my thirty-sixth year—1989 again—having dinner with my children's father in a little Vermont inn where I'd booked a room in the hopes of saving our marriage. The two of us, thirty-five and thirty-seven years old. Our children five, seven, and eleven. My husband had set his fork down and looked at me from across the table (John Kenneth Galbraith sat at the table next to us; Why do I always remember that part?) to deliver the news: "I don't want to be married to you anymore."

More moments I supposed I might never survive: When I was nineteen years old—May 1973—and the man I believed I'd love forever put two fifty-dollar bills in my hand and told me to go away and never come back, and the many months that followed when I begged him to speak with me again, to give me another chance. The fall I published a book about what happened when I was eighteen—1998 now—and just about every critic in America condemned not just my book but me. "The worst book ever published," the *Washington Post* said. "*Exploiter . . . kiss and tell artist . . . big mouth . . . the Monica Lewinsky of writers.*"

And worse: my Ethiopian daughters when I said good-bye to

them in April of 2011, turning their faces away as I reached to embrace them. The fact that I understood why made this no easier.

There was an e-mail once from Africa—October 2001—where my seventeen-year-old son had been traveling by himself for the better part of six months. "Malaria." No phone number. No further e-mail contact. A car accident for my son Charlie in 1999—a policeman at the door. Another car accident, 1997, Audrey this time, her tin can of a car hitting black ice on a New Hampshire road, spinning 180 degrees into oncoming traffic, the car crumpled, my daughter's glasses flung so far that the next day, when he visited the scene, it took her father half an hour to locate them in the snow.

She survived that one with a broken collarbone and stitches down the back of her head that still gave her trouble when it rains. Charlie was fine. Willy too. My parents died.

Money lost. Jobs that didn't work out. The farm I'd bought when young, gone to my ex-husband. All of those lesser sorrows than the one consuming me now.

"THERE IS A tumor in your pancreas." If ever there is a moment, outside of wartime, that qualifies as sufficiently disturbing as to inflict post-traumatic stress disorder on a person, that brief stretch of minutes Jim and I spent in that doctor's office when he told us the news would qualify.

I didn't want this to happen, but I couldn't stop it: The next day, and the day after that, and for weeks and months and no doubt years, though it's too early to tell about those—I would play those minutes over in my head. Or random pieces of them, that came to me at unexpected moments of my day, and in my sleep, even. One would skitter across my consciousness like a rat in the night, then disappear again, but only temporarily. I might be putting away groceries or driving to the bank, making the bed or grinding coffee beans; they came to me as I watched Jim shaving or carrying out the trash, climbing into his car, lacing his shoes for our walk. I might be reading, or listening to a song, or picking up the mail, and there it was again, in flashback form, but terrifying as it had been the first time.

Borderline resectable. My father died of this. Things we can do to make you more comfortable. Six months.

You want to cover your eyes when they come into your brain, these random fragments from the worst twenty minutes of your life; only it's not your eyes that let them in, or your ears either. They've taken up residence in your brain.

The white jacket. The plastic chairs. Jim shaking his head. My hand reaching for his. Him, polishing his glasses at this of all moments as if there were some mistake here that cleaning the lens might correct. Or maybe just to have something to do besides scream.

Not that he would have. He did not even cry, though I did.

There are things a person can do for PTSD, they tell us now. You go to a therapist who's an expert at this, and you focus your mind on the very moment that torments you most, the one that keeps coming back, that you can't get out of your head, and as you do this, the therapist has you look at her finger and follow it with your eyes as she moves it back and forth. This has something to do with the Rapid Eye Movement stage of sleep, when it is said that our most disturbing experiences are processed in the brain. I have known a few Vietnam vets who have been helped by this technique, and a few people who aren't vets for whom this Rapid Eye Movement therapy proved to be a good thing.

Those twenty minutes in the doctor's office that day were our Vietnam. Nothing would take them away.

37.

We learned a surprising fact. The tumor had probably begun to grow ten years before this.

A picture of Jim from 2005—in Rome with his children, laughing and eating ice cream cones in front of the Sistine Chapel. Even then it had taken up residence in his body.

It was there that night at the Lark Creek Inn, as we sat across the table from each other telling our stories. It was there as we sucked down our oysters in Point Reyes and danced in the kitchen and made love in Budapest. Long before we met it had been there—cells gradually multiplying, tentacles wrapping themselves around that vein. What if we'd known when it was smaller? That was the thing about tumors of the pancreas. Mostly, you only found out they were there when it was too late to do anything about them.

Then, not long after, you died.

It was November 14 when Jim and I received the diagnosis. Home again from the hospital that day, we had staggered up the stairs and lay in each other's arms for the rest of the night. I read him my wedding vows. He read me his. We wept and at some point finally we fell asleep.

When morning came, it took a moment to remember what we had learned the day before. But for Jim the reminder was unmistakable: The pain was constant now, and terrible, as I realized it probably had been for weeks before. He just hadn't told me.

We had to let our children know about the cancer—hard calls, though we delivered the news with as much optimism as we could muster. I told other close friends too, but we were keeping the diagnosis under wraps to the broader world of Jim's community at that point.

"Nobody's going to hire a litigator with cancer," he said, though I also knew Jim would never mislead a client. In those early days after we learned the news—just at the moment his business has started picking up—I'd heard him on the phone with some prospective client, explaining that he would be going through chemotherapy soon, and couldn't commit to the case.

There was a surgical procedure Jim needed—not the Whipple at this point but a less involved surgery, the first of many. This one called for the insertion of a stent in his bile duct that would relieve some of the pressure caused by the tumor. But a person couldn't get this surgery until his bilirubin count went down sufficiently, and so every day Jim and I made the drive to the Kaiser hospital in Walnut Creek, fifteen minutes from our house for a blood test.

This was only the beginning, of course. We knew there would be all manner of procedures and treatments ahead—though we could have had no idea how many, for how long, how hard they would be, how much worse the pain could become. We knew Jim would be receiving chemotherapy (this meant another surgery, for the insertion of a port) but this too had to wait until the stent was in place. Meanwhile, Jim was suffering a lot of discomfort (*Discomfort.* There was a euphemism).

Just the week before, Jim had tackled a long bike ride. Days later, I could tell from his face that the pain was constant, and grave.

While there remained no question that he had cancer of the pancreas, we learned that there were two different kinds of pancreatic cancer, adenocarcinoma and neuroendocrine. Though both were terrible, neuroendocrine cancer of the pancreas offered a little more hope. Now he needed to undergo a procedure that would confirm, definitively, which kind he had.

Ten days earlier, it would have been bad news to learn Jim needed gall bladder surgery. Now it would have been good news to discover that all he had was neuroendocrine pancreatic cancer. Not that it wasn't still life-threatening. Steve Jobs had died of that one. Neuroendocrine pancreatic cancer was bad, just not quite as bad.

It turned out that Jim adenocarcinoma. The bad one.

38.

Here was another thing I was coming to discover. Though the diagnosis we had received not even two weeks before was close to a terminal one, it was not the prospect of death we dwelt on. There is no way, I think, for a person to get his brain around the likelihood of his own imminent and painful death—and keep his mind there on a twenty-four hour basis. The same may be true for the woman who loves him.

So we set our sights on more direct and immediate obstacles, and with few exceptions, getting through those was as far as we chose to look. We did not look at—or even, I think, imagine—the prospect that Jim would die. We focused our energies on whatever extraordinary measures would be required to keep him alive, and in spite everything—the grim statistics, the look on the face of the doctor delivering the news that first afternoon—we chose to believe that we could do this.

In the pop psychology of the medical realm, this approach is generally labeled "denial." I view it differently. Our way of dealing with Jim's diagnosis was never a conscious choice, but a way of thinking we embraced within the first hours after learning the news because it allowed us to carry on.

When you are bailing water in a sinking boat with a hole in the bottom, you have to believe there's a chance you might make it to dry land—or why keep bailing? The belief that Jim might survive the cancer sustained us; it made it possible to put forth the efforts we did in those first days, and all the ones that followed. If some viewed this as "denial," or evidence of pathology, I preferred to see it as an extreme and unquenchable brand of optimism.

The thing about hope is that it provides the motivation to try. Our first step was clear. We knew we wanted to leave the Kaiser medical system and seek out another medical facility, other doctors, who might offer us more than that first physician's virtual death sentence. This also meant locating a new medical insurer. (Here came a new definition of good luck: Jim's diagnosis was received in the month of November, and not February, or June, or August. In the newly instituted world of Obamacare, November had been designated an open enrollment period. Thanks to this, we could shop for a provider that would cover treatment by any doctor or facility we chose, despite the cost, and regardless of a pre-existing condition. Jim's premium would be high, but given the kind of treatment we knew we'd be embarking on, it would be a bargain.)

The morning after we got the news, I began my research into alternatives. I got up at five now to start placing calls to the East Coast, gathering information about the kinds of treatment offered at Mass General, Dana Farber, Mt. Sinai, Johns Hopkins, UPenn. As the sun made its way across the country, I shifted my focus to facilities in the South, the Midwest, and then Texas. By the time nine A.M. rolled around, when they started answering phones at offices in L.A. and San Francisco and Seattle, I had already filled pages in my legal pad.

I made lists of clinical trials, and when I read about one that sounded promising, I got to work constructing a way we might move to the city where it was taking place (Philadelphia, Miami, Pittsburgh). I gained access to papers generally unavailable to the layperson on new research into pancreatic cancer—immunotherapy, gene therapy, proton therapy. Bent over our kitchen table, I worked to decipher the language, so far from my own vocabulary. Leaned up against the wall: three separate white boards that I once used to map out my novels. Now they displayed my lists of calls to make, addresses to mail Jim's scans, phone numbers to follow up on.

It was grueling and often discouraging—because the truth was, researchers had come up with very little that appeared promising. But the alternative of sitting still and letting grief overtake us—grief, and then death—would have been so much worse. Sometimes days went by in which I didn't wash my hair or change my clothes, and sometimes I found myself on the phone with my three yellow legal pads in front of me and a separate receiver on each ear, so I could speak with one medical facility while on hold with another.

I became an unrecognizable person over the course of those early days. Or maybe just the same person in unrecognizable circumstances, which sometimes gave me the appearance of a crazy person, probably. I'd be partway into a conversation, and suddenly realize I was talking at double speed. When it got too late to make any more phone calls—the East Coast offices closed down, and then the West—I stayed hunched over my laptop planning the next day's assault on the tumor. Even lying in bed, even when the lights were out, I couldn't stop thinking about it.

One thing I did not do, after that first day, was cry.

What Jim was doing over those first days and weeks is harder to say. He took a lot of blood tests—the crucial number being something called his CA19-9, which measured the levels of tumor antigens in the blood. We took some comfort in the fact that although Jim's CA19-9 was well above normal, at 135 it wasn't nearly as high as those of some cancer patients, which sometimes spiked into the thousands.

He spent a lot of time in his office. He actually tried working on cases. But I think it was also, for him, a nearly full-time occupation dealing with the pain. He had drugs, of course. Hydromorphone.

Oxycodone. But he used them sparingly. "I don't want to get addicted," he said. Addiction—a kind of problem that suddenly seemed like good news, because to have an addiction problem means you're alive.

But physical pain was only one piece of Jim's story, though it was the part he occasionally allowed himself to acknowledge. Nothing hurt more, I suspect, than the emotional torture of what he was attempting to absorb and navigate in those first days of recognizing that just about every single dream he had envisioned for his future was slipping away. This, he kept to himself.

39.

Another aspect of my research—less science-based, but crucial for keeping our spirits from sinking into the abyss—had to do with seeking out people who had been diagnosed with pancreatic cancer like Jim's who had survived, people who were alive and doing reasonably well after a space of a couple of years or longer. I was on a mission to find role models for Jim.

These longer-term survivors I located (four years out and not dead yet; five, seven) might not represent anything more than a single-digit percentage of the curve, but I wasn't looking for statistical efficacy, I was looking for hope. I knew how the graph of survival percentages looked, dipping dramatically six months after diagnosis, and then continuing on a sharp downward course all the way to somewhere around the twenty-four-month mark, at which point it went nearly flat, hovering barely above zero. This was the norm, all right, but we were not going for normal. If there were even a dozen people out there who had managed to beat the odds, I wanted to talk to every one of them.

Each time I heard about a person who had outlived the life expectancy of a pancreatic cancer patient, I tracked him down. It was a small enough world that the same names sometimes came up. There was a woman in Southern California named Laurie, whom I must have heard about from six or seven different people that first week, who was active in the PanCan organization and website. She was going on eight years now since surgery. There was Robert in Miami—an attorney who'd experienced a recurrence of cancer within months of his Whipple surgery, but had managed to stay alive and active longer than anyone would have predicted. There was a man in Boston, Joe, initially told he would not qualify for the Whipple, who'd managed to have the surgery two years earlier and now played tennis three times a week.

There were more, of course. And because talking to these people offered more comfort than anything else at that point, I stayed on the phone a lot.

These were cold calls made from our kitchen where I now stationed myself for eight, ten, sometimes twelve hours a day— pacing the room as I talked, more often than not my sole form of exercise. I'd introduce myself, asking first if they'd mind telling me their story. Invariably, they took the time to do this—as, later, I would do the same for other newly diagnosed pancreatic cancer patients, or wives or husbands or brothers or sisters of pancreatic cancer patients. We might never have met and in most cases never did, but we recognized a connection deeper now than what I knew with most of my friends, through the shared experience of this most terrible disease.

I had my questions set: *When were you diagnosed? What chemo-therapy choices did you make? What doctor, what hospital? When was the Whipple performed? How long ago?*

When I heard "two years ago" or (rarer by far), "six," I felt a surge of hope. Then I wanted to know every single thing that person had to tell me so that I could report it all later to Jim.

"I never believed the cancer was going to get me," one woman told me. "A lot of people say how terrible the Whipple is, but I told myself the day of the surgery that this was the best day of my life."

I wrote down every word. I kept a notebook—one of my many— containing what they'd said. Evenings now, when I lit the candles and we sat down for dinner—one of the few parts of our old life we'd managed to hold on to—I took my notebooks out and read out loud to Jim the stories of the people I'd met over the phone. "Joe plays tennis three times a week," I said. "He plays eighteen holes of golf every Sunday."

We lived off of that. My goals now had become so much simpler and more basic: that Jim be alive two years from now. And five.

Maybe seven, I said. How much was fair to ask for without being greedy? Seven years from now, they'd have a cure. If we could just keep Jim alive long enough, he'd get to the age where you die anyway. Why not go for that?

40.

It was in the first couple of days after we'd received Jim's diagnosis that my film agent, Judi, told me about the man I will call Dr. Miracle. The mother of a friend of hers had been diagnosed with pancreatic cancer and was treated by him. Ten years later, she was still alive.

For a patient with pancreatic cancer, this was extraordinary. Within ten minutes of hearing the story Judi had told me, I was on the phone to Dr. Miracle's office. Two days later, we were driving to L.A. Jim was at the wheel still. Over all our time together—just three years at that point—he had invariably been the driver. He was determined that cancer would not change this. He chose to forego painkillers so he could take the wheel.

Dr. Miracle maintained his offices on the campus of a well-known medical facility. He was an outlier, and though well-known in the world of pancreatic cancer treatment, a highly controversial figure.

Even before that first day we met Dr. Miracle, I'd been warned about his manner. "I hear he's extremely unlikable," Judi had told me. "My friend says he's arrogant and dismissive and gruff. But her mother has been cancer-free for going on nine years now. She worships the ground he walks on."

Unlikable was fine, I told her. We weren't looking for a friend. I may even have allowed myself to believe that this doctor's apparent lack of geniality might serve as some additional indication of his brilliance, which could translate into his ability to cure a form of cancer most people regarded as virtually hopeless.

We took our seats in the waiting room and I looked around at the others there: a couple of very thin bald women and one man whose body appeared so wasted that when he stood up, he'd held onto the waistband of his pants.

My eyes turned back to my strong, handsome husband, his beautiful head of dark, grey-flecked hair, his arms lean but muscular. Then back at the scarecrow man.

Not Jim.

When it was our turn, an assistant led us into the great man's office, past a wall of photographs showing Dr. Miracle shaking hands with Katie Couric, Dr. Miracle receiving an award.

He was a large man who looked to be a few years older than we were. "The question is," he said, "do you want to get on the same old train or try a different ride? Because we both know where the other one's taking you."

He asked Jim almost nothing about himself—his symptoms, his current status, and certainly not anything about who he might be as a man independent of the tumor in his pancreas. He sized me up briefly, and then stared out the window.

For the next hour and a half, Dr. Miracle held forth on the sorry state of pancreatic cancer treatment in the medical establishment today and the absence of virtually any meaningful improvement in survival statistics over the past twenty years. One by one, he brought up the names, now familiar to me from my long days of research, of the key players at UCSF, Stanford, MD Anderson, Johns Hopkins, UPenn, Sloan Kettering. When he got to the name of a woman whose medical assistant I'd spoken with just one day earlier— the author of some of the most current papers on the topic of pancreatic cancer, who had a number of major clinical trials under way—his lip curled with contempt. To hear him tell it, it seemed to Jim and me, the leading oncologists in the field were united in what almost appeared to be a conspiracy whose aim was systematically over-seeing the swift and painful death of pancreatic cancer patients all over the nation and beyond, and—this was worse—to sabotage the work of Dr. Miracle. In his eyes, at least, one person only stood between Jim and virtually certain death. He was that man.

Dr. Miracle had a highly unconventional approach to treatment. First of all, he told us, most doctors were far too swift in recommending surgery. They'd administer chemotherapy for a few months, then go straight to the Whipple if they felt it possible. The problem here being that a Whipple surgery was so tough on the body that it would take months to recover from, which caused a dangerous and very possibly lethal interruption in the delivery of chemo.

What Dr. Miracle recommended was a much longer period of chemotherapy before surgery—a year, or longer—assuming that the chemotherapy was successful in shrinking the tumor sufficiently to make this possible, as he believed to be far more likely under his regimen. And the cocktail he used for his patients—though tailored to each one individually, he told us, based on consultations with one of the world's most eminent gene scientists—differed significantly from those delivered at other facilities.

He rattled off a list of drugs, whose names—unknown to me only two weeks earlier—had now become part of my daily vocabulary (Gemzar, Abraxane, irinotecan, oxaliplatin, and one with the bizarre but oddly apt name of 5-FU). But the treatment delivered by Dr. Miracle included one crucial drug in the mix that had not been mentioned by any other doctor or researcher whose programs and papers I'd studied over these days. Avastin.

Avastin had been around for a few years now, but traditionally only in use for patients with colorectal cancer. Dr. Miracle was the only one who used Avastin with pancreatic cancer patients, he told us, and it was because of this, he believed, that he was achieving such impressive results.

If we chose to pursue treatment with him here in Southern California, Dr. Miracle went on, Jim would embark on a program of weekly infusions of his cocktail, with deliveries of Avastin every other week, or three weeks out of four. Because Avastin was off-label for pancreatic cancer—meaning not identified by the FDA as an approved drug for treatment of this kind of tumor—there would be no insurance coverage for these infusions. A single one of which cost $6,000.

The price tag did not give me pause. Just the opposite. Though for some time now Jim hadn't been earning anything close to what he once had in his practice, and I knew he worried about money, the prospect that there might be a new drug for him—no matter what the price—filled me with hope and resolve. We already knew all too well—from those grim charts in which survival was measured in weeks or months—what we might expect from Gemzar/Abraxane or all the rest. No graphs existed for survival on Avastin. To us this meant that anything might still be possible.

By the end of our ninety minutes with Dr. Miracle, I was convinced that we must do whatever it took to get Jim this treatment, and Jim for his part seemed equally ready. The fact that it had taken us seven hours to make the drive from Hunsaker Canyon to this high-rise office, with its waiting room full of people so thin it was hard to tell if they were eighty or forty, was something we'd have to figure out, but we would. And we weren't the only ones. My research had already yielded the name of another couple—Liza and Art—who made the weekly trip from the Bay Area for the miracle of Avastin.

All we wanted to know was how soon Jim could start.

We stayed so long talking with Dr. Miracle that by the time we left everyone else at the office had gone home, including his assistant. The receptionist's desk was empty.

"How much did today's visit cost?" I asked the doctor—I, the one who carried the checkbook.

"Pay me whatever it was worth to you," he said.

I wrote him a check for a thousand dollars. More magical thinking: If Dr. Miracle's advice was worth more than any other doctor might charge, it must be the best.

41.

We would be back for the first infusion in two weeks. Just waiting that long was agonizing, but this was the amount of time Jim had to wait to get his bilirubin count down. Meanwhile, to support the Western medicine approach, we pursued additional forms of treatment out of a belief that Jim should have every single thing going for him that he could.

Though Dr. Miracle had displayed no interest in nutrition and diet as a way of fighting cancer—and kept a large jar of hard candy at the reception desk for patients checking in—I stopped baking the pies Jim loved and removed all sugar from our diet. To avoid additional stress, I suggested that we discontinue all discussion of politics around our house. I sent away for a CD of Jon Kabat-Zinn teaching meditation techniques and books about juice cures and the ketogenic diet and tracked down an organization whose focus was providing personal athletic training for cancer patients for the purpose of building their strength and endurance in preparation for surgery. If Jim was going to get the Whipple surgery—and we were determined he would—it was important that he build his body up for it, as much as he would if he were preparing for a marathon. More so.

I learned about a man with a practice in Marin County who had achieved impressive results with cancer patients. Michael Broffman was not a medical doctor, but for over thirty years he'd been a student of Chinese medicine. Now he offered consultations and designed herbal treatment plans for people with serious, life-threatening illness.

In times past, Jim would have been skeptical, and probably he still was—Jim, a lover of pure science, a man who held the view that Reiki and homeopathy made no sense, and even acupuncture was a dubious discipline—but he agreed to pay a visit to Michael Broffman's office with me, after first filling in a questionnaire many pages long concerning his health history and symptoms.

From the minute I walked in the door I liked the Pine Street Clinic, with its plant-filled windows and strings of Tibetan prayer flags hung from the ceiling and a wall of very old wooden drawers labeled with the names of herbal remedies. There was a little fountain and crystals, of course, and prayer bowls and nice rugs and comfortable chairs—Eastern music playing, candles lit. But beyond the New Age style of the place, I registered a seriousness about the work being done here too, and Jim must have as well because I saw from his face that he was open to what the next couple of hours might teach us, and holding out some hope—hope being hard to come by, these days—that something good might come of this.

We were led into Michael Broffman's office—a small, welcoming room filled floor to ceiling with books, most of them evidently in Chinese, though he himself was clearly American. He was a nice-looking man, around our age—a cyclist, evidently, as I learned from the clippings I'd seen in the hall commemorating his participation in various fundraising rides. A couple of large standard poodles sat at his feet.

"I hope you don't mind," he said, gesturing to the dogs, and we didn't. It turned out the poodles were cancer-sniffing dogs, trained to detect the presence of a tumor in people who might or very possibly might not know they had one. For years, the dogs had been an integral part of Michael Broffman's practice, he explained, but a problem had arisen: Sometimes, walking through the streets of his small town with them, the dogs would become extremely agitated when they passed some person on the street. Clearly, they had detected something in this individual that he or she may not have been aware of yet.

Enough had been written about these dogs by this point in the local press and beyond that the fact of their agitation and attention to a total stranger produced alarm. And though it might be said that their response led to that person's seeking out the advice of a doctor—and very likely discovering, when she did so, the presence of cancer—it was still a complicated thing for Michael Broffman to find himself and his dogs representing, to his fellow citizens, something like the Angel of Death.

So the dogs had been taken out of service, and by whatever means he'd accomplished this, they no longer identified the presence of cancer. Now, for instance—though we knew all too well that at this very moment a tumor was growing in Jim's pancreas—the dogs displayed no more attentiveness to Jim than they did to me.

Unlike Dr. Miracle, Michael Broffman had a warmth about him and a manner that suggested he might actually be interested in Jim, and not simply Jim's pancreas. I leaned forward in my seat—yellow legal pad in hand as always—not wanting to miss a word.

He took out Jim's questionnaire and a thick sheaf of notes he'd made on the case. For an hour he went through a long and diverse range of possible treatment protocols—some involving diet, some supplements, some mushrooms and Chinese herbs. He was not one of those alternative medicine purists averse to chemotherapy—in fact, he was familiar with Dr. Miracle, and was currently working with at least one other patient being treated by him (though as open-minded as Broffman was about Dr. Miracle's brand of treatment, the same could not be said of Dr. Miracle for Broffman). His goal, he told us, was to use as many tools as possible to address the disease that had taken hold in Jim's body, with a realistic awareness of how difficult this one would be to eradicate.

When our visit was over, I had pages of notes. We stopped at the desk in front, where we bought a vast assortment of herbs and dried mushrooms. It felt good buying them, as it always did now, when I identified some new food or vitamin or herb thought to possess cancer-fighting properties. As much of a long shot as it may have been, that a handful of mushroom powder or turmeric-and-Reishi-mushroom capsules could wage war on a deadly cancer, taking those supplements and capsules served the purpose—if it did nothing more—of relieving our sense of powerlessness. It had been nearly intolerable to leave Jim sitting there knowing that inside his body at that very moment—while we awaited the first infusion of Avastin—the cancer cells were multiplying.

Among the many recommendations of Michael Broffman, one offered a beautiful simplicity, and unlike what Dr. Miracle was offering, required no vast expenditure of cash. Michael Broffman spoke of the need to restore the flora and fauna in Jim's digestive system that no doubt had been eradicated by the strong antibiotics Jim had been taking for infection. We needed to repopulate Jim's gut, he told us. Now he would tell us how.

"Eat good dirt," Broffman told Jim.

Through a mutual friend in Berkeley, I tracked down Michael Pollan, author of several books I knew well on the subject of organic food. I called him up to ask where he'd go in the Bay Area to locate the best dirt.

"There's a farmer in Petaluma," he told me. "Bob grows the best organic vegetables around. He hasn't let a single chemical touch his land in over thirty years."

I called Farmer Bob. I was not the first person to seek out the curative properties of his dirt, evidently. Not infrequently, people suffering from some form of illness or other that had required them to go on extreme antibiotic regimes had shown up at his farm. Sometimes they just sat down right there in the field to pull up a carrot and chomp on it.

I liked the idea of making the trip to Petaluma to procure our dirt, but we were also pursuing so many other things at this point—interviewing oncologists, visiting a nutritionist and an exercise therapist, taking those daily blood tests to monitor Jim's bilirubin, and more. No worries, Bob told me; one of the young people who worked at his farm made a run to Berkeley three times a week to deliver vegetables to Chez Panisse. He could leave a box of root vegetables for me at the restaurant—beets, carrots, turnips, parsnips, the kind that hold dirt—with none other than Alice Waters as the go-between.

Two days later, we stopped by Chez Panisse to pick up our good dirt, attached to a boxful of very good root vegetables. Under other circumstances, of course, I would have washed them first, but that was before. That afternoon we sat outside together under the dangling pods from the wisteria vines, filling our stomachs with carrots, dirt and all. We were like two characters in some fairy tale I hadn't read, one that must exist somewhere, seeking the secret potion, the magic bean. Maybe it was right there, attached to a carrot. Maybe it would be found in the smoothies I concocted daily now in our Vitamix, filled with nuts and chia seeds and organic berries chosen on the basis of their antioxidant level.

More likely, it wasn't. But believing it might be got us through our days.

42.

The bilirubin number went down, and the infusions began. (Though first there was a surgery—a minor one, by comparison—to place a port in Jim's chest. Now, when I reached over to touch him in the night, there was a hard plastic receptacle just below the skin, for receiving the chemo.)

We made our first trip back to Dr. Miracle's office the week after Thanksgiving and wrote the first $6,000 check for the magic Avastin. That night, Jim felt sick, but it felt good knowing that we were no longer simply leaving the cancer cells to attack him. We were attacking back.

Our lives after that took on a rhythm unrecognizable from before. There were the infusion weeks, and the off-weeks—those seven-hour drives to Southern California, trips to the oncologist in Pleasant Hill for check-ins. In between, and despite the sickness caused by the chemo, Jim tried to carry on some semblance of a normal life, disappearing into his office when he could to work on cases, though with an awareness that if any new client asked him to take on an estate fight, he'd be morally obligated to turn her down. "I wish I could help you," I heard him say, on the phone, "but I've been having some cancer treatment that's got me a little laid up at the moment."

Every day began with the making of his smoothie, with the goal that he be filled with as many immune-boosting herbs and supplements as I could get into the Vitamix my son Will had sent us when he learned about the diagnosis. I laid them all on the counter: frozen berries, banana, nuts, coconut oil, pea protein, chia seeds, kefir. Jim hated Boost, but sometimes I added that too, for the extra three hundred calories. He might not finish the drink—usually didn't—but I'd follow him around with it over the course of the morning, or whirl it up in the machine a second time, and a third, augmented with new ingredients. In a manner not so different from how, at age seventeen, I'd been obsessed with keeping weight off my own body, now my obsession was putting weight on Jim's—or more realistically, keeping him from losing any more. Sometimes, if he was in his office, or reading his Kindle in the living room, I'd set a tray down with bowls of nuts and slices of cheese. "If you could just eat ten cashews a day," I told him, "that would add on five hundred calories." I knew the numbers from my own days as a teenage anorexic. I kept a running tally every day of where he stood.

Always before, I had loved it that Jim had such a firm, fit body for a man his or any age. He'd been a runner all his life, and a cyclist, and had always been lean. Lying next to him on the bed, I could make out every rib bone.

But his lean physique no longer served him well. He had no reserves. His weight dropped from 145 to 135, then 125, then 120. Somewhere over the course of those days, I developed an odd new habit when walking down the street with him: If I saw a man with one of those bellies that men of his age so often possessed, I'd think, "How lucky he will be if he gets cancer. He could lose fifty pounds and not be in trouble."

Sick as he was now from the chemo, Jim still headed out to the gym almost every day to work out with his trainer, Eddie, lifting weights, climbing a rope, riding a stationary bicycle to build his stamina. We knew he'd need it.

A single goal remained unceasingly in our sights: to shrink the tumor sufficiently that Jim might qualify for the Whipple procedure.

"The tumor," I called it—never "Jim's tumor." I never wanted to take possession of that 2.5-centimeter mass in his pancreas. If anyone was listening, it didn't belong to us. "The Whipple," I called the surgery now. We were on a first-name basis with what may well be the toughest kind of surgery a person could undergo. And there was nothing we wanted more than that Jim might qualify for it.

43.

Days passed. Jim was feeling the effects of the chemo all right—
but this was good news, in a way. I liked to think that the
same thing that was knocking him out was knocking out the cancer.
There were clumps of hair on the floor of the shower now—his
beautiful hair—and his fingers were starting to get numb, and so
sensitive that he could no longer take a carton of anything cold out
of the freezer, or even open the drawer. Whatever I cooked for him,
he had no appetite.

Still, we continued to go through our days in a manner that
approximated our old lives—allowing ourselves to pretend a tragedy
was not taking place. We still started our day, before the sun came
up, in the hot tub out under the live oak tree. Every morning we had
our coffee together, then sat side by side at the kitchen table reading
the news and, in Jim's case, playing online Scrabble.

How do two people get through the day, when one of them has
a tumor inside his abdomen that may be killing him, and the other
is simply consumed with grief? We installed new light fixtures in
the bathroom. We invited friends for dinner and took long drives
and listened to music, watched *Downton Abbey*. We played ping-
pong and worked on memorizing poems—"The Love Song of
J. Alfred Prufrock" for Jim, "Dover Beach" for me. Between visits
to doctors, we took our walks when Jim was up to it, to the place
down the road—blocked off by a gate we chose to climb over—
that led to a few miles of hillside trails some rancher had donated
to the county, that almost nobody knew about but the people like us
who made their home in the canyon. Sometimes we heard coyotes

howling off in the distance, and one time we saw a fox. Jim brought his camera along, snapping my picture. I picked up pieces of owl scat, looking for mouse skeletons.

We made a point of talking about other things besides cancer on our walks—scientific discoveries Jim had read about, plans for our garden, trips we wanted to take—the most imminent being to my house on the shores of Lake Atitlan in Guatemala, where for almost a year now we'd been planning a Christmas gathering with my three children and one of his, along with all their partners. "No way I'm missing that," Jim said, heading out to work with his trainer.

A singer we both loved, Richard Thompson, was playing at the Freight and Salvage in Berkeley, and though this was taking place shortly after the infusions got under way—the pain constant, not to mention the sorrow—we had tickets, and decided to go.

The Freight is a relatively small, intimate space, and our seats were right near the front. This particular night, Richard Thompson had announced that he was playing all requests. Though we did not ask for any particular song ourselves, the very first one he played was our favorite.

The song is called "1952 Vincent Black Lightning." It's about a young, wild motorcycle rider named James who meets a woman named Red Molly. "That's a fine motorbike," she tells him. "Red hair and black leather," he says back. "My favorite color scheme."

He gives her a ring. He robs a store, and gets shot doing it. Red Molly is called to his bedside, and with his last breath, he gives her one last kiss before handing over to her the keys to his motorcycle.

I had always loved that song, and played it for Jim when I first met him. You could call it a melodramatic story, probably, but I was always a sucker for stories of big romantic tragedy. I just didn't want to live one.

★   ★   ★

ANOTHER TRIP TO Southern California. Just a month since the diagnosis, Jim's weight was down to 120 pounds, but that didn't stop him from doing his pushups every night with me alongside him, and sometimes he still did pull-ups on a bar we'd put up over our bedroom door. "You know the great thing about losing all this weight?" he said to me. "It's easier to pull myself up now."

Only it wasn't, of course. The cancer was never out of our minds, and he was hurting more than he liked to tell me, but he still headed out to his office when he could to work on a case and edit photographs from one of our previous adventures, and on Tuesday nights, if he was feeling up to it, he drove to his Storkzilla practices in the city. One night we drove to Sausalito together to the home of our friend Jerry for a day of playing rock and roll, and dinner after, gathered around the table with our friends. Everyone told Jim how good he looked. Baldness became him, they said.

Driving to doctors' appointments—there were so many of those—we tried resurrecting our Wanda and Buddy routine and Jim's Topo Gigio imitation. We talked about my longtime resolve that we take dancing lessons together, and about inviting the guys in Jim's band to the house at Lake Atitlan when Jim was over this, to play music in the shadow of the volcano. At the end of every day, we slept naked in each other's arms, clinging to one another. One night the phrase came to me, with a whole new meaning: *holding on for dear life.*

At the point Jim was diagnosed, he had been seeing a therapist, as I was too. For Jim, this had marked a moment—possibly the first in his life—when he had felt able, finally, to explore his relationship with his father. Some of this he kept to himself, but sometimes, too, on therapy days, he had come home after wanting to talk with me about the work he'd been doing with Dr. Geissinger. He was excited and hopeful about understanding the ways in which that early experience of being terrorized, and his perpetual sense of himself as having fallen short of being the son his father wanted, had shaped other aspects of his life. He was looking in new ways at his relationships with his children, and his relationship with me.

Some real sadness accompanied these sessions with the therapist. But something else too, which was the possibility that he might at long last free himself from very old wounds. Both of us might.

It was one of the things marriage had made possible, I had been discovering: the safe harbor we seemed to inhabit that gave us courage to venture into rough seas and rocky places. It would have been a wonderful thing if we could each have done some of this work in our twenties or thirties or forties—even our fifties—but the important thing was that we were doing it now.

Then came the diagnosis. And suddenly, discussions of one's childhood injuries—parents who'd hurt us, marriages that failed—became another luxury we could no longer afford. We were fighting for Jim's survival now.

Jim still went to Dr. Geissinger now and then, but he worried about the cost of the visits. And anyway, there were just so many other appointments on the calendar. Every day, almost, another trip over the bridge.

I gave up my therapy. (Too expensive. Too costly of time.) Jim hung on a little longer. But as much as he liked talking with Dr. Geissinger—who had told Jim he no longer planned to bill him for their time together—he went to see him less and less. And finally, not at all.

It would probably have been a good thing exploring, with a therapist, what the cancer had done to our lives. But the cancer was taking everything we had.

44.

The end of the year approached. If the days were dark now, they were only going to get darker. Same thing that was true of our canyon, as we moved toward winter solstice, and the rain kept falling, and more and more of the small tasks we'd taken care of around our place went unattended as we struggled simply to get through another twenty-four hours.

We did not speak of death. All our focus went to shrinking the tumor so Jim could get the Whipple. And how best to accomplish that. The clock was ticking. We had to wipe the tumor out faster than cancer cells could grow.

The urgency that accompanied this knowledge never left us. Dr. Miracle had explained to us what it was about this particular form of cancer that made it perhaps the most dreaded form of the disease. Where some cancer cells are permeable, he said, pancreatic cancer forms a hard shell around itself that makes the tumor nearly impervious to chemotherapy. For treatment to be successful, these cells need to be *tricked* (this was the word employed by more than one of the experts with whom I spoke, and in the articles I studied) into allowing the elements administered in chemotherapy to gain entry into the tumor.

Something about the way these articles were written and the language of the doctors with whom we spoke led to an almost inevitable perception: that the cancer was not simply a highly unfortunate fluke of mutation, but an actively malevolent force within a person's own body, going to war with itself—as if the cancer had a personality, a nasty and villainous one. In the same way that I had projected onto the rat we still heard outside our bedroom window every night a kind of premeditated intention to destroy our peaceful home, now I saw the cancer cells that way—as possessing ill will, and even more than that, true evil, like Lord Voldemort or Darth Vader or the villain played by Javier Bardem in one of Jim's favorite James Bond movies, *Skyfall*: brilliant, sadistic, relentless.

But James Bond—the movie hero he loved best—had triumphed, and so would Jim, I said. In the face of all evidence to the contrary, I willed myself to believe this. And because I believed this, it appeared that Jim also did.

45.

It was a lonely business, fighting cancer. This one in particular. The word *pancreatic* left little room for anything good.

You didn't want to tell your old friends how it was. They'd sympathize, of course, but they wouldn't understand—or, if they did, that might be worse. "I don't want to be the cancer patient wherever I go," Jim said. But this was happening.

Then an unexpected group of new friends entered our lives. Sitting in the chair at my hairdresser's one day—my own faint attempt at carrying on some semblance of a normal life—I heard a woman in the next chair talking about a men's group in our town whose members were all fighting pancreatic cancer. When I got home I told Jim about the group.

It was not easy for Jim to reach out to these men he'd never met to announce the fact that was, for each of them, the single most awful aspect in each of their lives. Much as I had done decades before, when my children were very small, and I wanted to make sure they'd have friends, I contacted one of the men myself—Dan, a founding member—to tell him about my husband and urge him to drop Jim a note.

Dan sent a letter, with a long and detailed account of the many stages he himself had gone through since his diagnosis a few years back, when he was still in his forties. The devastation first, followed by months of grueling treatment that had seen his weight drop by seventy pounds. (This was more possible for Dan, who was a much larger person than Jim, and stood well over six feet.)

Dan had managed to undergo the Whipple, he wrote, and after

it there had been more months of struggle. But for Dan, the good news was that he had now returned to his normal weight, was working full-time, attending his kids' sports events and even playing some basketball.

The pancreatic cancer breakfast group—seven of them—met at a local restaurant every few weeks to compare notes on their treatment and share whatever they'd learned in their research about possible breakthroughs in the field of pancreatic cancer, and what clinical trials were on the horizon. That, and moral support most of all. Though none of these men possessed a medical background, they had all become highly knowledgeable about the disease and knew where all the cutting-edge work was going on. They could name every drug and its side effects. Everyone knew about Dr. Miracle and Michael Broffman and all the other players: Temblor at UCSF, Morton at Stanford, Wolfgang at Johns Hopkins, Gonzalez in New York. The gene therapy program in Arizona. The NanoKnife.

The morning he was supposed to meet with the pancreatic cancer breakfast group, Jim thought maybe he'd cancel, but in the end he went, after I nearly pushed him out the door. When he returned from that first meeting, he filled me in on each man's story. There were five of them—six now, counting Jim—all between the late forties or early sixties. All but one, whose cancer had metastasized, had undergone the Whipple procedure themselves. And even the one with Stage 4 cancer—the death sentence—seemed to be beating the odds, Jim reported. He was in a clinical trial and his tumors were shrinking. He and his wife had just returned from two weeks in Tuscany.

They were a terrific group of men—smart and highly informed, and likable, and every one of them in possession of a surprisingly positive attitude.

And of course we wished we had never had occasion to meet them. Same as they all no doubt wished the same of us.

46.

The breakfast club offered comfort and support, but it seemed to me that the thing most likely to offer Jim joy at this point was playing music with his friends. Rock-and-roll medicine.

So I called Jim's musician friends, inviting them to our house for a Sunday afternoon music jam to be followed by dinner of seafood paella, a specialty of mine. Every one of them said yes—Jerry and Rich, the two lead guitarists; Tony, the accordion player; Tucker on ukelele; Gary on keyboards and Allan on drums. Wives too, I said. We would finally get to have, at Hunsaker Canyon, the kind of big, noisy dinner with friends we'd pictured that first day we visited on Jim's motorcycle, when the property first came on the market and the wisteria was in bloom.

As usual, Jim worried more than he needed to about making everything perfect for this gathering. Sick as he was from chemo, he had taken out the leaf blower and then the vacuum cleaner, and then got to work on the French doors.

"You don't need to do this," I told him. "These are good friends." Maybe it was his father's training—a childhood spent on yard work and chores, and punishment if things weren't done just right—that made it impossible for Jim to leave dirt on the patio or brush in the yard.

The day before the party, I made four pies and drove to three different stores getting the best seafood for the paella. I wanted not just shrimp and cod and clams and mussels this time, but also scallops and crab and calamari tentacles and lobster claws to decorate the platter. When I got home, my arms were weighed down by bags that Jim insisted on taking from me and carrying in, though I knew this was not easy for him now. That night he set out his three bass guitars and arranged the music stands, rearranging the chairs for the wives, setting out the charts for songs. I assembled the ingredients for margaritas.

The morning of the party, when Jim got out of bed, I watched him standing there. He was studying his hands as if they were no longer attached to his body. Sometime in the night, his fingers had gone totally numb from the neuropathy. There was no way he could play his bass.

We held off a few hours, hoping the nerve endings might come back to life. Jim went back to bed, sicker than I'd seen him since the first days following the diagnosis.

At ten thirty I called Tony, asking him to get the word out to the others. There would be no rock and roll at our house that day.

"I feel like a jerk," Jim said—the old habit from childhood of taking on responsibility for anything that ever went wrong. "I've spoiled everything."

I dismantled the big outdoor table we'd set up and carried the extra chairs back out to the garage. Then though it was not yet dark, I climbed into bed next to Jim and we watched three episodes in a row of *Downton Abbey*—the furthest we could get away from our lives that day, and a million miles away from "Stairway to Heaven."

Later again—dark now, Jim asleep with his laptop open, his rock-and-roll jeans still laid out at the foot of our bed—I carried the seafood out to the yard. I had tried without success to give it away, though I probably could have tried harder, and in different circumstances I would have. As it was, I flung the whole mess into the woods for the animals. First the mussels, then the clams, the scallops, the lobster even, the crab. I could have frozen the stuff, of course, but I had no stomach for any of it anymore.

I pictured how it would be later, sometime between now and dawn, when the animals in the canyon discovered what was there—the feast attended by raccoons, deer, and who knew what else—maybe mountain lions and foxes. We might hear the coyote howling on the hill that night. But no rock and roll.

47.

Almost ten months before this—before cancer, and bilirubin counts, and endoscopies, and Avastin, and 5-FU, and neuropathy—we had made the plan to gather as many of our children as we could at my house on Lake Atitlan for a big family holiday together, our first with the children. All three of my kids—Audrey, Charlie, and Willy—were up for the trip, along with two of their partners. Those plane tickets had not come cheap, but never mind. It was a dream for us, to be together with at least some of the children this way.

After Jim was diagnosed, when the kids asked if we were planning to cancel Christmas, we told them no way. We'd be there. But as the month wore on, and the chemo began taking effect—Jim's beautiful hair gone, along with so much else—we realized it would be impossible for us to make that trip.

My younger son and daughter and their partners still flew to Guatemala. Jim and I spent a quiet Christmas alone, though on New Year's Eve, we dressed up and headed across the bridge to a party. Jim was as handsome bald as he had been with hair, though in other ways his face had changed dramatically. Not just because it was thinner, and more lined; even when he smiled for the camera, there was a look in his eyes that didn't used to be there. Studying pictures now, I realize there was a look in mine too.

48.

In January we began to question the wisdom of continuing to make our trips to Dr. Miracle. Partly this had to do with discussions Jim had with members of the breakfast group, a couple of whom had consulted the miracle doctor themselves at various points along the way in their treatment. We'd been reading about Avastin, and it was hard to know what to make of these articles, but as much as we wanted to believe that this doctor had hit on a way to attack adenocarcinoma of the pancreas as no others had, I could find no evidence in the medical literature that those $6,000-a-week infusions made any difference in the outcome of the disease. In my telephone conversations with pancreatic cancer treatment facilities around the country, when I mentioned who was treating Jim and recited his treatment protocol, I would register a slow intake of breath on the other end of the line, the measured words that almost invariably followed.

But for us the deciding factor in our decision to discontinue the Avastin had been something else. Early on, when Jim had first gone to Dr. Miracle, I had asked his chief medical assistant if she could provide me with the names of patients he'd treated who'd survived for over five years, post-Whipple, other than the one I'd heard about from my agent, Judi. Recognizing that she would not be in a position to give out their phone numbers, I asked if she'd let these patients know how much I wanted to speak with these long-term survivors and give them my phone number.

One called. One only.

I asked again. Still waited.

Then I asked to read any papers Dr. Miracle might have

published on his treatment protocol. He showed me a draft of one, unpublished.

After that first visit when we'd signed on for treatment, Dr. Miracle never had time to address my questions about Jim's treatment. Whereas on that first day in his office, he had spent over ninety minutes with us discussing his approach to treatment and the reasons why every other oncologist in the field was doing everything wrong, now he ignored my messages. Once I rode all the way to L.A. with Jim in the hopes that I'd have more luck getting Dr. Miracle's ear if I showed up in person rather than calling, but that time, when I'd asked if I could have a few minutes to speak with him before my husband's infusion, the assistant had come back to report that it was an unusually busy day. A conversation of even the shortest duration would not be possible.

One of the people with whom I discussed the choice to leave Dr. Miracle—though we never met—was Liza, another wife of a man with pancreatic cancer, who was also making the weekly trip to L.A. from the Bay Area and shelling out the three-times-a-month Avastin check. Liza agreed with me: Dr. Miracle could be maddening, but she and her husband, Art, had made the decision— equally agonizing—to stick with his treatment regimen.

"How are any of us supposed to know what's the right thing here?" she said to me, over the phone. "We aren't doctors. And even the doctors don't really know. You can drive yourself crazy, thinking about all the things you might be doing, or the things you're doing that might be dead wrong." *Dead wrong.* There was a phrase for you.

After much debate, Jim and I concluded together that his odds were better in one of the more mainstream pancreatic cancer programs—so long as it was the very best. We canceled the next trip we'd had planned for L.A., with the resolve that we would go anywhere, spend whatever it took getting there. We just needed a doctor—a team, actually, not a lone cowboy—whom we trusted.

What to do, what to do? I could talk on the phone all day with people at pancreatic cancer programs around the country, read papers, haunt the PanCan website, call up pancreatic cancer survivors—or the widows of those who had not survived—hearing about where they went, what drugs they were given, which surgeon performed their Whipple. But in the end, all we could do was trust our instincts.

"Boatmen on the River Styx," Jim called the surgeons and oncologists—these gods you sought out, in search of the elusive cure. Not even the cure, really—just the chance of getting a green light for the Whipple procedure. I did not ask myself this other question: Suppose it didn't even matter where you went, or what drugs they treated you with, or what berries you ate or did not eat, or whether you got CyberKnife radiation or immunotherapy—whether the surgeon had gone to Harvard or Stanford or Penn? What if this cancer were simply so deadly that the person you loved was going to die anyway?

We were in the world's most high-stakes gambling event, where you got one card to play—one shot—and if you chose wrong, you died. You might die anyway, but that was another story. We weren't going there.

49.

I heard about another possible miracle worker. His name was Dr. Ronald Weiss, and he practiced medicine in New Jersey. Though he had received conventional training in Western medicine, and for years had worked with patients in a hospital setting, Ron Weiss had gradually shifted his focus—a little at first, then more and more, and now totally—to the philosophy that no better form of treatment existed than eating the right foods and eliminating everything else but those foods from one's diet.

Unlike most physicians who tended to put so little emphasis on nutrition and diet, Ron Weiss had long been a believer in healthy vegetarian eating. But for him the turning point had come many years earlier when, just as he was completing his own medical training, his father had been diagnosed with Stage 4 pancreatic cancer and given months to live.

Though at the time Ron Weiss was very young—just starting out in his practice of medicine—he resolved to seek out a way of helping his father that went beyond what the doctors had offered.

With nothing to lose, he put his father on a strict macrobiotic diet, eliminating all animal proteins. He augmented this diet with a number of foods and spices he believed to possess specific cancer-fighting properties. (Now, he said, he knew about far more of these foods, but even then he was aware of a few. Turmeric. Berries with high antioxidant content.) In addition to animal proteins, he eliminated all sugar from his father's diet—also oils, salt, and virtually anything that might have enhanced flavor.

"Pleasure is a trap," he said. "Pleasure leads to consumption of unhealthy foods."

Ron Weiss's father was in his seventies by this point, and never one to abstain from meat or salt or sugar. But he had gone along with his son's experiment. And when he did an amazing thing had happened. His health began to improve.

Twelve months after the diagnosis of pancreatic cancer—his weight stabilized, his energy restored—Ron Weiss's father returned to the office of the doctor who'd given him the death sentence. When the doctor saw him, he reacted as if he'd seen a ghost.

Ron told us his father had lived another year after that, subsisting on an adapted form of the macrobiotic diet. Eventually the cancer returned, and when it did it had killed him swiftly. Still, Dr. Weiss believed that healthy eating had given his father an extra two years of good quality life. (Not exciting dining experiences, but never mind. As much as I loved food, and loved cooking, I would have agreed to subsist forever on kale and pomegranates if it would have kept Jim alive.)

This experience had formed the beginning of the practice Dr. Weiss had built, focused entirely on food as medicine. Eventually, he'd left his mainstream medical practice, bought a farm in northern New Jersey where he oversaw the cultivation of organic crops, assisted by a full-time organic farm manager and a dietician named Asha who shared his passionate commitment to curing illness through diet. They had recently opened their doors to a range of patients suffering a variety of medical issues from obesity to heart disease to cancer.

I had read this much in an article online. That was enough to convince me that Jim and I needed to speak with this man.

It was seven P.M. on a Saturday night the first time I called Ron

Weiss to ask if he could help. This would have been ten P.M. Eastern time. But sixty seconds after I left my message he called me back.

We talked for over an hour. By the time we rang off it was decided: Jim and I would fly to New York City that coming weekend, borrow my friend David's car, and drive to northern New Jersey to stay at Ron Weiss's farm, Ethos. We'd spend a week there, learning how to prepare foods that could help Jim, and receiving an education in Ron Weiss's brand of medicine.

Dr. Weiss wasn't a salesman, but he told us he would make it his mission to lower Jim's CA19-9 count sufficiently over the course of those few weeks that Jim might open his mind to a natural approach to the treatment of his cancer. No doubt the prospect of getting a chance to cure, in Jim, the very cancer that had killed his father, contributed to Ron's passion for helping Jim.

"I'm not going to promise you anything," he told us on the phone that first night. "All I can tell you is that I'll give you everything I've got. I've waited twenty-two years for the chance to apply what I've learned since my father's death to another pancreatic cancer patient's situation. I believe I can help you."

We booked our tickets to fly east. By the time we arrived at Ethos Farm, Ron had devoted days to reading up on the chemistry of pancreatic cancer cells and foods that might be best equipped to combat it. He had put together a long list of herbs Jim was to consume in massive quantities, three times a day, along with the more standard macrobiotic fare. Some of these foods took so long to prepare—and so long to eat, because of the quantities Jim was required to consume—that it seemed as if our entire day was spent chopping, preparing all those bitter herbs and organic vegetables and then chewing the giant pleasure-free salads we prepared in bowls as big as troughs—only to resume preparation for the next meal almost as soon as that one was finished.

We were the only patients at the Ethos Health Center that week, and among the first patients there ever, which meant that we received the virtually undivided attention of Ron and Asha. From early morning to the end of every day, we worked with those two— me, alongside Jim, living on the same diet. Sometimes we'd listen to a lecture on some aspect of the diet, or on the importance of meditation. Other times we'd participate in a cooking lesson. There was no salt in anything we ate. No oil. No wine to accompany our meals. No coffee.

For our part, we were not going to abandon chemotherapy. But Ron asked us to give his diet one month. "Let's measure your blood levels and tumor markers before we begin treatment, and again four weeks later," he said. "I believe we will see significant improvement."

Once again, committing to one course of treatment over another felt like a huge gamble. We could not afford to lose valuable time treating the cancer. But after long conversations with Dr. Weiss, Jim and I decided to see what might be possible if Jim gave himself an extra week off of chemotherapy while adhering to the diet. This would place him two weeks beyond the normal interval between most chemotherapy infusions, which felt like an acceptable space of time to give the alternative treatment a try. Not a lot of time to witness improvement, but Dr. Weiss believed that even in such a short time, Jim might begin to feel better.

Looking back on our decision now to interrupt chemotherapy for those two weeks, I ask myself if this might have been a moment— or one of them—when we made a fatal call. What might it have meant to Jim's prognosis that we stepped away from the chemotherapy as we did? Much as the Norway rat outside our bedroom, whose footsteps we still heard in the night, had wised up to the workings of every trap we'd laid out, I could see the cancer cells mutating new ways to render themselves invulnerable to every form of chemotherapy drug we threw at them. Was that December the month some rogue cell made its way into Jim's liver?

Still, it felt good to be putting something healthy into Jim's body instead of filling him with poison. Knowing, too, how little in the way of hope the world of mainstream medicine was offering us, it was impossible not to feel drawn to exploring a different route from those already proven to offer only the barest possibility of success.

I liked Asha and Dr. Weiss. His belief in the form of treatment he practiced was passionate and informed by a great deal of research, though research outside the mainstream. All that week we spent in New Jersey I carried around the book he recommended to me—*The China Study*—reading passages out loud to Jim when something struck me as particularly important and persuasive. "Listen to this," I'd say, and reel off another amazing fact about the curative properties of a particular herb, and the cancer-promoting properties of sugar, or—conversely—the machinations of the drug industry.

In all our many consultations with Dr. Weiss that week, he did not weigh in on the advisability of undergoing the Whipple procedure. But one conversation we had stands out for me. It happened near the end of our time together.

"Perhaps, if you feel good about the results you get by living on this diet, you may opt not to have the Whipple procedure after all," he told us. "Even if it becomes an option, as it well may."

At the time, I supposed that Dr. Weiss was suggesting his diet might actually cure Jim's cancer on its own, without benefit of surgery—and this sounded unrealistic and rash. As much credence as I might give to the benefits of turmeric and blueberries and all the rest of the foods Ron and Asha had offered up to us, it seemed impossible to suppose that a food—any food—could eradicate a form of cancer as deadly as this one.

Much later, I thought back on what Dr. Weiss was saying to us that day. This time it struck me differently. I think he might have been trying to convey something else to Jim and me, besides our need to believe that this diet of his might cure pancreatic cancer. Very gently—because it would have been hard if not impossible to deliver this assessment in plain, hard language to the people we were then, who were still so desperately attached to the dream of a cure—I think he may have been suggesting that we might actually do better bypassing Whipple surgery and adhering to his diet not as a way of permanently eradicating the cancer, but as an alternative to a brutal procedure whose odds for saving Jim's life struck him as impossibly low.

PERHAPS HE WAS quietly suggesting that it might be wiser to get a good year or two in, without surgery—as his father had, eating in a manner that could slow down the growth of cancer for as long as possible, with the hope that Jim might actually manage to feel good for a significant portion of that time.

If he had said this to us at the time, I could not have accepted his words. In our innocence and desperation, we had chosen to view "getting the Whipple" as akin to reaching the promised land. Ron Weiss, who had no doubt seen plenty of patients in the aftermath of that eviscerating procedure, knew better—as we would too, one day.

When the week in New Jersey was over, we flew home, but for some time we kept to the diet Ron and Asha had given us. Because pomegranates were a crucial part of the program they'd designed for Jim—and pomegranate season was ending—we made a trip to the Berkeley Bowl and bought up every single pomegranate they had in the store—over a hundred of them—that we stored in the backup refrigerator we had, whose function we had initially envisioned as keeping beer cold for parties.

Now when you opened the door of that refrigerator, all you could see were pomegranates.

I lost fifteen pounds that month. Jim, who had nothing to lose, lost twenty.

As for the rest: Jim's tumor markers did go down a little on the Ron Weiss diet, though not as dramatically as we'd hoped. It is definitely true that we both felt surprisingly good after a month of eating this way, though we also missed the pleasure of food as something more than pure sustenance.

But at the end of six weeks of living on the diet, Jim threw in the towel. "If I keep living on these salads I'll fade away," he said. His weight was down to 108.

That night we grilled him a steak and made a Caesar salad with Parmesan cheese, egg yolks, anchovies. I shared in the meal, along with a bottle of cabernet, and after, we ate pie.

We still tried to keep up with the pomegranates. But we couldn't get through them fast enough. We'd open one up, and instead of beautiful little red jewel seeds, we'd find the fruit rotten.

So one night we carried what was left of the pomegranates outside into the same field behind our house where I had thrown away the seafood I'd bought for the paella party that never happened. One by one, whooping and laughing, Jim and I flung what was left of our pomegranate stores into the woods.

The animals in our part of the canyon ate well that season, even if we didn't.

50.

Our quest sent us east. We wanted to interview surgeons and their medical teams at the three top Boston hospitals: Dana Farber, Mass General, and Beth Israel Deaconess. On each of the three days a different surgeon, a different interview.

We both liked the surgeon we met at the first hospital we visited, a man whose reputation was well-known to me from my research, who had performed hundreds of Whipple procedures. In the weeks leading up to this trip, I'd spoken with a number of his former patients, all of whom spoke highly of him.

"You only get to talk to the ones who are still alive," Jim pointed out.

After that visit, driving back to New Hampshire where we were spending the night, Jim and I agreed that we could not imagine a better surgeon.

The next day we met with a second surgeon, and had a second meeting with the great Boston pancreatic cancer specialist, Dr. Brian Wolpin, whose name came up a lot in my telephone research, to hear his analysis of Jim's scans. With two strong candidates for our surgeon now, Jim was tempted to forego our meeting with the last surgeon, Dr. James Moser, at Beth Israel Deaconess Medical Center.

"We've come this far," I said. "We should hear what he has to tell us." So we went for our third interview.

DR. JAMES MOSER was what my mother would have called a cool customer, but warmth and sense of humor were not near the top of our list of requirements for the person to perform Jim's Whipple surgery, assuming he would be able to have it in the first place.

Dr. Moser was in his late forties, probably, handsome and trim, with silver hair and a confident manner that displayed little in the way of emotion. This may have been a good thing for a man who spent his days meeting with patients suffering from a form of cancer that would kill the vast majority of them. Sitting in the waiting room awaiting our appointment, studying the other patients with consultations scheduled that day, I reflected on the statistics. Twelve patients waiting their turn. With luck (there was that word again) half would qualify for a Whipple. Of those six, four would die.

Please God not Jim.

When it was our turn to see Dr. Moser, what I noticed first were his hands. They looked just how you would expect a man's hands to look who spent the majority of his waking hours in the operating room rerouting the gastrointestinal systems of pancreatic cancer patients—perfectly manicured nails and long elegant fingers that looked as if they had never touched a garden tool or tinkered with an engine. Skin soft as a baby's.

He sat across from us, this man who—if we chose him as our surgeon, and if he agreed to perform the surgery—would literally hold Jim's life in his hands. I would have set a sack of gold coins at his feet if it made the outcome any different. Promised him anything.

He did not dwell on the prospect of a cure. What he said that afternoon was that he had studied Jim's scans, and believed Jim had a reasonable shot at getting the Whipple. "I can get the tumor out," were Dr. Moser's words, spoken with more confidence and assurance than either of the others we'd met on this trip. He had performed hundreds of Whipple procedures, he said. This one would be more complicated than most, due to its location, but he could take it on.

Hearing his words, the two of us had felt close to euphoric. New definition of good news: getting to have surgery that would totally alter the configuration of your entire digestive system and leave you with severe difficulties digesting food for the rest of your life.

We left the hospital that day filled with optimism, and the pure, groundless faith, borne of absolutely nothing but the need to believe this, that for us the story would be different. Nothing had gone wrong yet. As long as that remains so, you can still believe that anything might be possible.

Over the months that followed, Jim would return to Boston several times for scans—performed in Boston, rather than at the local cancer center where he received his infusions, because the Moser team wanted to study the images taken by their own equipment. Then would come a procedure called CyberKnife in which the precise location of the tumor—what was left of it, after chemotherapy—would be mapped radiologically, and attacked, over the course of a week, by a series of robotically programmed doses of radiation.

Once this had been done—assuming all else went as Dr. Moser hoped—Jim would be ready for the Whipple procedure. After that would come a period of recuperation requiring close monitoring—meaning we'd live in Boston for at least two months before returning home.

HOME. A PLACE we loved. So why was it that we chose to go so far away for treatment?

At the time, when friends asked us this, I told them that we were looking for the best hospital in the country for Jim's surgery, the best surgeon—and it is true that Boston offered superlative treatment. But where we lived, in the Bay Area, we had two world-class medical facilities within an hour's drive: UCSF and Stanford. So why did we feel the need to uproot ourselves as we did?

I think now that it was more magical thinking. Though we didn't say this to ourselves at the time, the choice to seek out treatment three thousand miles from home was another way we allowed ourselves to believe that we had tipped the odds further in our favor. If Jim traveled farther, he might do better. If surgery in Boston required more of us, surgery in Boston might offer us something more than what the more obvious path might yield. Jim's survival, for instance.

AFTER THAT FIRST consultation with Dr. Moser and the decision to go ahead with the Beth Israel team, we returned to our New Hampshire hotel that afternoon with a sense of excitement and resolve. The Boston oncologist, along with Dr. Moser, had recommended that Jim go on the most demanding form of chemotherapy—Folfirinox. "You're young," she told Jim. "And in good shape."

Bring it on, we said. If Folfirinox was tougher than the other chemotherapy drugs—if it would be harder to tolerate, and make Jim sicker—this stood as simply one more way that our outcome would be different from the more typical outcomes for pancreatic cancer patients.

Jim was tougher than most people. So was I. If our treatment was brutal, it was more likely to work.

"Our treatment." This was how I spoke now. Same as I said later, to a friend—without even thinking about this—"We're on Folfirinox now." And, "We're getting CyberKnife radiation."

I—the woman who had called herself a solo operator for twenty-five years, now saw myself as so inextricably linked to the man I had married that there was no way he could suffer from cancer without my doing the same. I had cast my lot in with Jim. That Fourth of July weekend when we spoke our vows with the fireworks exploding over our heads had not been the real moment when I crossed the line from single life into marriage. But I had crossed it now, though the landscape we traversed, that brought me to this place, was the most desolate I'd ever known.

This was marriage. Not the romantic dream anymore. But the bedrock.

51.

We spent one last night in New Hampshire before flying home to California. When I woke up that day, an unlikely thought came to me.

The weather had been frigid all week. But no snow had fallen—or at least, only the thinnest dusting the night before. Though I had lived in a warm climate for over two decades by now, I knew what this meant. Perfect conditions for skating.

I called an old friend who still lived in my hometown to ask if she had extra skates. Then the two of us headed out together to the old Mill Pond.

We laced up our skates. The ice was glass that day, with no one else out. Twice we went round the circle the way we had as children. Then I pointed to the frozen river that lay beyond the circle.

"What do you think?" I said to Morgan.

We took off down the river, blades slashing through the thin layer of newly fallen snow, sun hitting the frost in a way that made the whole world glitter. Cold as it was I took off my hat and let my hair fly behind me, racing as fast as I ever had on skates, racing as if something were chasing me, and in some ways it was.

In my head, I could hear Joni Mitchell from the *Blue* album, my favorite. *I wish I had a river I could skate away on.* Slash, slash. Blades on ice. Wind whipping my cheeks. Blood racing. The sound of ice expanding, that sounded as if the whole glassy surface might be giving way. Keep moving fast enough they'll never catch you. Keep moving and you won't fall in.

52.

As promised, the Folfirinox was rougher than the previous chemo, but Jim never complained. In late February, a new round of tests revealed that Jim's tumor markers—his CA19-9 numbers—were going down. This was the best news we might have gotten, and an indication that the chemo infusions had been shrinking the tumor. When he returned to Boston for his next scan, this was confirmed. The scan after that one was even better.

Still, there was seldom a day without some problem, and most of them required calls to the oncologist or the nurses. Four times now, since Jim's diagnosis, we'd had to race to the emergency room when Jim was suddenly doubled over, or painfully constipated, or suffering some other of a long list of mysterious symptoms and troubles. As much as I hated our trips to the ER, I had come to dread holidays and long weekends, knowing that when one of those rolled around, our access to the doctors we counted on would be curtailed. More than once, I had found myself counting the hours through a holiday weekend, waiting for the specialist we needed to come back on duty.

Still, we kept trying to carry on with our lives. In January I went to Lake Atitlan to host my annual writing workshop there. I'd gone by myself, leaving Jim to make a Boston trip on his own—staying with our friends Jason and Karen in Brookline—but after, he joined me at the lake, and we spent two full weeks there between infusions.

Those were some of our good days. The good days among our bad days, anyway. A whole new category. Jim's hair was growing back, and he had put on a little weight. Though we no longer set out to climb the volcano as we had the year before, we still walked into the village every afternoon to buy vegetables in the market and paddled the kayak, and prepared meals together that we shared on the patio overlooking the lake. In seasons past, Jim had swum in the lake with me. Now he took photographs of it.

My editor Jennifer and her husband, Peter, joined us for the second week, and when Jim learned that Peter had ridden a motorcycle in his youth, the two of them rented a couple of Kawasakis and took off on them for the day. Nights on the patio we sat out late talking about rock and roll, and on the last night we set off a fireworks show with the plan that next year Jennifer and Peter would return, and Peter and Jim would outfit a raft with fireworks for an even bigger display to light up the lake.

Jim and I discovered something on that trip to Guatemala. As much as we loved our home, and as hard as we'd fought to buy that place less than a year earlier, now it felt good to be away from there. Everything that surrounded us in Hunsaker Canyon reminded us of how we'd imagined our lives would go there, before. Everything reminded us of everything we were at risk of losing, if we hadn't lost it already.

It was an illusion to suppose that by getting on a plane we could escape what was happening in Jim's body. Still, whenever we left home, the heaviness lifted. It was easier to pretend, when we were in New York, or New Hampshire, or Lake Atitlan, that what we had left behind us was not simply our home, but Jim's diagnosis.

We had to go back to the U.S., of course. As we boarded the boat that would take us across the lake to the car that would bring us to the airport, and from there to San Francisco, I knew it was all about to start up again: the infusions and the blood tests, the piles of bills on our dining room table, new ones arriving daily. I thought of the look on one doctor's face as she had said to me, when Jim's most recent stent had failed, that perhaps we should insert a metal stent, even though doing so would require him to be on antibiotics for the rest of his life.

"The rest of his life?" I said. How could a person's body withstand an unending course of antibiotics?

She had paused then.

"Well, it's not like we're talking about . . ." she said to me. Then stopped herself.

We got home in March. A week later—with one more infusion behind us—my editor at *Travel + Leisure* called me up to see if I'd like to do a story for him on the Lake District of Chile.

It had been months since I'd written anything more than a Facebook post. My novel, that I'd believed to be nearly finished when I set it on my desk the previous November to accompany Jim to the hospital for what we thought might be a diagnosis of gallstones, had sat untouched since that day. The cup of coffee I'd been drinking that morning, before we took off for the hospital remained by my computer monitor in my abandoned office all these months later with a thick skin of mold over the top. Now I said yes to the assignment and booked our tickets to Chile.

53.

As we did before, we had to fit this trip in around the timing of Jim's Folfirinox infusions. To fit in the maximum time for our trip, we'd get on a plane the afternoon after he'd received treatment, and then return home the morning of the day he was due for his next one. He looked sick enough at the gate where we waited to board the plane that they allowed us to preboard, as most airlines did now, and we both knew Jim would probably be sick on the plane too—but as Jim pointed out, he'd be sick wherever he was, so why not on a plane headed to a marvelous destination?

He always seemed better once we arrived wherever we were going. This time the trip would last for twelve days. We would stay at two different luxury hotels in the Lake District and spend a night or two in the capital city of Santiago. I held out some hope that the high-quality meals would allow Jim to put on a few pounds.

In Santiago we visited the home Pablo Neruda had created for his mistress at the time, Mathilde—who would later become his third wife, and the inspiration for many of his most passionate and romantic poems. At the Neruda house, I bought a copy of *Veinte Poemas De Amor*—in Spanish on one side of the page, English on the other—to bring with us to the lake. At night I read them to Jim in both languages. Never mind that he spoke no Spanish. There was music in the sound of the words.

In part because of the poetry, but also because I shared a certain kinship with Neruda's style of making a home—crazily eclectic, funny, romantic, with an eye toward hosting friends and creating spaces for love—I became obsessed with the story of Neruda: the houses he and Mathilde had shared, and their love affair. Though time was short on this trip, I suggested we rent a car—a BMW convertible—and drive to Valparaíso, and from there to a spot on the coast called Isla Negra, to visit the two other Neruda homes. As usual, Jim was quick to agree, and quicker to take the wheel. We had only one day to make the trip, but Jim drove fast.

That night, after we'd taken in the last of Neruda's houses, we stopped into a little restaurant on a side street in Valparaíso. At the table next to us, a couple—easily thirty years younger than we were—talked on their cell phones for the duration of their meal. Sometime near its conclusion—with the man and woman still on their phones, neither meeting the eyes of the other—Jim pointed his Nikon in their direction to capture the image. There was no need for him to say it: He would never spend a meal with me speaking on the phone, any more than I would.

"What a waste," he said, taking my hand as we headed back out into the night.

Next morning, we made our way to the Lake District. The first hotel had been a perfectly maintained gem of 1950s modernist architecture overlooking a lake and a volcano not completely unlike the one we knew well from our days in Guatemala. One night we descended the steps to the lakeshore. Side by side, we lay together on the dock, looking up.

"The Magellanic Cloud," Jim said, pointing to a spot in the blackness above us. "We never get to see it in the Northern Hemisphere."

"I always wanted to lay eyes on that constellation," he told me. And who was I, a woman who never even knew until now that the Magellanic Cloud existed, I told him.

That week, we caught a salmon in the Pucon River, but it jumped out of my hands and back into the water. We rode horses into the Andes on Chilean saddles so well padded that even Jim, skinny as he was now, felt no discomfort. Nights we ate trout from the lake and drank Pisco sours and later Jim set out with his camera at midnight to shoot the night sky from the unfamiliar upside-down perspective—long-exposure shots that required him to remain very still for a long time, which he was good at. We talked about coming back to Chile—next time, to the Atacama Desert, where the view of the stars was one of the best on the planet, and Patagonia. Talking about the future made us feel that we had one.

For our last day in the Lake District, one of the guides at our second hotel—this one an adventure lodge—had suggested a number of hikes of varying degrees of difficulty. The one we chose, Mt. San Sebastián, was the most challenging, he told us—a climb that would bring us to the top of a twelve-thousand-foot peak in the Andes. Very few guests at the hotel—including the hotel owner himself—had ever made it to the summit. But we would, we said.

This was the toughest climb I ever attempted, and for Jim, who had once done Mt. Whitney, up and down, in a single day, the second hardest. Only this time he was heading out on the trail with five rounds of Folfirinox in him.

Several times along the way, I thought I couldn't go another step. I made a bargain with myself: *Just get to the top, and you'll know you are strong enough for whatever lies ahead back home.* Meaning undergoing the Whipple procedure, of course. Or loving a man who undergoes the Whipple procedure. No incision in my case, but what lay ahead for me would cut deep too.

There were a few places on the trail where I had to get down on my hands and knees, the climb was so rugged and steep, and it stretched for hours. For his part, Jim sometimes seemed to be moving in slow motion, like an ancient pilgrim, but he never stopped. A couple of times, I looked up at his thin body moving through the trees, the ever-present camera strap around his neck, the back of his head under his baseball cap bare of the hair I'd loved to stroke. "Remember this moment," I told myself.

We made it. From where we stood, at the highest point of Mt. San Sebastián, we could see all the way to Argentina.

It was almost dark when we got to the bottom of the mountain, and we had run out of water. We could have made it with our empty bottles at that point. We were ten minutes from the car.

The only reason I can account for what happened next is that we were just so crazed from exhaustion our minds no longer worked clearly.

Our guide offered us a sip of water from the stream flowing past us on the trail. We took it.

Four days later—home again in California now—we were both hit by a powerful case of stomach cramps and diarrhea. For me, this lasted just twenty-four hours. For Jim, it was much worse.

He was diagnosed with a parasite called cryptosporidium, an affliction easily curable with antibiotics for the healthy population but life-threatening to anyone with a compromised immune system.

At daybreak on Easter Sunday we placed an emergency call to an infectious disease specialist at Beth Israel. He prescribed antibiotics, but he told us it could take weeks or even months to eradicate this infection.

That was time we didn't have. For however long the cryptosporidium lingered, there could be no further treatment of Jim's cancer. And no Whipple procedure. Climbing that mountain might have cost us everything.

Only it didn't. Luck came now in the form of Jim's intestine clearing of the parasite in record time. As soon as he was better—back up to 135 pounds, amazingly, and feeling good after a six-week break from chemotherapy—we flew back to Boston for another scan.

This time, the news from Dr. Moser stunned us. The tumor had shrunk by 50 percent. He was ready to operate.

54.

We spent the day before the surgery at Fenway Park, and the Red Sox won. After, at a bar across from the ballpark, we had oysters to celebrate, and when we finished our usual dozen, we ordered another dozen, and another dozen after that.

"It's an odd thing," Jim said. "Tomorrow I'm electing to have a surgery that will gut me like a fish. I know it's going to be a long time before I feel this good again, if I ever do. Right now all I want to do is go off and live my life with you instead of checking myself into that hospital.

"But this is the last train out of the station," he said. "I'm going to be on it."

55.

We were at the hospital before the sun came up. I stayed with Jim for as long as they let me, while they did basic tests and got him ready.

Dr. Moser came in to say hello—wearing his scrubs now. "There's a point in the surgery around the three-hour mark," he told us, "when we'll have Jim's abdomen open and I can see what's going on in there. Sometimes, when you're doing a Whipple, this is the moment you discover that the cancer's more advanced than you thought, and you can't move forward with the surgery after all."

And if that happened? What then?

"We sew him up and send him back to the ward. We'll know we tried."

As always, Dr. Moser was confident. He told me he'd get a nurse to call me from the OR when he got to that point, so I'd know if they were going forward with the surgery. "I'm feeling good about this one," he said.

After I said good-bye to Jim I headed to the waiting room, knowing it would be a very long day. The room where I'd spend it—if luck were with us—was fluorescent-lit, lined with hard plastic chairs that faced each other, with a scattering of magazines and a reminder on the wall concerning the importance of hand sanitizer. On the opposite side of the room, a family had gathered—a man in his early sixties like me, and four young people around the ages of my children and Jim's. They were engaged in cheerful-sounding small talk—about their jobs, the Red Sox. As for me, I didn't feel like talking to anyone.

I had brought a book with me but I kept reading the same sentence. The family across from me played cards.

Around four hours from the time I'd settled in for my day of waiting I got a call from one of the OR nurses. "We reached the tumor," she said, as a person might when describing a war maneuver carried out behind enemy lines. "Dr. Moser's going in."

Hours passed in which I mostly sat, unable to read my book or eat anything. On the other side of the room, the sixty-something-year-old father and the young people with him were unwrapping sandwiches from the hospital cafeteria and laughing. The twenty-somethings were sharing funny stories about their mother—the kinds of stories my children might reminisce about (in my case, this would involve how messy I was when cooking, my habit of acquiring musical instruments I never learned how to play, my bad driving). It was the kind of talk a family engaged in when idly passing the time, with not a whole lot of stress going on. If not for the institutional décor, you could have thought they were enjoying a family reunion.

From my side of the room, there was nothing but worry. My own children and Jim's were nowhere near. Friends had volunteered to sit with me, but I preferred to be alone, I told them. I did have my laptop, and found a surprising measure of comfort reading the messages that poured in on my Facebook page from people I'd never met who'd been following our story over the months, telling me now that they were praying for Jim. From Japan and Colombia and Australia and France, they wrote to me. "We're with you," they said. Perhaps they were. I may even have felt it.

Dinnertime now. In the waiting room, the family across from me had brought in food, but I wasn't hungry. The various members of the family were just opening their Styrofoam containers when a woman approached them, bent to speak with the father, a hand on his shoulder. The daughter leaned in, and the son, and the two others

I had come to realize from our many hours sharing this room must be their partners.

Suddenly, the room was spinning. The food scattered. The father sat there, hands to his face, shaking his head, but the children were weeping, then wailing. Someone stood up, staggered, dropped to the floor. They all rushed out then—food wrappers and bags abandoned.

It could happen that swiftly, the end of life as we knew it. But time could also creep so slowly that even a minute seems endless.

It was close to midnight when the call came, this time from Dr. Moser himself. "This was the toughest Whipple I ever performed," he said—adding, with his typical brand of self-assurance, "there are probably only five surgeons in the country who could have performed this one." He being one of them, of course.

They got the tumor, and took thirty-eight lymph nodes, he told me. It would be another few days before the pathology report, but things looked good so far.

Then I made my way down the hall to the recovery room and found the bed with Jim in it, almost unrecognizable from that person I first met, not even four years earlier, at that restaurant in Marin County, where I kept waiting for him to suggest that we order something and he never did.

For so long, I had been fearful of getting too close to this man, letting him love me, letting myself love him back. And even when I did, I had been so reluctant to put that big diamond on my finger, and more so, to make the commitment it symbolized.

Romance was one thing. Marriage another.

Now there were tubes coming out of him. His eyes were closed, his mouth open. Gone, the dashing hero at the wheel of the Boxster, the sharp dresser who liked to meet me after work in the city for seafood at Sam's. Once such a handsome man, he looked a hundred years old right now, but he was alive. I took my place by the bed.

"I'm his wife," I told the nurse—*wife*, a word it had taken me a good year (also a bad one)—to utter as I did now.

"He's very confused," she said, adjusting one of the monitors, the beeping machines, the bags of IV fluid. "He keeps saying the surgery was a failure. Maybe you can convince him it wasn't."

Jim was heavily sedated still, but he opened his eyes as I approached the bed. Seeing him lying there as he was now, a person wouldn't have thought he could say anything, but he did.

"I'm screwed," he told me. "I'm totally screwed."

I took his hand. Stroked it. Bent over close to whisper in his ear.

"You're OK, Jimmy," I told him. "Dr. Moser says it went great."

"I'm screwed," he said again. Almost angry this time, that I didn't believe him.

"That's not true," I said. "You need to believe me."

Later, we would joke about this. When the anesthesia had worn off and he was in his hospital bed, sitting up partway, with his glasses on and his Rolex, his Kindle at his side. But that night he looked me straight in the eye with a ferocity I had never experienced from him before—he, the man who had never spoken to me with anything but tenderness in his voice. "If you're lying about this, I'm going to sue you," he said to me.

"You're going to be OK," I said. "You have to believe me."

56.

The operation had lasted fourteen hours. Over the course of this time Dr. Moser had removed the tumor, but this was not the whole of it.

Along with the tumor went a part of Jim's pancreas. Also his duodenum, also his gall bladder, part of his large intestine, part of his stomach. These were reconnected in a manner that bore no resemblance to the original design of his or anybody else's digestive tract. In addition, because of the particular placement of the tumor in Jim's pancreas—the way it had wrapped itself around a vein (there I went again, seeing the tumor as some malevolent force, imbued with human qualities, central among these an active intention to destroy my husband), the vein itself had to be removed. To replace it, Dr. Moser had harvested—*harvest*, there was a word for you—a replacement from Jim's neck. His jugular, in fact. In other circumstances, this itself might have qualified as major surgery. As it was, the jugular transplant was the least of Jim's issues.

The day after the surgery, when he was out of intensive care, Jim could sit up a little, though he was still heavily medicated and it would be days before he could eat regular food. We had been staying at the home of our friends in Brookline—playing cards with their sons, staying up late with Jason talking about politics and the law. But now I moved into the hospital. The nurses set up a cot for me next to Jim's bed, though later, after the first few days, I abandoned the cot and slept beside him in the hospital bed.

Because my babies had been born at home, I'd never spent a night in the hospital, and except for an outpatient surgery one time,

I'd never experienced a major health issue. I had steered clear of doctors' offices, never even went for checkups. But that June the hospital became my world.

It's a whole other way of living. Always, in the past, I'd spent as much of my waking hours outdoors as I could—particularly in summer, and particularly summer in New England—but now whole days went by sometimes that I didn't set foot outside, or even know the weather. We lived not by the sun or the stars that we never saw anymore, but the rhythm of life on the sixth floor of Beth Israel: waking at five or six—though who was to say what getting up meant anymore? We were up every three hours through the night, when the nurse came in to take Jim's vital signs and hook up a new IV of pain medication. I learned to put a piece of cloth over the computer that sat mounted on the wall across from the bed, glowing blue through the night, with Jim's medical records—his long list of prescriptions, notes from the medical team—displayed for whichever nurse was on duty.

All night long we lay together, in a state close to but not completely the same as sleep, as shadow figures moved in and out of the room performing their tasks. Sometimes it was taking Jim's vital signs, sometimes the administration of painkillers. Always that light glowed, and I could hear the sound of the air that pumped through Jim's special mattress, almost like breathing, or an endless series of sighs.

At seven the night nurse left and the day nurse took over. Then came the orderlies, the dietician, the women bringing in the trays of broth and Jell-O and later, Boost. Not yet on solid food, Jim was dropping weight fast, but we'd been prepared for that one. Some days there was a problem with the incision—fluid leaking, a repair required. Some days there was an issue with his drains. Always, there were issues with digestion. That part never changed, and never would.

As weeks passed—Jim discharged from the ward, admitted again, discharged, admitted—we came to know all the hospital regulars, the nurses and the doctors, the medical students on duty when Jim needed more painkillers, or a drain appeared to have come out, and I rang for help at three A.M., or four, as I often did. They wandered in from the dark hallway and took their place by the bed. Daytime and nighttime blurred.

Among the nurses, we had favorites, and it would be small things as much as large that determined this. Some understood better than others how to lift Jim's head so it didn't flop back on the pillow, or they'd show particular care removing his socks. There was an art to taking blood, particularly from the arm of a person as thin as Jim, whose veins had been pierced as often as his. The greatest art, perhaps, was maintaining a presence of quiet, benevolent invisibility. Jim and I spent nearly every hour of every day together, but hardly ever got to be alone. I longed for that.

Over our days in the hospital—that summer, and for all the hospitalizations I didn't know about yet that lay in our future—we talked a lot with the nurses. One of Jim's nurses had been a punk rock musician on the Lower East Side of Manhattan back in the early days of CBGBs (but went to nursing school when he realized he'd have to come up with college money for his kids). There was a Filipino woman, a nurse's aide and single mother, working nights and going to school days to be a full RN; the traveling nurses, who moved from city to city, touching down at a different hospital every three months; the young Jamaican woman—she'd be on leave soon—pregnant with her first child, whose nickname for Jim was "Handsome." More than the doctors, it was these nurses whose presence determined whether a day was good or frustrating.

At some point over the course of the morning, the doctors would make their rounds, and I was so anxious never to miss this moment that I didn't leave the room for anything until they got there. This visit would include half a dozen medical students with Harvard insignia on their coats, along with an intern and resident, probably. Dr. Moser, the man we always wanted to hear from, would lead this group, and when they got to Jim's room—our room— they'd form a semicircle around the bed, listening while the surgeon examined Jim's abdomen and spoke about his case.

We got used to the strangeness of having his body serve, for the assembled group, as the object of daily discussion and instruction. Dr. Moser would point out the incision, the positioning of Jim's drains, the particular issues of his case. There was a long scar on his neck for instance, from where the vein had been removed. This had altered his voice, though the doctors were hopeful that would be tempo- rary. Meanwhile, he'd need a surgery to inject Botox in his vocal cords. And possibly another vocal surgery after that. Jim also had a hernia—not atypical for a Whipple patient. And there were ques- tions of fluid retention, possible infection (always a fear). There were so many things that could go wrong, we learned. So few that could go right.

Jim's daughter, Jane, rode the bus from Brooklyn to spend a day with him. She had recently become engaged, and Jim was happy about that. We talked about when the wedding might be—not till the next year, it turned out. She was not a person who subscribed to the concept of having her father give her away, but he would be there, of course.

He'd be stronger by then. He'd have put on some weight. I knew how Jim loved wearing his tux, but this would be a Brooklyn wedding. No tuxedo. It would have needed major alterations now anyway, so just as well.

I had thought at first that I'd use this time to explore the museums of Boston—the Isabella Stewart Gardner and the Museum of Fine Arts, both within blocks—but apart from occasional lap swims at the Brookline Y, I discovered I didn't want to leave Jim. Mostly, we spent our days side by side in the bed together, reading and working on our laptops, watching movies, checking the political news. Donald Trump had announced his candidacy for president, but nobody was taking this seriously.

Our world got smaller, with occasional bulletins from the outside. The Giants were having a bad year. The Red Sox were having a good one. The guys in Storkzilla wanted to know when Jim would be home. They were short a bass player. For a while, there was talk that Jim might be back for a show in July. Then it was August.

The summer dragged on. I lived in the hospital and dreamed of writing at my desk in Hunsaker Canyon, dreamed of swimming in a lake instead of a pool. Sometimes I asked myself what had become of my life. It was not a question Jim ever asked about his own. Not out loud anyway.

57.

Now comes a critical moment in our story, though how critical did not become apparent until much later. This may actually have been the moment when two people more clear-eyed than Jim and I were capable of being could have recognized how everything would turn out, though would I have wanted to know this? Probably not.

Five days after the surgery, Jim was allowed to go downstairs and sit outside on the bench in front of the hospital. It was early June in Boston, and the tulips were out, the sun was shining, and it was warm enough that Jim wore nothing more than his hospital gown, though for modesty's sake he had put on a pair of sweatpants underneath. Later, as the weight kept falling off of him, I would have needed to bring a pillow down with us for him to sit on, because the bench was hard for a person with so little fat on his bones— little, and then none. But that day he looked like himself still. His hair had come back, and he had grown a beard, which looked good on him. I joked that he now resembled that devastatingly good-looking guy we used to see in Dos Equis advertisements, The Most Interesting Man in the World.

We were sitting on that bench together taking in the simple pleasure of the sun on our faces when we spotted Dr. James Moser walking down the street toward us—just returning from lunch probably. Evidently nobody was getting a Whipple at Beth Israel that day, because he was wearing a suit.

It was always a great moment when we got to talk with Dr. Moser. You always knew that his time was in short supply, and we hungered for his words, and any information he might have for us. There was no space in our communication for pleasantries or even emotion. But that day he was actually smiling.

"We got the pathology reports back," he told us. This was the analysis of those lymph nodes they'd taken during the surgery.

From my many hours on the phone with pancreatic cancer patients and their widows, I knew this was often the moment when you'd learn if the person you loved was going to live or die. My new friend Pam—unknown to me until she'd come to the hospital to meet me just before Jim's surgery, but instantly a friend—had described to me, though not to Jim, the moment when she and her husband, Mike, had sat in the office of their surgeon at Mass General when he broke the news to them, a week after Mike's Whipple procedure, that of the eighteen lymph nodes he'd taken out, fifteen were full of cancer.

Mike had held on far longer than most: nearly four years after the surgery. But the day they'd heard the results of his pathology report had been the moment when they'd known it was only a matter of time before the cancer would come back, and when it did it would kill him.

Dr. Moser sat down next to us on the bench. I leaned in so as not to miss a syllable. We had lived through a few of these times now—moments when it felt as though our entire future were about to be laid out for us in the space of a sentence. It seemed that time stood still.

"The results look good," he told us. "Your margins were clean. Out of the thirty-eight nodes I removed, thirty-six were cancer free."

Good results. For a world-class surgeon, that must have meant an elegantly executed procedure. No doubt Dr. Moser's skilled hands had gotten into places others could not have reached. There had been the matter of that one particularly challenging artery in Jim's pancreas, I knew. To remove the tumor had required Dr. Moser to cut perilously close. But he'd accomplished this. For a surgeon, this must have constituted success.

Good results, for Jim and me, meant something different—that my husband might be cured. We might get our life back. We might yet raise olives, and grandchildren.

Hearing the news of the pathology report that day, I started to cry with happiness. Jim was smiling. It seemed, at that moment, as if the worst might be over.

Now Dr. Moser was shaking Jim's hand. I put my arms around Jim, in the way I'd learned to do since the surgery: cautiously, with an awareness of all the places in him that hurt, which were most of the places. All our focus on those thirty-six clean nodes. Whatever the story was with those other two lymph nodes, the main thing was that our surgeon appeared happy, so were we.

I think now that those two lymph nodes were the real story that day. Even if there had been only one lymph node containing evidence of cancer cells, it would probably have been enough to tell us all we needed to know: There was cancer in Jim's body, and sooner or later it was likely to make its way through his lymphatic system. We might have more time, or less, but I think that day on the bench outside Beth Israel, our surgeon delivered something close to a death sentence. We just chose not to hear it.

58.

The term for follow-up chemotherapy administered after surgery is "adjuvant." It was crucial, Dr. Moser said, for Jim to embark on eight weeks of infusions, as soon as he was strong enough. He spoke of Folfirinox —the same form of chemotherapy we'd opted for in the months leading up to surgery.

"It's an unconventional choice," Dr. Moser told us. "Jim would be one of the first to do this. But I think he can handle it."

What kind of odd new reality had we entered, that the idea of filling Jim's veins with a form of treatment regarded as the toughest and hardest to tolerate, the most toxic, should land on our ears as good news? But it did. If there were a chance that one cancer cell remained in his Jim's body—and evidently, some did—I wanted it eradicated.

We believed we could accomplish this. Nights in bed, lying side by side or in each other's arms the best we were able to in the post-surgical world, I reminded Jim of our successful summiting of Mt. San Sebastián, and his of Mt. Whitney before that. He was a long-distance runner. He was an Eagle Scout. As small a percentage as might exist of pancreatic cancer patients who'd beaten the disease, the percentage of men who made it from Webelo to Eagle Scout was smaller, I had reminded Jim. What did that tell you?

These were the times I went back over, for him, the stories of the men and women I'd talked with on the phone over the last nine months who'd managed to survive, cancer free, for years after the Whipple. Laurie in Southern California, Robert in Miami. Ruth Bader Ginsburg (our favorite). There was Dan, the founding member of the men's pancreatic cancer breakfast club, and all the others in the club, getting on with their lives.

"Remember Joe, the one who plays eighteen holes every Sunday?" I said, as we lay in the darkness. I had just called him that morning to tell him about Jim's surgery, and to ask how he was doing.

He was doing great, evidently. "He said to tell you that come fall, when we're back in Boston, you two are playing eighteen holes." And get a load of this: in honor of Pancreatic Cancer Awareness Day this summer, Joe was going to be on the mound at Fenway, throwing out the first pitch.

"Next year, that's where I want to be," Jim whispered. "Out on the mound, baby."

59.

More days passed in Boston—in Boston still, because the pancreas team wanted to keep a close eye on Jim—and slowly we began to see what life might look like after a Whipple procedure. (What it was for now, anyway. We were still able to hope that what Jim was going through might be temporary.) When a new complication arose—as they did, daily—we could tell ourselves, "We'll just get through this one." We had not yet recognized that complications were not simply temporary setbacks. They were our way of life.

I won't list them all. The drains, the twice a day Lovenox injections to prevent clotting, the leak that required another surgery, the hour-long visits to the bathroom. The diarrhea, or constipation, the stomach pain, the back pain, the hernia, the vocal damage that had required first one surgery on Jim's vocal cords, then a second. The rows of pills on the breakfast tray. The hospital socks to reduce swelling, the face masks, the sterile gauze, the inflatable pillow, the ascites in Jim's abdomen, the chills, the neuropathy.

One day, during an examination, Dr. Moser reported that Jim was suffering from something called Portal hypertension. A look came over his face when he said this, but at the time this didn't seem so significant. There were so many other things going on. Hard to keep them all straight.

Four times that summer, we had to race back to the hospital. Every time we did, there was first the wait for admission in the ER— each time with the same maddening round of questions requiring one of us to rattle off the history of Jim's treatment from the beginning, list the medications he was on, answer, again, "Is your husband allergic to any medications?" I got so good at this that the nurse taking it down would sometimes ask me to slow down.

We had to stay close to the medical team, but we managed a couple of short trips out of town—to New Hampshire for a visit with my daughter and her boyfriend, where we helped to paint the new house whose purchase had been made possible, in part at least, by Jim's tough lawyer letter on their behalf.

From New Hampshire we drove our rental car north to Maine for lobster and pie on Becky's porch—trying to recreate the times we'd known there in summers past, though everything was different now. Months before this—back in the spring, when the news of the steadily shrinking CA19-9 numbers had filled us with ambition for our lives—I'd once again reserved a week for us at the cabin on Silver Lake that we'd rented the past three summers and vowed we'd return to forever. We ended up forfeiting our reservation—not the first canceled plan, and far from our last.

But we could spend a few nights in Maine at Becky's cottage on Mousam Lake, I said, for our ritual of corn from the garden and pie on the porch. It was summer. I could finally swim.

That afternoon, sitting on the porch looking out at the water but no longer able to enter it, Jim saw blood coming out of the drains in his belly. I called our medical team in Boston, while Becky's daughter, a cancer survivor, lifted Jim's shirt to study his wound.

Everything felt fragile now. The corn had been a terrible mistake; it kept Jim up that night, back and forth to the bathroom with pain so bad that it was almost a relief returning to Boston next morning. What we wanted now, more than sunsets or a screen porch or the sound of loons on the lake, was the safety of doctors close by.

60.

Finally, as summer neared its end, we were allowed to fly back to California. We had one final conversation with the team at Beth Israel, who had revised Dr. Moser's initial plan to treat Jim with Folfirinox, opting instead for a gentler form of chemotherapy, gemcitabine.

I fought them on that. "What about Folfirinox?" I said. What about Dr. Moser's words to me that day on the bench outside the hospital, "If I were in your shoes, I'd want Folfirinox"? If it was tougher, it was better. Bring it on.

In the end, we went with a modified version of Folfirinox called Folfox for Jim's adjuvant chemotherapy. The doctors agreed to this, but warily.

"You need to be careful," Jim's Beth Israel oncologist told us. "If the chemo is too hard on Jim, he'll have to interrupt treatment, and that would be more serious than not having had it in the first place."

They told us we should wait as long as twelve weeks for Jim to begin treatment back home. "The important thing is making sure he's strong enough to withstand this," the Boston doctors told us, "and that you get the first dose in before twelve weeks have passed."

But we were impatient and ambitious. Neither one of us had been able to put out of our minds those two lymph nodes that had been revealed in his pathology report to contain cancer cells. We wanted to get on with the process of knocking them out.

And Jim was looking better. Putting on a little weight even—back up to 128 after dropping to 120, following surgery. Our oncologist back home, examining him when we returned to California, offered the opinion that Jim was ready to begin treatment at the six-week mark. We went for it.

It is easy, from the distance a year brings, to revisit all the choices we made and ask, might things have gone differently if we'd made different decisions?

In late August, five days after he began treatment with Folfox, Jim became so ill he had to be hospitalized. Either as a result of his lowered resistance from surgery combined with the chemo, or perhaps as a direct result of being in the hospital—a breeding ground for bacteria—Jim came down with the C-difficile infection. As he had with the cryptosporidium, only far worse this time, he was suffering from such massive bouts of diarrhea that he dropped ten pounds over a weekend with no sign of a letup. Ten pounds. Then twelve, fourteen.

The doctors gave him antibiotics, vancomycin. This seemed to get the C-diff under control, though we also knew that once a person has contracted C-diff, it frequently returns.

Meanwhile, Jim was due for another round of Folfox, but because of the infection, it was postponed. First by one week. Then two.

Finally he could get chemo again. Two days after the infusion the C-diff came back.

This time we were ready for it. I had read a series of articles about a form of treatment for C-diff whose results were far superior to those patients experienced when treated with vancomycin. This was fecal transplant: a procedure that called for the insertion, into the digestive tract of the affected patient, of fecal matter from a healthy individual, for the purpose of repopulating the gut with flora and fauna that might fight the infection. It was a concept not so far removed from our practice, back in the previous fall, of eating dirt. But more radical now, and more powerful.

The doctors who'd been treating Jim had shown no interest in fecal transplant, so we sought out a gastroenterologist in Oakland who specialized in this. The waiting list to see him was so long that the next appointment stood two months out, but I told the receptionist my husband couldn't wait that long, and when she held firm on the dates, I asked to speak with the doctor himself. The next day we were sitting in Dr. Stollman's office.

Neil Stollman was a warm, open, approachable man—just the kind of person I might have expected for one who had ventured into the territory of fecal transplant. No doubt his years of performing a procedure that many in the conventional medical world still regarded with distaste had contributed to the air he had of irreverent humor. "My own daughter's embarrassed by what I do," he said, laughing. "But I know it saves lives."

"This C-diff could kill me before the cancer has a chance," Jim told him.

Neil Stollman nodded. "No shit."

When I told him that I'd been so desperate to help Jim—and so fearful that time was running out that I'd prepared homemade fecal transplant capsules, using myself as the donor, Dr. Stollman displayed no sign of shock or censure.

"I'm not going to give you a hard time for being a do-it-yourselfer," he said. "A person who's been intimate with the patient is often one of the best donors." Still, the method he prescribed for fecal transplant made use of certified fecal matter provided by a lab in Cambridge, Massachusetts, which would be conveyed to Jim through a procedure roughly akin to a colonoscopy.

By the time we had made it to Dr. Stollman's office, Jim was down to 108 pounds and dropping more every day. Neil agreed to see him for the procedure the next morning.

Within eight hours of receiving the fecal transplant, the diarrhea was gone. By the next morning, color had returned to Jim's face.

He could eat again without running to the bathroom. The next day his weight was up two pounds. By the end of the week he was at 116—a number that sounded good to us now.

We called the infusion center. Jim was ready to resume chemotherapy, we told them.

No more chemo, they told us.

"Unfortunately," the oncologist explained, "in a situation like this one, where chemotherapy has been severely interrupted not once but twice, its effectiveness has been compromised. When the administration of chemotherapy is inconsistent, the body has an opportunity to develop resistance to the chemicals. It would no longer serve you to receive further infusions."

Here came those malevolent cancer cells again, straight out of a Hollywood action movie. They'd gotten a taste of our secret weapon, and now they were onto us.

We called our team in Boston then, to revisit the decision, but our Boston oncologist took the same position the one in California had. There would be no more chemotherapy for Jim. Then, or ever again.

"Maybe it's good news in a way," Jim told me that night, as we uncorked the wine and lit the candles for dinner. "Now we just live our lives for a while without all these trips to the cancer center."

We knew better, of course. There were those lymph nodes haunting us—the two out the thirty-eight Dr. Moser had excised from Jim's abdomen, the ones in which the pathologist had registered the presence of cancer cells.

I tried not to think about them, but I did.

61.

When we first returned from Boston, we had assumed that Dr. Moser and his team would continue to serve as Jim's primary medical team, supported by the local infusion center where he'd received treatment earlier. But it swiftly became clear to us that it would no longer work to have our oncologist and surgeon three thousand miles away. After checking out a number of options closer to home, we made an appointment with the top Whipple surgeon at UCSF—not for further surgery, but for oversight of Jim's case. Most important, we had to choose a new oncologist. We made an appointment with Dr. Eric Nakakura, the top UCSF pancreatic surgeon, and Dr. Andrew Ko, regarded as one of the top pancreatic oncologists in the Bay Area.

As we had so often, we made our way across the bridge for what I now recognized would be a full day of sitting in waiting rooms, undergoing tests, conferring with medical assistants, answering the familiar round of questions about medications, procedures, surgical history, and finally seeing the doctor.

Jim began the day with blood tests and scans. It was a few hours later when we got to the specialists. First Nakakura. Then Ko.

The first twenty minutes of our visit with Dr. Ko felt routine, predictable—a recounting, despite the presence of the file of Jim's treatment to date, culminating in the Whipple in Boston.

Then Dr. Ko looked down at Jim's file, and back at us.

"So, the appearance of these soft tissue nodules on your scan strongly indicates the recurrence of the cancer," he said, as blandly as if he'd been offering commentary on the Giants' performance that summer, or the weather. Instead of a death sentence.

Soft tissue nodules? Recurrence?

This was not the first time I had the sensation that the walls of a room were closing in on me, the floor giving way. A sick feeling came over me, the taste you get when you think you might throw up.

"From the Beth Israel scans taken after your Whipple," Dr. Ko was saying, "it appears that these nodules were present back in July, but they are more easily detectable in this current scan."

I reached for Jim's hand. Always, in these moments, my first response. *Here I am. Where are you?*

It seemed to me that Dr. Ko had surprisingly little to say about this situation. If we had been less stunned, I would have taken out the notebook I always carried for our doctor visits and begun to question him, but now I could only study the wall behind the doctor's cool, pleasant face. To look at Jim's would have been too hard.

We didn't say much driving across the bridge. But by the time we got home I recognized what I had to do. Get back into my old research mode, take out the white boards, get back on the phone. There were some clinical trials going on that sounded promising with an immunotherapy drug called nivolumab, a place in Arizona we'd heard about from one of the men in Jim's pancreatic cancer breakfast group, and a clinic I'd heard about recently in Germany where they treated Stage 4 pancreatic cancer patients with some protocols not approved in the U.S. By the next morning, I would have Jim's file and his scans on the way to Germany via FedEx.

Most of all, I wanted to know what they'd have to say about this in Boston. It was too late on the East Coast to speak with anyone there the day we'd learned Dr. Ko's assessment of Jim's cancer, but the next morning at six I was on the phone to the Moser team, driving into San Francisco to pick up a copy of Jim's most recent scan, express mailing the incriminating CD to our radiologist and Boston oncologist, and to Dr. Moser himself.

Five days passed then while we waited—filling the space with middle-of-the-night episodes of *Downton Abbey*, candlelit meals neither one of us felt like eating. Finally came the call from Joe Mancias, the radiation oncologist who had overseen the Cyber-Knife procedure on Jim. Hearing his voice, I gripped my phone tight and pressed it to my ear. Jim was filling the birdfeeder but I didn't call him in. I'd take in the news first, myself, then tell him.

"We've all studied Jim's scans closely," Dr. Mancias began. I had stopped breathing. "We discussed this at length." Then he told me that he and his colleagues were in agreement. They had concluded unanimously that there was no recurrence of cancer. What the doctors in San Francisco interpreted as nodules was scar tissue. The team at UCSF—as skilled as they were in performing a Whipple—were simply not familiar with the kind of Whipple Dr. Moser had performed on Jim, he told me.

I put down my phone. I walked over to Jim and put my arms around him. "We're OK after all, Jimmy," I told him.

OK for that day anyway.

62.

That September, my son Charlie was getting married—the wedding to take place in Baja, Mexico, with his brother and sister and their partners coming. Jim wanted badly to be there—for Charlie, whom he had grown to love, and also for me. But the C-diff had left Jim way too vulnerable. There could be no traveling.

So I made my way alone to Mexico, sharing a house with my children's father, a man with whom I had once been in a state of so much bitterness and anger that just being in the same room was difficult. This was behind us now. He'd had his own struggle with cancer in his family. His son Taj, my children's half brother—but to them, simply their brother—had battled a rare form of liver cancer a few years earlier, but was now doing well. No doubt Taj's cancer had changed us all.

For both my ex-husband and me, I think, it was our big losses that had allowed us to make our peace. Jim's cancer had made me a sadder but kinder person, and certainly a more forgiving one, same as I suspect Taj's cancer had done for Steve. For all these reasons, I think, when our son spoke his vows, my children's father had reached out for my hand, and later that night we danced together.

But I longed for Jim's presence at the wedding. In the years after my divorce, before Jim and I got together, I had attended a hundred events on my own, and I'd grown accustomed to that. The previous three years had changed me, however. I wanted my husband by my side for this one. Now I called him from the rented house in Mexico, looking out at the ocean.

"Remember our wedding?" I said. It felt like a million years ago, but the number was two.

63.

That fall I grew to understand a profound truth about the way most of us view illness, in our culture anyway. It was the way I used to view illness too. People got sick, then they got treated, and they got better. If on occasion someone died—my father, of pneumonia—they were probably old, or they had a car accident. If not—as with my mother, dead of a glioblastoma just after her sixty-seventh birthday—they were certainly the exception.

As much as I had learned about pancreatic cancer and the devastating nature of the disease, in many ways I had continued to look at Jim's illness through that same lens for a surprisingly long time. He had gotten sick, and then sicker. But eventually we'd emerge from whatever crisis was afflicting him and he'd start to get better. Even after three trips to the emergency room, even after six trips, I held on to that picture.

So did many others. To most of the people who followed our story—all but those who had known someone with pancreatic cancer—the fact that Jim had gotten through the Whipple surgery signaled a victory. Wherever I went now, well-meaning friends would ask if Jim was "better yet," as if it were only a matter of time before this would be so. Facebook friends sent wishes for "a speedy recovery"—a phrase I came to hate, though I didn't fault anyone for employing it. We ourselves, though we lived with the diagnosis, somehow failed to recognize the inexorable pattern of steadily downward motion.

If either of us had ever done anything as simple as to create a graph charting the numbers of times we had to rush to the hospital, the space between visits, the bouts of diarrhea, Jim's weight, we could have seen it in starkly visual terms. On any graph, the line would have gone relentlessly downward. Maybe that's why we'd never made one.

Here was the truth, though Jim was not yet able to see it, and I did nothing to encourage that he might: Jim never felt good anymore. The only question was, how bad did he feel?

Then there was the other part—the fact that Jim could no longer receive chemotherapy. Talking about that would have been like talking about the possibility that one day North Korea might launch a nuclear attack. What was there to do about it? What was there to say?

He tried working, but practicing law was almost impossible now. Though Jim still addressed, as best he could, the needs of his old clients—from cases he'd signed up months before, mostly—the phone inquiries about representation went unanswered, the updates from California Estate Practice unopened. He still paid for a gym membership, but never went anymore. He had given up therapy. The Triumph sat untouched, as did his bicycle. Largely because he was unable to receive more chemo, his neuropathy had retreated somewhat, but he hardly ever drove into the city Tuesday nights for Storkzilla practice.

Still, the hardest thing was not the pain in Jim's gut, or the neuropathy, or the hours he spent in the bathroom. It was what happened to his brain.

He said it didn't work as well as it used to, and this was so. He could still talk about science and politics, and he always wanted to hear my stories. He was reading the manuscript of the book I'd finished before the diagnosis now, in an effort to help me get back to work, and had marked the manuscript with copyediting suggestions—good ones. But a cloud of fog enveloped him too and he forgot simple things. He lost his phone. Lost his keys. His glasses.

His laptop, even. He knew it was happening, and the fact that this was so terrified him more even than the cancer.

I Googled "chemo brain" and, out of the belief that it would be less alarming if he could recognize the reason for what was happening to him—and the prospect that it might reverse in time—I read out loud to Jim what the Mayo Clinic had to say about the phenomenon.

Meanwhile, I made lists for him every morning now: tasks to take care of. Calls to make. In all the important ways, I told Jim, his mind was working fine. He could still beat his old circle of opponents at online Scrabble most of the time. We could still have our talks over dinner about politics or music or books, or our children. He had his same wry, subtle brand of humor. Most of all, he still paid exquisite care to every single thing related to me. But when I asked him a question now, he took a long time to answer. Everything had slowed down.

"At least I can still make you laugh," Jim said.

64.

Jim had his pancreatic cancer men's breakfast group. I had a new group of friends too. Wives of pancreatic cancer patients. Wives and widows.

One was my friend Pam, in Rhode Island, who had come to the hospital to meet me a few days before Jim's Whipple surgery to lend support, her own husband having died the summer before. Then there was Deborah, known to me only over the phone and e-mail, and sometimes text messages exchanged from waiting rooms in doctors' offices. Her husband, Bob—a man she adored—was a pediatric physician who'd been diagnosed the year before Jim, and underwent the Whipple at Johns Hopkins. The surgery had seemed to go perfectly, but within weeks it turned out the cancer was back, this time in the lining of Bob's abdomen. Since then he'd been surviving on a feeding tube in the care of Deborah, his funny, wildly loving, and infuriated wife, an RN. "It would have been better if I wasn't a nurse," she told me. "Then I could just be his wife. That part sort of gets lost now."

For Pam, who lived alone now, it was easier to talk, but with Deborah there was always the problem of not wanting our husbands to hear us, so we snuck off to talk at odd hours of the day and night, when the men were asleep, mostly. I hid myself away in the gypsy caravan behind our house to call her, as if I were carrying on an affair.

Nobody understood my life now more than another woman who was living it. I yearned for her voice as a person in other circumstances might for a lover. Sometimes we shared medical reports. Sometimes despair. On occasion we allowed ourselves to imagine a time, one day in the future, when the four of us would meet over dinner somewhere—a great meal, served up with a pile of Creon pills, and a bottle or two of red wine. We imagined how we would look back on these days we were living, the bullet we'd dodged. "Remember that tumor you had?" "Remember that awful surgery?"

We were two women who might have known better—she a doctor's wife and a nurse, I a tireless online researcher. But against all evidence to the contrary, we held on to hopefulness.

"Like you," she wrote, in one of our almost daily e-mail exchanges, "my husband is the air I breathe, and how we are going to get through this and come out the other side smiling is a mystery to me. But somebody is going to be writing an amazing article about them in some medical journal someday, I just know it. Don't let anyone tell you otherwise."

As many friends as we both had, there was no explaining this to any of them. A woman I'd never met who lived three thousand miles away understood. Sometimes she felt like my sister. Sometimes my twin.

"I press my hand to his warm, sleeping abdomen, where I imagined his pancreas to reside," she wrote one day, "and I will the cancer be gone, be smaller, be merciful to Bob. From my heart through my hand." While she was doing this in Syracuse, I had been doing the same in Lafayette.

We shared the details of our endless visits to medical facilities too, of course. Johns Hopkins. Beth Israel. UCSF. As awful as it was, a certain comfort could be found in knowing someone else walked the same path. The details of specific procedures differed, perhaps, but the bottom line was the same. There was in each of our lives a man we deeply loved, whose body was under siege from the most terrible cancer, and our days were consumed with the struggle to get him through it. With very little left over for ourselves.

"Bob was not able to have his feeding tube inserted through his abdominal wall, which we have now tried to do four different times and different ways," she wrote, from Baltimore. "Too much scar tissue. So we came home with a little tube down his nose, through his stomach and into his small intestine. Resumed his adjuvant therapy Thursday—miracle poison—and it's been a long weekend of watching him be racked with sharp muscle pains, aching joints, headache, and general terrible malaise. Grateful for feeding tube, because he won't eat a bite and I'm convinced he would have starved to death at the rate we were going. He's a very handsome man, but 'skeletal' doesn't really suit him."

"Yes on all counts," I wrote back, too tired myself to document the particulars.

65.

ecause so much of Jim's pancreas had been removed, his body no longer created the enzymes necessary to digest food. He could not eat a bite without taking a pill first—Creon or Zenpep, depending on which manufacturer you went with.

These pills were made from the digestive enzymes of pigs, and they didn't come cheap. But as we would learn, on the one or two occasions when Jim found himself without his Creon and tried to eat anyway, failure to take the pills before eating even the smallest amount of food led to terrible pain. More than once, we found ourselves somewhere—heading over the Bay Bridge or to a party, suddenly realizing we'd left the Creon at home. Nothing for it then but to turn around and go home.

I learned to keep spare pills in my wallet. Also emergency Dilaudid.

I don't think Jim experienced a single meal since his Whipple surgery that was totally free from pain. We had a set of rules, of course, concerning foods that would be easier or more difficult to digest. But even when he followed the rules—and he always did— you never knew when something he ate would make trouble, and when it did he could be up all night suffering the consequences. Where, in earlier times, I had always seen our dinners together as one of the best parts of our day, it was difficult now not to approach every meal with anxiety. Still, I still dressed up for our dinners and put on music and lit the candles. We always shared a bottle of wine—a part of my day that I now looked forward to more than I should. I knew this, but I wasn't prepared to give it up.

Every night, as we sat down together at the table, I still took Jim's hand and closed my eyes before we lifted our forks, our silent prayer.

There was no need to ask what we prayed for, though I would add three words to the end of it.

Remember this moment.

66.

We returned to the gastroenterologist. He proposed a new diet for Jim, designed to vastly reduce the amount of fermentable food he took in, with the hope of creating less irritation in his intestinal tract.

It was called The FODMAP diet, and as he spoke my eyes scanned the list of prohibited foods:

No gluten.
With a few exceptions, no cheese.
No milk products. No ice cream or yogurt, cottage cheese, butter.
No onions. No garlic. No broccoli, cauliflower, beans, asparagus,
    beets, avocados.
No salad. No raw foods.
No apples, pears, cashews.

There was more. When the list was finished, I asked what was left.

Meat, of course. Fish. Some nuts.

As we sat there taking it in, a sense of loss overtook me. This was not the hardest news we had received in a doctor's office, or even close. But it was listening to Dr. Terdiman recite the rules of FODMAP living that brought me to tears as none of the rest of it had. A small, whining voice was muttering in my head—a voice I hated, but could not silence.

Let me out of here.

My losses were nothing compared to Jim's. Still I registered them and grieved each one as a small death—and whether I spoke of this or not, Jim knew it too.

"I'm so sorry," he said, same as he did so often. "This wasn't how I meant our life together to go."

67.

Our life together: What we had imagined. What we got.

In those early days after we met—the days Before—Jim would sometimes walk in the door at seven after his day's work in the city and suggest that we go out for sushi. Ten minutes later we'd be in the Boxster, zipping over to College Avenue, where we liked to sit at the sushi bar, not a table, to watch the chefs at work. Or he'd learn about some interesting new place in Oakland—Peruvian, Cajun, Fusion—and make us a reservation. We might drive up the coast for oysters on a Sunday. Or to North Beach for Italian food.

Still in my core a girl from New Hampshire who'd spent fifteen years living on a farm at the end of a dead-end road, I never ceased feeling the thrill of our glamorous California life. I loved putting on my high heels—never mind if they made me taller than Jim; he would only be proud of me—and riding the elevator to his office, or meeting him at the bar at Sam's or the Ferry Building. And to me, for a time, all of this—the good life, I called it—seemed like a not-insignificant part of our life together. I was having, in my fifties, a kind of experience I had not known in my twenties, thirties, or forties.

Sometimes, during those early days together, I'd ride BART into the city at the end of the day and meet Jim for dinner there—always dressing up for the occasion, and loving the sight of him walking through the door with his briefcase, heading my way. Once, and once only, on one of those occasions when we'd made a date to meet up after work at the Ferry Building oyster bar, I'd tried playing a game with him. Dressed for the part, I pretended to be a woman he'd never met, alone at the bar, striking up a conversation as a total stranger. With my hand brushing against his arm, I asked him provocative questions about what brought him to this place, and if he had plans for later that night. I rubbed my foot against his leg, as if I were a fast and dangerous woman, like someone out of a James Bond movie.

Jim had hated this game. Or rather, he didn't know how to play it. He was incurably old-fashioned, hardwired to be a one-woman man, with that woman being me. The idea of flirting with some stranger at a bar wearing a slinky dress—even if that stranger were his wife—left him deeply uncomfortable.

"Can we stop this now?" he said after a couple of minutes. "Can we just be us?"

He was a man who thrived on commitment, a man who wanted to be married. Married to me.

Before I met Jim, I used to study other people's marriages, but from the outside, with my face pressed against the window of a house I never entered. I supposed that a good marriage was an endlessly extended romance combined with a regular dose of fun. How many people got that?

Only then I did. I took vast pleasure in having this good, kind, witty, smart, handsome, and endlessly playful man (playful, so long as the play didn't involve that game at the oyster bar) who would take me out to dinner and do the driving after. I could plan trips to places like Paris and Positano—the place I'd hauled my three suitcases up that long run of steps, alone, the summer I'd sent Doug packing, when the old Italian man had called out his question to me, "Where is your husband?"

After all those years, I'd found him.

I also liked the part about getting up in the same bed every morning with the same person at my side—a man I loved—and sometimes going out for brunch together on Sunday mornings, setting the *New York Times* on the table next to the fresh-squeezed orange juice and the plate of smoked salmon and bagels while we divided up the sections, looking up from mine now and then to share some interesting piece of news, or to tell about some new movie that sounded worth seeing.

For me—a woman who had long feared marriage, and then late in the game discovered its pleasures—marriage to Jim had meant comfort, pleasure, safety, ease. Marriage—this one, at least—allowed for the ability to make plans, see into the future and know whom I'd be sharing it with. All that, combined with my usual round of solo adventures, at the end of which he'd be there to pick me up at the airport and take me out on the town.

Then came the diagnosis, and in all my years of envisioning a relationship, I had never imagined a life like the one we lived now. I had not seen myself sitting in some doctor's waiting room for the fourth time that week, standing in the bathroom injecting Lovenox into my husband's hip or buttocks—wherever I could find a little fat for my needle. Soon there was none.

Sometimes now, I was angry. Not at Jim, but at life. I moved through my days with a chip on my shoulder, ready to take on whoever got in the way of getting Jim what he needed. I needed to be tough now. I hated it that this was so.

Pancreatic cancer is not an illness a person can readily take on alone. There needs to be another person, preferably one like me— pushy, demanding, relentless, all the traits of mine that had been among my least attractive in some other context. Now my ability to push hard—the same thing I'd done to get us through the crowds at the Hardly Strictly Bluegrass festival—was the reason we'd gotten the Boston surgeon, the better health insurance, the fecal transplant, the second opinions. I was tenacious as a dog pawing the dirt for a bone.

Sometimes, when Jim was in the hospital, if his nurse that night was late delivering his pain medication, I haunted the nurses' station, checking my watch every thirty seconds to make my point. Jim was the lawyer. But I was the advocate. "I wouldn't be alive without you, baby," he told me. It was a heavy weight to carry, the knowledge that this might be so.

There was no going back. There was no place on earth I could run away to, where I could stop worrying about Jim.

Not all at once, but gradually, over the months, another revelation came to me: None of that other stuff, much as I'd loved it, was what made a marriage. Not restaurant dinners or romantic vacations. Not walks on the beach or visits to the wine country in the Boxster. Not oysters and martinis or moonlight over the Bay Bridge.

This was marriage. As uncomfortable and inconvenient and devastating as it might be to live as we did now, we inhabited this place together. I could register envy sometimes (daily, in fact) reading the Facebook posts of all those people I knew who were off taking trips and sailing in the bay, or visiting grandchildren. But comparing my life now to anybody else's would accomplish nothing.

And here was the other part. As much as I hated what had happened to Jim, and to both of us, I had never felt closer to him. I would like to think we would have reached this place without the discovery of a tumor in his pancreas, but I wonder if we would have.

It came to me one day in one of those doctors' waiting rooms, awaiting the results of some test or other, that I no longer viewed what we were doing now as some kind of departure from of our real life. This *was* our real life. I stopped thinking about the way I spent my days as an interruption of my work. This *was* my work.

As the months passed—endoscopies, infusions, blood tests, scans, hospitalizations, port flushes, infusions again—I could no longer fantasize as I once had about escape, because I could no more escape Jim's illness than I could escape my own skin. There was no separating Jim's story from mine anymore. Whatever it was that lay ahead, Jim and I would go through it together. Lying in bed next to him one night, I could hear the beating of a heart and no longer knew to which of us it belonged.

68.

That November we flew back to Boston for a scan to check—as always—on whether there'd been a recurrence of the cancer. It was an event we underwent often now. Each time, excruciating. Put the gun to your head, with a bullet in one of the chambers, and spin. Squeeze the trigger, see if you're still alive after. If so, you're free and clear for another three months, at which point you do it all over again.

We sat in the waiting room for close to an hour that day, and as we did so, I studied the people around us. It was never hard to know which person in a couple was the cancer patient. That would be the man whose neck was so thin now his shirt collar no longer touched his skin, or the woman whose pants hung like laundry on a clothesline, as if there were nothing inside them.

One in particular I remember—a woman a few years younger than Jim and me, from the looks of her, though it was never easy guessing the age of a pancreatic cancer patient. She was not a new patient evidently, because the staff all knew her. She had come with her husband and two daughters to receive the results of her most recent scan, or maybe an MRI. She sat there in her too-big Red Sox sweatshirt for a few minutes, holding her husband's hand. Then the receptionist called her in.

I knew about visits like this one by now—the little rituals you perform, sitting on your hard plastic chair while waiting your turn, the bargains you strike to receive good news. *If it could just be neuroendocrine . . . If his CA19-9 numbers can just be down under a hundred, if they will just tell us he can have the surgery, here are all the things I will do.*

Waiting for a verdict, praying for a good one. *Good* having taken on a new meaning, of course: *Good* was hearing no bad news.

Jim and I were still waiting to see Dr. Moser ourselves—Dr. Moser and Dr. Mancias and the rest of the team—when the woman in the Red Sox shirt emerged from her appointment. One look and we knew: The news she and her family received must have been the kind every pancreatic cancer patient dreads above all else, the moment they learn the cancer has returned following a Whipple procedure. Or maybe a scan had indicated the presence of a metastasis that would now preclude the Whipple. Either way, the family had walked in the room looking anxious but hopeful. When they left ten minutes later, the daughter was crying and the parents could barely hold each other up.

It was a scene—or a variation on a scene anyway—I relived on many occasions. We were like passengers on the *Titanic*, hovering in the frigid night air of the north Atlantic, all hoping to get into the lifeboat.

Not that, quite. We were all of us travelers on the same impossibly rugged path—one that made climbing San Sebastián look like a cakewalk—but at different stages in the journey.

Every now and then you looked up and saw one of your fellow seekers falling by the wayside. When you did, it had the effect of witnessing a glimpse into your own future. Your possible future anyway. Today we would be spared news like what that woman and her family received. But who knew what tomorrow would bring? Or six months from now, or twelve, if we were lucky enough to even be here twelve months from now?

I looked at that woman and her husband—he, the one in my shoes, me the one in his—then looked away. It was as if I'd heard the sound of footsteps on my own grave. Or that of the one I loved, which was almost the same now.

69.

Over the months that followed Jim's diagnosis, one of the things people often said to me—both friends and strangers alike— was that I needed to take care of myself too, while caring for Jim. I lost count of the number of times some well-meaning friend would cite the example of the passenger on a flight in which turbulence occurs. "You have to put the oxygen mask over your own face first, if you're going to be of help to anybody else," they reminded me. Then they'd suggest a pedicure or a massage. Maybe a walk around the reservoir. All good ideas, no doubt, though seldom if ever implemented by me. The sorrows that surrounded me would not have been diminished by a visit to a nail salon.

For me, as a person who had spent her whole adult life telling about her experiences, it was impossible not to be sharing this one. But that fall and winter, and the spring that followed, were not a time for writing books, or articles even. I could not write a novel, I discovered, because I was so consumed by the real-life story we were living. Every time I'd start to consider an idea, my brain would turn instead to some thought I'd had about a new treatment or drug or doctor who might conceivably be helpful to Jim. This happened enough times that after a while ideas related to my own projects and dreams no longer came to me anymore, almost as if my brain acquired the habit of short-circuiting creative thoughts because the impossibility of sustaining concentration would leave me too frustrated.

Still, I had not stopped being a writer. Writing about what happened to me had become, for me, the way I made sense of my life. And so, many times over the months, I turned to the unlikely community of readers on Facebook to share the story of what Jim and I were going through. One day, I posted a long meditation on what it meant to be a caregiver.

I was calling out into the darkness with an unspoken question, awaiting some word of response, same as I always did. "Is it just me?" I was saying. "Is there anybody else out there who understands?"

So one day I posted this on Facebook:

When a person you love is diagnosed with cancer, the sense of sorrow and fear—for him—is so vast and consuming that to speak at all of your own losses is likely to come across (to your own self, first, and maybe to others) as pretty selfish and narcissistic.

"What right do I have to complain about anything?" says the wife of the man with pancreatic cancer, "when my husband is facing the possibility of death and the virtual certainty of pain for months on end? Perhaps forever."

So, caregivers are supposed to put their own smaller sorrows aside. And mostly, we do.

But it has been my way—as a woman, but also as a writer—to speak of the kinds of human experience so many of us are taught to believe we should keep hidden. I am speaking here of those so-called "shameful" emotions like envy, anger, self-pity, vanity, pride—the moments I believe all of us experience in which we display our least heroic but possibly most human selves.

Over my many years as a writer, I have written about plenty of those moments in my own life: small vanities, large failures. I could name a few thousand inglorious moments I've chronicled over the years.

You could conclude from all of this that I am just a bad person. Or a deeply flawed, foolish and weak one, anyway, and no doubt I am all of those things on occasion. But it is always my hope, when I write as I do, that my words may reach someone out there—maybe some teenage girl, or some woman whose children don't speak to her, or some boy who can't tell his parents he's gay—who has experienced his or her own brand of shame over the failure to live up to the standards of perfection or selflessness or nobility or simple "normalcy" we aspire to, and the persona so many others around us work so hard to maintain. I'd like them to know they're not alone.

So I will tell you now that along with sorrow of the most profound variety over what Jim has been going through—and rage at the unfairness of it, for my husband—I sometimes grieve, and sometimes rage, on behalf of my own self too.

I think about the man or woman out there, reading my words, who may also be serving as the caretaker to a well-loved person as he or she confronts a devastating illness. I would never want to leave such a person believing—in the midst of his or her own struggle—that I am some kind of selfless hero who tirelessly tends to the needs of her ailing husband with no thought to any need of her own.

Sometimes I look in the mirror and the thought that comes to me is this shallow: Cancer has added ten years to my face. Sometimes I register impatience at how slowly my husband is walking, or the fact that he is too cold to have dinner outdoors the way I'd like, or the fact that we've had to cancel some plan I was looking forward to a lot because he isn't up to it. Sometimes I want to jump in the car and drive away.

I never do. But I think these things.

I will now say what some people in this situation may feel unable to admit. I believe that however much we love someone, and despite the pledges we have made to her or to him, none of us gives up our individual personhood. I am Jim's wife, Jim's partner, the one he counts on to be here in his darkest moments—and I will be that person for as long as he needs me—but I am also me, the same person I was for the fifty-seven years before we met. Same as he is, at the end of the day, his own autonomous and separate person too.

The voice of that woman I was, who used to be in charge of her life, and is now ruled by an illness that does not reside in my own body, has not disappeared. It calls out sometimes, and sometimes it practically screams: *What about me? Where did my life go?*

Nobody understands this better, by the way, than Jim. Who grieves for my losses as he grieves his own. More so, sometimes.

One of the hard parts of these past nine months—not as hard as watching the man I love in pain, and certainly not as hard as being that man—has been the loss of something very dear to me: my freedom to do the work I love. More than anything—more, even, than my friends, or my children—the constant for me over the last forty-some years has been my ability to sit at my desk, open my laptop (or, before that, face my typewriter) and write.

I need to work. Lucky for me, I also love to work. And for close to a year now, it has been almost impossible to concentrate on anything besides pancreatic cancer for more than an hour or two at a time. Frequently less. Anyone who has ever loved and cared for a person with a serious illness will understand what I mean.

At the point we received Jim's diagnosis last November I was nearly done with the revisions of a novel due to be published the following spring. Then everything stopped in our lives—Jim's work, my work, so many of our plans—as we got to work fighting this disease and figuring out how best to vanquish it. Months passed in which I did not set foot in the room where I write. All that long, hard winter and well into the spring I did not open the manuscript of my novel.

In the end I managed to finish it. But I don't think I'll be starting anything else for a while. My mind is somewhere else.

I wish I could say I never complained about this to my husband.

But I did. Because he is not simply the reason for my sorrows, but the man I go to when I need to talk about them.

This morning as I write we are back at the hospital to clear one of the frequent blockages Jim experiences in his bile ducts. (Next week it will be something else.)

And I—a woman who used to say she couldn't take an hour off for lunch—now interrupt my life, day after day for cancer. No, I do it for Jim.

Sometimes I rail against all this—rail against cancer, rail against hospitals, rail against the loss of my freedom to work, my freedom to go swimming in New Hampshire last summer, my freedom to be happy and carefree with the man I love, the disappearance of our dreams. But the larger truth is, I am here. This is not the experience I wanted, but as with every other experience in my life, I do not intend to sit this one out, or to pretend for one moment that it isn't happening.

This is my life, and at the end of the day, I don't want to miss a minute of it.

70.

For many people, it turned out, that Facebook post touched a nerve.

Though my words appeared nowhere but on Facebook, and to nobody but the readers who found me there, the reaction to my words was intense. A great many readers, including many who'd never visited my page before, shared the post. Many people wrote to thank me for my words, and—if they were living the life of a caregiver themselves, or had done so in the past—for acknowledging a truth too seldom mentioned in the world of cancer treatment.

But there were others who expressed shock and anger over what I'd written. For a woman whose husband was suffering a life-threatening illness to admit to resentment or frustration was unacceptable, as it had been even to one of my dearest friends. Some people who wrote to me in the aftermath of my posting those words chastised me in particular for how guilty I must be making Jim feel when I spoke of the losses in my own life, brought about by his illness.

Maybe I'll never know the truth. But what I believed to be true was the same thing I had believed all my life, long before Jim's diagnosis. Long before knowing Jim, I believed in telling the truth about what was going on in my life. No experience is so terrifying, I've always said, once you turn on the light, and take a hard, clear look at the thing that most terrifies you.

There could be no pretending to Jim that I did not miss my old life—consumed as I was with my worries about his.

All I knew to do about that problem was to talk about it with the person closest to me in the world. That would be Jim.

We had shared so much over our time together. Now we shared this.

"I know how hard it is for you that you aren't writing any books at the moment," he told me. "But one day you will tell this story."

71.

A letter in the night from my friend Deborah, known to me only through the connection of e-mail and the telephone, and the shared experience of loving a man with pancreatic cancer. From the time stamp on the e-mail I gathered she'd been up at three A.M., as I often was on my own coast.

"Isn't this the strangest pickle we find ourselves in?" she wrote. "I've done a lot of thinking about the word 'hope' in the last sixteen months, and am no closer to a definition that I can internalize and live with than I was the day Bob was diagnosed. Few diseases present the unwilling participants so little hope, right out of the gate. I have been looking for hope for so many months now, and some days I no longer even know what to hope for. Surgery was what we hoped for, and we got there. And now we're here, not exactly where we expected to be. Have you figured out 'hope' yet? And if so, would you mind sharing?"

PACIFIC GAD AND ELECTRIC was working on the power lines over our house, and to do this, they had employed helicopters that now hovered overhead eight and sometimes ten hours a day, their propellers whirling, engines roaring so loud that if Jim and I were outside in our spot on the patio at the end of the day—our oasis— we'd have to yell to make ourselves heard to each other. Because the normal power to homes in Hunsaker Canyon had been shut off, a generator was also operating nonstop. Even in the middle of the night, we could hear it.

The whole thing rattled my nerves in a way that nothing we had known over the previous twelve months had. One day I placed a call to the number PG&E had provided for the person overseeing the project. "You'd better hope there isn't a Vietnam Veteran living on this road who suffers from post-traumatic stress disorder," I told her, "because if there is he might just put a gun to his head."

Ten minutes later a police car pulled up, with three officers who wanted to speak to my husband, investigating my call.

"Do you consider yourself at personal risk?" one of them asked Jim. (Well, yes, there was this problem of pancreatic cancer, he might have told them. But no, he was not afraid of his wife.)

"Do you have any firearms in the home?" one of the other two inquired of Jim. (Yes again. Jim's rifle and shotgun from target practice in the Owens Valley, along with various old guns he hadn't taken out in years, but he was wise enough to shake his head.)

I wanted to say something, but my guard dog stopped me. This was no time for registering opinions about noise pollution and its effect on the psyche.

"Let's go to Guatemala," I said to Jim, after the police cars pulled away—still yelling over the roar of the hovering helicopters.

So we did.

This time there was no more hiking, and no more making pizza in the pizza oven, now that Jim no longer ate gluten. No swimming, no making love. Still, we could sit on the patio and remember when we'd done those things, and pretend to each other that we'd do them again. It would be easy to call this behavior denial, or just plain delusion. But for us, as much as we tried to live in the moment, part of the moments we experienced now required a belief in our future together. Travel—sometimes on planes, sometimes just in our imaginations—provided that.

Did I actually suppose that cancer wouldn't find us in Guatemala? Or on the barge trip we'd hoped to make through the canals of Holland, or in New Orleans, where Jim's old friends Al and Susan urged us to visit, or to the little cabin we used to rent on Silver Lake?

Some people, looking at the list of all the places we went to since Jim's diagnosis, and the longer list of places we tried to go— might suppose we were attempting to pack in as much living as we could while this was still possible, but it was never a burning need to experience some place or another that sent us out into the world. Sometimes being in our house just felt too sad.

There sat the Jeep that was going to bring us to the Owens Valley together—the engine idle for so long now that we would later learn (but only when we went to sell it) that rats had built a nest there. There sat the outdoor ping-pong table where we'd pictured having a daily match with each other—with full knowledge that the only way I'd ever get a point off of him would have been for Jim to play left-handed. There was the music room, where Jim would have played with his band on Sundays, and the office where he would have practiced law, the long table where we had pictured our children gathered round—or friends—for big, happy meals and after, music and conversation late into the night, and if they drank more than a person should, there was the gypsy caravan out in back, where they could sleep it off. And there was the pergola where the wisteria had bloomed that first day we rode Jim's motorcycle to check out the house—though there too was the rat, whose resistance to every effort we'd made to get rid of him had come to feel like some kind of curse.

Hunsaker Canyon represented everything we'd thought we'd make of our life together. Much of it abandoned. Hunsaker Canyon was also the place we'd returned to that day we received the diagnosis, the place where the two of us had experienced the greatest devastation of our lives. We had worked so hard to get that house but as much as we loved our home, there was a certain relief in driving away from it.

72.

A week after we got back from Guatemala, Jim returned to Boston to check in with the doctors at Beth Israel. Five months had passed since the surgery, and they wanted him to have not simply another scan but an MRI.

Jim wasn't afraid of much, but one thing he hated was tight, closed spaces. I had seen him choose not to get into a BART train, coming home from the city, if it looked too crowded. Even an elevator sometimes made him uneasy. But an MRI would be harder than those.

The first time he tried to have one, he panicked, and they had to shut the machine down. They rescheduled for a few days later, but this time he took Valium. I was back home, so a friend who lived nearby—a former writing student who'd offered to help—agreed to bring him to the hospital for the procedure and, later, to pick him up.

When he got out of the MRI, Jim was still heavily drugged. Forbidden to eat for all the hours leading up to the MRI, he was hungry, so she brought him to the hospital cafeteria, where he'd ordered a big meal.

He took a few bites and got violently sick. In his drugged state, he had forgotten to take his Creon pills—those enzymes crucial for digestion now—and my friend had known nothing about the requirement that he do this. She drove him back to Jason and Karen's house, where a full night passed before the worst of the pain of his mistake was behind him.

Suddenly the thought came to me, what would happen if some

crisis occurred—a strike maybe, or a world financial collapse or a war—that left us unable to procure Jim's pills. He could not take a bite of food without them.

"We need to begin setting extra pills aside," I said to Jim—I, a woman for whom the prospect of a world financial collapse or a war now signaled one thing above all others: the prospect of a Creon shortage. I added this to the long and growing list of assignments on my yellow legal pad: *Stockpile pig pancreas enzymes.*

73.

An e-mail from my friend Deborah in Syracuse.

"The mourning never stops for some loss or another," she wrote. "Even little things. Bob doesn't make the coffee anymore. (Stab through my heart.) I am so weary of begging Bob to drink that I truly could just scream. My day is disorganized into ten-minute intervals of fielding phone calls from bat-shit crazy Medicare zombies, running to pick up meds (that someone got wrong—more phone calls and trips back to pharmacy), keeping feeding tube running, meds, meds, meds, 'what can I get you?' 'how do you feel?' 'does anything hurt.' On top of taking out the trash, feeding the animals, scheduling appointments, making hotel reservations, why hasn't this scan been ordered yet (more e-mails to appropriate providers)?, maintaining the cars, paying the bills, keeping up with laundry, kids, friends.

"If we both make it through this goat rodeo, it will be a wonder if we're not BOTH stoners! Right after Bob got sick, everyone who walked into the house brought some kind of pot, which we have stashed for the time being. But it calls to me on a regular basis. I feel like I can never let my guard down, as some shit is always just about to hit the fan. You know what I mean."

And I did, of course. Though for me, what beckoned was wine. Two full glasses every night now, and once I'd finished the second, it seldom felt like a bad idea to pour a third.

74.

Jim started every day on his laptop. He loved news from the world of science, and reported to me whatever discovery had been made, especially if it concerned life in our little solar system or beyond it, in the galaxy. Then, though it generally made him mad, he'd turn to the news of the political world. Donald Trump's name was in the news a lot now, though it was still impossible to believe that anything would come of this.

But more than any of the rest of it—politics and science or online Scrabble—what occupied Jim now were websites devoted to fast cars. More and more, that fall, I would find him studying some online write-up about a particular new model. He loved his Boxster, but it was old—no longer as responsive as it had been once, and the mechanism on the convertible roof no longer functioned. The Boxster sat under a tarp now, as it had for months, leaving Jim with a 2007 Prius as his daily driver. Hardly a car to suit a man with a James Bond persona—Don Diego, The Most Interesting Man in the World.

Jim knew all the great models of fast, expensive cars, and studied the statistics about them, read reviews from *Car and Driver*, not to mention the biography of Elon Musk, creator of his all-time favorite vehicle, the Tesla. That one was out of our price range, but it seemed to me he should have the pleasure of sitting behind the wheel of a vehicle he loved to drive. He'd worked hard all his life. So much was gone. Here was a pleasure still within reach.

"We can sell the Prius," I said. "Let's get you a new car."

Jim pointed out the practical realities, though he didn't have to. He was hardly earning any money as a lawyer anymore. I'd run up a major charge-card debt while Jim took cash from his savings every month for all our medical trips, and everything else. We were burning through money, throwing cash at cancer.

At another moment in our lives, our finances could have looked like our big problem, but at this one I gave little thought to dollar signs—not because we had an abundance of money, only because we had a far greater abundance of trouble. If a moment presented itself in which a few extra dollars could help get us through the day, I was seldom reluctant to spend them. If Chilean sea bass at $29.99 a pound could provide a little pleasure—after five days of hospital meals—was I going to conclude it was too expensive and opt for canned tuna instead?

That afternoon I accompanied Jim to the BMW dealership. My idea, not his.

More prudent types—which would be just about everyone we knew—might have opted to lease a car there, but I urged him to buy one outright. I wanted Jim to have a picture of a future with miles ahead, and road trips with me. It made no sense, but the magical-thinking part of me chose to believe that if we spent enough money, we might actually buy ourselves a future.

We did not purchase an absolutely new BMW. The one Jim chose, encouraged by me, was a 2015 model, with eight thousand miles on it. But it was a top of the line M3, with a sunroof and a Harman Kardon sound system and heated seats and Sirius radio and a special set of sensors in the front that showed you, on a screen by the steering wheel, exactly how much space there was in a tight parking spot, or whether some obstruction lay behind you, backing up.

I didn't even ask the price of the car. It was Jim's business, Jim's money, and later, after he'd filled out the paperwork, it made me happy to sit beside him in the passenger seat (bare feet on the dashboard, my usual position) as he drove that car home.

When we reached Hunsaker Canyon, he had sat in the driveway, his head resting on the steering wheel. "I'm crazy," he told me. "I should never have spent so much. I could be dead in a year."

At that moment, I would have done anything to fend off despair. Pull my clothes over my head and run naked around the car, waving my hands. Crank the Sirius XM radio to top volume, blasting Guns N' Roses. Set fire to a hundred-dollar bill.

"This is a perfect vehicle for us," I told Jim. "You can take curves fast in this car, and sleep in the back on our road trips." On the BMW lot, we had actually put down the seat and stretched out side by side in the back to see if we could sleep there. We could.

"I'm going to load the sound system with rock and roll," Jim told me, patting the leather dash with the Harman Kardon speakers. "Then I'm going to bring you to the Owens Valley in this car, baby."

75.

I had my fantasy too. Jim thought about cars. For me, it was houses.

My whole life, I'd been on a quest to find my home. I thought I'd found it in Hunsaker Canyon, but then cancer sent me back into flight, searching for something I could not even have named. A safe place to hang my hat, where trouble couldn't reach me.

Some years before, in my early days with Jim, I'd bought a little shack that sat on the shore of a pond in New Hampshire, on a half-acre of land with an outhouse. Nothing great, but for me it had represented my toehold in the place I still considered my true home, though I hadn't lived there for twenty years. It was typical of Jim, and the way he accepted me and my choices for my life, however odd, that he never questioned this purchase at the time, though it never made any sense. When did I think I was going to spend time in this cabin of mine? Where was the money coming from to fix it up? Two questions he never asked.

Two years after I'd bought the place, when we were scrambling to come up with the down payment for our place in Hunsaker Canyon, I'd sold my little shack—at a loss—and the money had made the purchase of the Hunsaker Canyon house possible, though Jim had contributed far more than I did.

That fall something possessed me to make a Google search for "Lakefront properties, New Hampshire." I had less than three thousand dollars in my bank account at the time, and little prospect of more anytime soon—having barely worked for over a year by this point. Looking at New Hampshire real estate was a little escape, I told myself. When things were roughest, I dreamed of swimming at the New Hampshire lake house of my dreams.

A lot of listings showed up in my e-mail then, but I never saw a house I loved. Most of them sat on tiny pieces of land, with neighbors on both sides and a postage-stamp piece of beach. Inside, they tended to look the same. Home Depot cabinets, low ceilings, tiny dark bedrooms. Those houses all cost way too much, and I didn't want them anyway.

Then sometime in late October, a listing showed up that was different from all the others. This house sat on two and a half acres of land on a dirt road with no nearby house on either side and a long strip of beach on a small, beautiful lake that did not allow motorboats. The house itself had been built in 1900, with a wide porch wrapping around two sides. Inside, the walls were old pine, and the kitchen looked as if nothing had been changed since around 1955, which was probably the case. The property had remained in the same family for fifty years at least.

The house itself sat on a rise overlooking the lake. Down at the water there was a boathouse with a deck. I knew right away that if this place were mine, that boathouse would be where I would set up my writing desk and where I'd sleep.

Where Jim and I would sleep, I said.

The price on this house was lower by far than any other I'd looked at. And one more thing: It was a twenty-minute drive from where my daughter Audrey lived. Twenty-five minutes to the little town of Harrisville, where Jim and I were married. My friend Danny lived nearby, and other old friends too. The farm stand where I'd always bought our corn back in the days I'd lived on our old farm was five miles down the road.

I had no money and no borrowing power. Still, I developed a little ritual. Every afternoon around five, usually before dinner when Jim was taking a nap, as he did more and more these days, I'd head up to the writing studio where I no longer wrote anything. Glass of wine in hand—wine, an essential part of my day by this point—I'd open up the website of that house on Whittemore Lake and click through the pictures.

I got to know that place so well I could have drawn a blueprint. I had studied the old gas stove in the kitchen, the ugly flowered couch in the living room, the rocking chairs on the porch. I could have told you the china pattern of the teapot in the hutch.

I asked Danny to drive by the place for me. "It faces west," he told me. "Good sunsets. Totally quiet except for the loons."

I was still only dreaming, but it was a comforting dream. I asked Danny to call the Realtor. The afternoon of his visit to the house—late November by now—he called me again.

"There's not one thing you wouldn't love about this house, Joyce," my friend told me.

In late December, I clicked on the website of the New Hampshire lake cottage. Flipping slowly through the familiar images on the screen, the thought came to me. "What if one day I click on this website, and the property's been sold?"

It was five o'clock on the West Coast. Eight P.M. in New Hampshire. Still, the listing agent for the house had picked up his phone. I named a price, many thousands of dollars lower than the one being asked for the place. A crazily low figure.

"I'll get back to you," he told me.

Ten minutes later he did.

When I shut down my laptop and went to make our dinner, Jim was sitting in the kitchen, reading the political news. "I just put an offer in on that house," I told him. Weeks earlier I'd shown him the pictures, but hadn't mentioned the house since.

"They accepted it."

He did not miss a beat, my husband. "That's really great, baby," he told me. Except for one time I had proposed that we get three puppies from a particularly irresistible litter at the SPCA, I cannot think of a single moment in our time together when Jim ever told me not to pursue what I had my heart set on.

I wasn't clear where the cash would come from, but I had a little time to work that out. My long-delayed novel was set for publication that February, and though the money I'd get when it did was spoken for a half-dozen different ways, I now saw it as going to the down payment on our New Hampshire cottage.

In those first weeks after I signed the purchase and sale agreement, Jim and I talked about the place now and then, though with a certain vagueness. Once, sitting on the couch together at the end of the day, he asked me to show him the pictures again.

"That's where I'll smoke my cigar," Jim said, indicating the porch. The rocking chairs. He liked my idea of sleeping in the boathouse, he said—and though it was too small to hold anything bigger than a single bed, for us a single bed was enough.

"I bet there'll be trout in that lake," he told me. "I'll bring my rod."

76.

We invited twenty-seven friends for a holiday dinner. I would have been happy setting up tables made out of old planks laid on sawhorses, Jim preferred a less funky look. He was this way about most things, though never about me. I was always rough around the edges, and he never showed any indication that he had a problem about that.

So he made a trip to Ikea and came home with twenty chairs, then spent the next three days assembling them. He bought two long Ikea tables and matching wineglasses. Then he took out his vacuum cleaner.

We set the tables up in our living room end to end so they stretched almost the entire length of our downstairs. I'd always wanted the kind of life that allowed for big gatherings like this one. Of our children, only my son Willy would be at the dinner, but there would be plenty of friends.

I cooked for days, and it felt good doing something that had nothing to do with cancer. Before the meal got under way, I had asked that we go around the table one person at a time to speak of what we'd been most grateful for in the year that was now drawing to a close. I had worried a little, suggesting this, that hearing what everyone had to say might go on so long the gumbo would get cold, but I needn't have worried.

Every person's words were a revelation: Alice, diagnosed with breast cancer, was grateful for her dog. Katherine, who'd lost her home in Oakland and had no idea where she'd be living ten days from now, was grateful for the friend who'd offered her couch.

Sally, whose son had been very ill, expressed gratitude that he was slowly recovering. Hal, who'd spent three months in Syria and Greece serving food to refugees, was grateful for having gotten to be there.

When it was Jim's turn, he did not speak of the cancer or the surgery, or the pain. "It might seem strange to say this," he said, "but these have been the best years of my life."

"*Buen provecho*," I said. Good appetite. (Not easy to accomplish, when you've undergone a Whipple procedure.)

We raised our forks and began to eat.

77.

We kept trying for a normal life, but its definition had changed. Every day started with pills—so many different pills that to keep track of them I made a chart, and almost every day required a trip to CVS. If it was a prescription for painkillers we needed—Hydromorphone, the Fentanyl patch—this was likely to be a complicated process, and might require trips to multiple pharmacies before we found one with enough pills in stock to fill the prescription, or a pharmacist able to assist us. One time the pharmacist kept the two of us waiting for an hour, grilling Jim on why he needed the refill so soon, placing calls to the doctor.

"She's treating you as if you were an addict," I whispered to Jim.

I paced the aisles of the store. The pharmacist was doing her job, I told myself. Still, I could feel the rage overtaking me. Not just for the hour at the pharmacy, but all the hundreds of hours before this one spent on trying to keep Jim alive, keep him out of pain, or just get him through the day.

It happened a lot now: Times I went into town on errands—bank, post office, Trader Joe's, and always the drug store—and nine times out of ten the cashier ended our transaction with the words, "Have a good day." Or (this was a Friday phenomenon): "Do you have plans for the weekend?"

The cashier inquiring about my day didn't know me. The girl behind the counter at the dry cleaner's didn't care. But the question— "How's your day going?"—always served as a reminder of all the ways my day was not going well, the weekend plans we used to have, and never did anymore. I let myself imagine all the ways I might answer the cashier's bland, meaningless question: "I'm having a terrible day. My husband has had diarrhea for a week. My weekend plans? I'll probably drop in at the emergency room and maybe stay up all night Saturday, watching five episodes in a row of *House of Cards*, to help my husband get through the pain."

One time I actually lectured a bank teller when he asked about my day. He meant well. It just didn't occur to him—lucky man—that a question like that, asked of someone like me, presents only two options. Either you give him the real answer—a guaranteed conversation stopper—or you lie.

I had already dealt with the "how's your day going" question three times in a row by the point Jim and I got to the CVS that afternoon to fill his hydromorphone prescription. Three times that afternoon I had said my day was going fine. But it had taken something out of me too. All that bland disapproval of our real lives had left a bitter taste in my mouth.

I had planned on buying a hairbrush along with the pills. It was in my hand, and no doubt I was gripping it more tightly than a normal shopper might hold on to a plastic brush. The unfairness of everything was making my temples throb.

I looked at Jim—leaned against the counter, looking weary—and at the couple in front of him, with their purchases of sunblock and toothpaste, a child wanting a toy car his mother told him he didn't need because he had one just like it at home, a pregnant woman buying vitamins. I was angry at them too and angry at myself for the fact that this was so. It wasn't their fault that they got to spend their morning doing regular family errands, which did not include filling a prescription for opiates.

That plastic hairbrush was still in my hand when they finally called us up to get our pills.

I could feel it happening then: the crack, breaking loose. A small, not-very-dramatic act of rebellion, enacted at the counter of the Lafayette CVS store. I took out my credit card, but I did not set the brush on the counter with the rest of our purchases.

I didn't conceal it. I just didn't pay for it.

Back in the BMW with his medication, I told Jim, my Eagle Scout husband, what I had done. In some other moment, he would have expressed shock. He would have gone back in the store himself to pay, probably. As it was he just sighed and put his key in the ignition. This cancer had brought us to so many dark places we would never have imagined ourselves going. The fact that it had turned me into a shoplifter was the least of those.

78.

December brought more digestive issues for Jim. More wine for me. The FODMAP diet was helping a little, but Jim was still losing weight, and worse than that, he was losing muscle.

I haunted the supermarket searching for things Jim might be able to eat. Two trips a day sometimes, hours in the kitchen concocting dishes that might appeal to him, though I threw away as much food as we consumed.

I went back to the pot dispensary where I'd procured a card months before, studying the strains of marijuana that might help Jim get through the nights. We paid a visit to a new nutritionist. I started setting out an extra shot glass of MCT oil for Jim with every meal, to help put weight on him, and bringing him protein shakes multiple times a day, though these sat next to his chair largely untouched. Jim's old clothes fell off of him now, but every day or two a box arrived with a new pair of pants or a shirt in the smallest size. Not lawyer pants anymore. These were sweatpants, and even the small ones hung on his body.

Another of the men in the pancreatic cancer breakfast group died—the third, since Jim had joined the group.

Something was happening to Jim's muscles now that seemed to bear no relation to the food he took in or the supplements I pressed on him. Jim's forearm was so thin I could almost encircle it with my hand.

"I need to start working out again," he told me, and so before bed every night I joined him for planks and pushups, counting out loud how many we did. But the number kept getting lower. We still walked our trash cans to the end of our driveway, Thursday mornings, for pickup. But when they were particularly heavy, I'd suggest putting the can in the back of the BMW instead of walking it out to the road, and Jim didn't argue.

The beautiful BMW. Our road trip car. Mostly we drove it back and forth to the pharmacy, and to deliver those garbage cans up to the road.

Still, when John Prine came to town that month, we got on a BART train to hear him and held hands when he sang our song, "Glory of True Love."

"There has to be music," Jim said. "Give up that one and you're dead anyway."

79.

We put up a Christmas tree. But for the four days surrounding December 25—on the run, as usual—we went to New York City.

It was a trip that almost didn't happen. At the airport in Oakland, preparing to fly out, I'd been given a TSA clearance that allowed me to sail swiftly to the front of the line, but Jim had not, and the holiday line was so long it was clear he'd never get to the front in time to board our plane. "I know it's not your style, Jimmy," I told him, "but you need to pretend you're me. Push hard and cut through the line. You can play the cancer card."

In all the months he'd never done this, but now, to please me, he did. Over and over, as he pushed apologetically through the line, my soft-spoken husband repeated the words, "I'm so sorry, but I'm a cancer patient. I have to get on this flight with my wife."

And he did.

From the first time I came to New York, on a bus with my mother, at age ten, for the 1964 World's Fair, I had loved this city. Every time I came here, my heart beat quicker. I moved fast through the streets, wanting to take in as much as I could in my time there. No time to stop. No time to waste. Too much to see.

Like me, Jim had always been fast on his feet. He was the man who could zip over to the law library to find a relevant citation of a case and back to the courtroom in the space of a twenty-minute recess—but by this point every block we traveled took a long time. Every stop proved costly to Jim. And I moved at his pace now. We sat on park benches a lot, stopped in often at coffee shops. Never mind the coffee part. This was about the bathrooms.

It was a very different kind of trip from our New York adventures in the past, when Jim had followed my lead as I raced around the city all day, hopping on and off subways and walking sixty blocks at a time, ducking into galleries and clubs, riding the subway to remote parts of Brooklyn or the Bronx. This time we took in little in the way of museums. But there was a show of Picasso sculptures at the Museum of Modern Art, and we were not going to miss that one.

The show featured sculptural works made over the course of the artist's long life, from his early twenties to his nineties. It was this part that moved me most that day: the wild exuberance of the works Picasso made in his tenth decade of life and the extraordinary good fortune he'd known, to have not only lived that long, but to have lived that long making art to the end.

What could be better than that? Despite my mother's death at sixty-seven, I always pictured that I would live a long life too, and once Jim and I got together, this was my vision for the two of us. I had seen us as a very old couple one day, like those couples I'd studied so often over the years, still holding hands into their seventies and beyond. Now, as we studied the Picassos, I realized how much more modest my hopes had become.

"Let him live to seventy," I had said that first stretch of months after the diagnosis, though not out loud. *Let us travel to Italy. Let him get to see his grandchildren.*

Let him know a day without pain, I said now. *Let him sleep through the night.*

On Christmas Eve we attended a midnight mass at the Cathedral of St. John the Divine. From my spot in the pew, I watched as Jim—an Episcopalian who'd stopped attending church before I met him—made his way to the front of the cathedral to take communion.

Seeing him up there by the glittering chalice, bending his head to receive the wafer, his beard almost all gray now—still bearing a resemblance to The Most Interesting Man in the World—I realized how much thinner he had become than I had allowed myself to take in up to now. When you live with a person every day, you're less apt to recognize the changes in his body, but that night I saw it.

A couple of years back—in our Before days—Jim had taken a photograph of the two of us on some hike—just our shadows on the ground, elongated in the way shadows get at the end of the day when the sun lies low on the horizon.

He looked like a shadow person now. Almost a ghost—a figure not so different from the one on the cross in the sanctuary.

OUR LAST DAY in New York was Christmas, and the streets were surprisingly empty, the temperature unseasonably warm. I had gotten up before Jim, and because I knew he'd be staying in bed another couple of hours—in bed, then in the bathroom—I took the subway to Bryant Park. Later, we'd have breakfast together, and then head to the airport for home, but first I rented skates and for an hour circled the rink. Except for one or two skaters, I was alone on the ice. It was a kind of rehearsal.

80.

Deborah in Syracuse checked in again. Her husband, Bob, was going downhill fast and it was terrifying, reading her notes to me, to look into my own possible future. Still, I could not look away.

"Having a rough go of it here, and have been back and forth to Hopkins so many times I can't even remember when or why at this point. Complications are too numerous to even try to recount.

"I wish with all my heart this was not happening to him, or Jim, or anyone else for that matter, and I certainly have no idea how I would be if the tables were turned. Some days I find it so annoying I can hardly stand to be in the same room with him and then I feel guilty if I go get a damn manicure. I don't know whether this level of depression (has started on Zoloft, with no obvious effect yet), apathy (on Adderall—if I took as much Adderall as he is on I'd be out washing every car in the shopping mall parking lot around the clock) and general withdrawal from the world is specific to pancreas cancer or not, but it surely sucks. This brilliant mind has ground to an alarming halt. He is not reading, writing, listening to music, watching movies, or visiting with friends. All he does is sleep. He is such a thinker—always thinking up the next study, the next article to write, the next book to read or painting to paint and it is so distressing to watch his mind go blank. One day he asked me what our phone number was.

"He's got a feeding tube, has had two drains (which just got removed here) that had to be flushed and measured twice a day, dressings to be changed, meds around the clock—you know the drill. I love this man to bits, but I am so angry that he has abandoned me. He is so diminished, I was thoroughly expecting the oncologist to say on Wednesday that the disease had run rampant and we were at the end of the line. At which point I was going to regret every prodding, pissed-off word I've said to him in the last two months. When he didn't say that, I got even madder. How much sense does THAT make?? If you tell me you know exactly what I mean, I will do the following:

A. Worry about you
B. Prop you up best I can from afar
C. Know we'll be friends forever"

IN JANUARY I got on a plane again, alone. I was headed to Guatemala to teach my memoir workshop at Lake Atitlan, as I did every January, with the plan that Jim would meet me afterward. Once I had looked forward to these times on my own, but now I hated to leave Jim.

One other thing about that January: I gave up drinking wine, possibly not forever, I told myself. But for now anyway. For months I had told myself I'd do this, but every other time my abstinence had lasted no more than a couple of nights. "My life is hard enough," I told myself, as I uncorked the zinfandel. "I deserve this." Jim took Dilaudid. For me, the drug was wine. But lately the thought had been coming to me, that maybe the wine was making my life harder. Or would, eventually.

Giving up my drug of wine that January was a big deal. But maybe because I was away from Jim then—and away from the constant presence of illness and pain—I found it easier than I had anticipated, doing without alcohol. I was swimming a lot and teaching my workshop. Jim's situation was the same that it always had been, but having that brief reprieve from witnessing it on a twenty-four-hour basis allowed me to sleep through the night for the first time in months.

For eight solid days, at the lake, I lost myself in other people's stories, though late at night, when I was done leading the workshop, I'd call Jim back home in California. One night, after I was done filling him in about my day, I could hear him drawing in his breath before he spoke.

"I have a little news," he said, his voice steady and even. "I got back the results of my new blood test. It looks like my CA19-9 has gone up."

The tumor markers. The number every cancer patient feared. They weren't conclusive, but seeing them rise was never good news. I felt the impulse then, to pour myself a drink. Felt it, and resisted.

Some months earlier—after the soft tissue nodule scare with Dr. Ko, Jim had chosen a different oncologist at UCSF, Katie Kelley, whose specialty was liver cancer, though she treated pancreatic cancer patients as well. Now I wanted to know what Dr. Kelley had to say.

"I'm not too worried at this point," Jim told me. "Katie says that sometimes, all an elevated CA19-9 means is that you've got inflammation in the gut, and we knew that already."

We moved on to other topics. What good did it do to speculate or play out disaster scenarios? I told Jim about the workshop, and about an orchid plant Miguel and Mateo had found in the mountains for me, and about the pizza our friend Henry had made that night. After we said good night, I stepped outside to look at the stars.

When the workshop finished, I was scheduled to teach in San Miguel de Allende. Jim would meet me there, and we'd spend a few days together in Mexico, and then return to the lake for a few more weeks. Back in December, knowing her wedding was coming up in the spring, I had suggested that we buy his daughter, Jane, a ticket to come spend a week with us at Lake Atitlan. This might be the last time, for a while anyway, that Jim would have a chance to spend time with his daughter on her own. That was how we put it to each other, at least, and to ourselves.

On Valentine's Day, in San Miguel, Jim woke up with a fever so violent that no blankets could warm him. Friends drove us to the emergency room.

We spent the day there getting tests. Jim had some kind of infection, but the doctor there concluded that the antibiotics would get it under control, and by the end of that day it appeared they had.

We might have flown home to San Francisco, but once the antibiotics kicked in, Jim was feeling better, and he didn't want to miss Jane's visit. Nothing mattered much more to him than repairing what had been, for years, an uneasy relationship. Things had seemed good since the diagnosis, and he wanted to shore up the good feeling that existed now. I was happy about the visit too. Jane had asked if I'd bake pies for her wedding—and though the event was taking place three thousand miles from the kitchen where I generally baked, and pie for a hundred people was a lot of pie, her request seemed to signal good things in our relationship, so I told her yes.

After the scare in Mexico, Jim and I met up with Jane at the airport in Guatemala City and made our way to Lake Atitlan. In the back seat of the car with the two of them I studied Jim's face as he studied his daughter's: how happy he was that she was there.

We spent four good days with Jane. Jim was tired, but he felt good, or as good as he ever did at that point—the infection apparently behind him. Our conversation was full of plans for the wedding, set for the end of April. Earth Day. We'd be there, of course.

The day after she left, the chills and fever—rigors, the name for this—returned. This time it seemed clear to me that we needed to go home. I got online to buy plane tickets, and within twenty minutes our bags were packed and carried to the road, where the driver I'd called was waiting to bring us to the airport.

The whole drive there I held Jim's hand. "It's going to be better once we're home," I said. Always one more thing that would make the difference.

By the time we reached the airport, Jim was disoriented. A person observing him might have imagined he was drunk, or on drugs. Well, he was on drugs, of course. He was always on drugs. But this was something else.

I checked our bags. By the time we reached the security gate Jim was more dazed than ever, but he had to go to the men's room, he told me. I hovered by the entrance, picturing Jim on the floor inside, unable to speak Spanish—the men around him supposing he had simply consumed too much Ron Zacapa. I was just about to find someone to go looking for him when he emerged. He had no idea where he was.

"We need to get to the plane now, Jimmy," I told him,

Jim needed me to hold him up, so I left our bags at an airport restaurant. Once I got him settled safely at the gate, I'd run back to get them.

Two heavy carry-ons. Two backpacks. My ukulele. His Cuban cigars (not strictly legal to bring into the country, but no one ever checked).

I dragged the bags down the long airport corridor, out of breath, heart racing. When I got to the gate, two airport security officers were sitting on either side of Jim.

"Is this your husband? He is a very sick man."

They would not let us on the plane, though I was begging. "It's just to Miami," I said. It seemed like a better idea to get Jim partway home, at least. But the security officers shook their heads.

I took Jim by taxi—Jim, and all our bags, retrieved from security—to a private hospital in Guatemala City recommended by a friend. Jim sat in the back seat, shivering, as I wrapped myself around him.

At the hospital, they put him in the ICU. It was an infection again, and a bad one.

He stayed five days at the Hospital Herrera Llerandi, where doctors identified the particular bacterium in Jim's body from blood cultures and treated him with IV antibiotics that saved his life. By the fourth day, he was sitting up in bed and discussing the Rolling Stones with our gastroenterologist, a guitar player. He was worried that his hair had grown too long at this point, so I found a hair-dresser willing to come to the hospital and give him a trim. "Your husband has such good hair," she told me, as she packed up her scissors.

We were OK again—the infection not totally eradicated but under control. Flying home was not possible until Jim could complete a course of intravenous antibiotics, so we returned once more to the lake, and every day an American nurse we'd found in the village came over to give Jim an injection of more antibiotics.

The plan was for Jim to go on ahead of me back to San Francisco, to see his doctors there while I stayed on another two days to close up the house. Standing on the dock the morning the boat came to get him—the fishermen already out with their nets, the sun just coming up over the volcano—I kissed him good-bye as he stepped into the lancha and watched as it disappeared around the tall rock bluff.

"I'm going to start practicing law again, baby," he told me, over the phone that night, from back in California. He had a couple of new estate-planning clients. He was setting up meetings with attorney friends in the city to let people know he was back. He was going to get back to the gym. And then there was Jane's wedding to think of, less than two months away.

Two days after Jim got home—the night before I was due to return, myself—the fever returned. It was close to midnight when he drove himself into San Francisco and checked into the emergency room at UCSF Parnassus, which was where I found him—in a room on the fourteenth floor—when I got home myself the next day. There was the familiar IV pole beside him again, with more antibiotics dripping into his veins.

We thought he'd be there a day or two.

81.

I had briefly supposed it was good news when they told us that Jim was suffering from an infection again. At least this wasn't cancer.

But this was not just any infection, and it was not just one. On the white board in Jim's room, the doctor heading up the team on his rotation had written down the names of the bacteria attacking Jim's body: Streptococcus. Pseudomonas. Micrococcus luteus. Enterococcus. Stretched out on the bed next to him as I was now for most of every day, I had them memorized. Also the names of the attending physician and the nurse on duty that day, the Special Instructions, and Goals for the Day. (*Walk down the hall. Eat solid food.*)

Jim had a private room, but it still felt crowded with the IV pole and the monitors, the chair for visiting doctors and medical students. They'd brought in a chair that folded into a cot for me, but most nights it sat vacant. I preferred to climb in alongside Jim in his hospital bed. Thin as he was, fitting the two of us into that bed was not a problem.

As a person with no health issues of her own—a broken or breaking heart didn't count—it was an odd thing to be living in a hospital. We had a wonderful home back in Hunsaker Canyon, with our music and our garden, the birds, the stars. But it felt better just staying with Jim in the hospital than going back and forth between that world and this one.

When I walked out the door, I'd be hit with all the busyness of the world carrying on without us. News of the presidential primaries, oversized images of the San Francisco Giants attached to lampposts, e-mails about upcoming events Jim would not be attending at The Family—Storkzilla rehearsals, wine tastings, Ladies' Night. I'd see the buses barreling down Market Street, daffodils coming into bloom, joggers along the bay, signs announcing the imminent reopening of the newly expanded SFMOMA, an event Jim had been talking about since we first met. It was all too much—all these signs of life, all those reminders of what we used to do, where we used to go, Before.

I remembered registering this same sense of amazement that long-ago summer I cared for my mother when she was suffering from the glioblastoma that killed her, and I was spending my days at her bedside. How could people be sitting in cafés, drinking wine, picking up dry cleaning, heading off to the symphony—arguing with their husbands at the supermarket over which cut of meat to buy? Biting into their sandwich without taking a single pill. Pedaling their bicycles. Walking their dogs. Looking bored. So few held hands. Didn't they know how lucky they were? If my husband had their husband's pancreas, we'd never complain about one thing ever again.

Mostly I stayed away from the world of the healthy people, that spring. I preferred to stay in the room with Jim, up on the fourteenth floor—alongside him in the bed, under the covers even, watching shows together on his laptop (the O. J. Simpson miniseries, a documentary about Keith Richards) or comparing our observations of that day's nurse. We still took our walks when he was up for it— down the hall to the window with the view of Golden Gate Park, or to a set of stairs where we practiced going up and down. Ten steps. Seven. Five. This was our world, the fourteenth floor. Growing smaller all the time.

82.

He knew I had a terrible sense of direction, and got lost regularly—even in the seemingly familiar territory of the hospital. He worried, when I'd head out to the cafeteria, that I might get lost. So when he could, Jim got out of bed and—still attached to his IV pole—walked me to the right elevator.

He was not wrong that I needed his help: I had lost my way in this place more than once. One time, when I was slow in returning to the room—caught up in a maze of corridors—my cell phone rang. It was Jim, sounding worried. "I thought I'd lost you," he said.

"That won't ever happen," I told him.

83.

A week passed, and then two, and the infection hung on. Scans
of Jim's abdomen had revealed a whole cluster of abscesses
in his liver collecting fluid and breeding bacteria, like craters on the
moon. Every week now, he needed a procedure to drain the fluid
again. Gallons of it.

He needed another procedure to insert a stent in his bile duct.
Another procedure to remove the port that appeared to have bred
its own infection. Each time he needed surgery required twelve
hours of fasting beforehand and a trip to the third-floor operating
room, where we would sit in the hallway for an hour or two—three
sometimes—waiting our turn. Then came the recovery room. Then
the trip back to the fourteenth floor, where Jim could eat again, if the
nurses had remembered to set the Creon on the tray beside his food.
Sometimes they did, but now and then they didn't, and if they'd
neglected to set those Creon pills on his tray, it didn't matter how
many hours Jim had fasted or how hungry he might be. He'd have
to wait for the pills, and I'd go into battle mode, procuring them.

Something happens to a person when he lives in the hospital for
a certain period of time. Maybe it's the lack of sunlight, the lack of
fresh air, or just living in a world of other sick people and doctors.

Jim's fingernails went gray. His eyes took on a watery cast. His
hair, which he always took such good care of, was matted. His body
filled with fluid, so his belly—always so trim—now stood out like
that of a woman in her ninth month of pregnancy. His feet swelled
so much that the skin cracked, and I borrowed size-thirteen shoes
for my size-nine-and-a-half husband. (The only pair I could locate

were bright green, borrowed from a friend with large feet; I brought him a pair of sweatpants he had back home in the identical shade. "Look," he said. "Now I'm an elf.")

Still, he was getting out of this place. "I'm going to be there for Jane's wedding," he still told me daily. Three weeks to go. Plenty of time.

We booked a flight for the two of us. We'd get to the city with a couple of days to spare so I could bake all those pies.

Two weeks away. Ten days. Eight. Jim was still on the IV, the bacterium still mutating every couple of days, his abdomen filling with fluid in between procedures to drain it.

All our doctors knew the wedding date now. "We'll do our best," they said, but the looks in their eyes told me what they really believed.

"I have to be there," Jim told them.

With six days to the wedding, we made a new plan. A shorter trip to New York. I'd buy the pies instead of baking them. We'd use Jim's airline miles that we'd been saving for an Italy trip to fly first class, to make the flight less arduous.

He kept trying to get well enough to travel. Every afternoon, if he didn't have some surgical procedure, the two of us would make our way to a staircase at the end of the hall—Jim in his Maine Media Workshop baseball cap and the yellow paper gown he had to wear, identifying him as a patient with serious bacterial infection. Very slowly, for the next fifteen minutes, we'd go up and down a flight of steps together—*up, down; up, down*—as I held his hand and counted. He wanted to be strong enough for Jane's big day.

In the end, I flew alone to Jane's wedding—the second wedding I'd attended on my own in eight months. I left the hospital on that Friday morning and landed that Friday night, with fourteen pies waiting for me at the best pie shop in Brooklyn. The night of the wedding party, I read the toast Jim had written for Jane. The truth was, Jim had needed help writing this. He knew what he wanted to say to his daughter, but putting the ideas together was hard for him now.

The night of the wedding I brought my laptop with me so Jim could Skype in from his hospital bed, but when I reached him, he couldn't say much, and when I told him I'd bring the laptop over to Jane and her new husband, so they could Skype with him, he seemed not to hear me.

"I have to go to sleep now," he said. His voice seemed to be coming from someplace farther away than California. The bottom of the ocean, maybe.

I flew back to San Francisco the next morning. When the plane landed, I went straight to the hospital. I climbed into the bed next to Jim to show him the photographs of the wedding. One, of his three children all together, he studied for a very long time, saying nothing.

There had been a time when we talked of grandchildren. We didn't do that anymore.

84.

More days in the hospital. Five weeks. Six. Jim slept a lot now, though it was never a deep sleep, and seldom for long. Very often, when he fell asleep, he'd have his laptop in front of him, and a cup of the herb tea in his hand.

Two times that season, when he fell asleep, he had spilled the tea onto the laptop. Both times the hard drive had been wrecked, requiring the purchase of a new computer.

"I'm giving up tea," he said.

FOR MONTHS, JIM had been taking Dilaudid for the pain. First twice a day, then three times. Now it was every three hours, and if the nurse was five minutes late delivering the pills, I raced to the nurses' station to remind her.

The drug made his mind blurry. We could still talk about things (the Republican primaries—Donald Trump no longer a joke; a Netflix documentary we both loved about Keith Richards). Sometimes we listened to music, and sometimes we read, though concentrating for more than a few pages was difficult. My sister—often a distant figure in my life over the years, but a comforting presence these days—had taken to sending us poems she liked. I read these out loud to Jim. One of our favorites, by Jane Kenyon, a poem written when she herself was suffering with the cancer that ultimately killed her, was called "Happiness."

Sometimes, in our hospital bed together, we watched the final season of *Downton Abbey*, whose sponsor's ads—for Viking River Cruises—we loved as much as the show.

"I'm taking you on one of those, baby," Jim told me.

He was still funny, and his capacity for tenderness and love remained unaltered. But he had lost a lot of his old sharpness, and he knew it.

"You have no idea," he told me one afternoon, "how it feels when your brain stops working the way it used to."

Still he was holding on to life—every scrap of it he could keep in his grasp. At the photographer's golden hour—near sunset, when the light was best—he'd make his way slowly down the hall on the fourteenth floor with his camera. His destination was a window that looked out over Golden Gate Park, the place where, in Octobers past, we'd run like a pair of maniacs from one stage to another trying to catch every act we could at the Hardly Strictly Bluegrass festival. Now, wearing the yellow paper gown announcing his infection, Jim held his iPhone up against the glass and pointed it toward the San Francisco skyline and the sun going down over the Golden Gate Bridge. I conjured images for him of our old, good days.

"Remember those oysters we had outside in Marshall, with the fresh bread and the wine?" he said. "That first cold beer we got after the Gulf Haggas hike, when the police were going to arrest us for drinking from an open container?"

There was that night in Guatemala, Jim at the wheel of our rented Jeep, driving in near-total darkness on that crazy road to Semuc Champey as a fire raged above us.

"Remember that time," I said, "when we drove home so late there wasn't one car on the road and I took my shirt off on Mt. Diablo Boulevard?" We'd been in the Boxster, with the top down. "Remember the time we went to the Jean-Paul Gaultier show at the de Young Museum, and after, I got you to dress up in my black leather pants and that metallic silver shirt, with the boots?"

This would be Jim, my Brooks Brothers man. The man with a closet full of identical white shirts and navy blue striped ties. He had actually let me take his picture in that getup, and he had looked very good in it.

I had put on a black bustier that night, and my other pair of leather pants—gold ones—with hot pink feather-trimmed boots I'd found in a Goodwill store, along with every piece of dime-store jewelry I owned. Out on my deck in Mill Valley, we shared a bottle of wine and pretended we were Paris hipsters, but when it was dancing time, we'd chosen our John Prine song, "Glory of True Love." At the end of the day, that was more our style than Gaultier.

There is a history of secrets a couple shares, and short as our time had been, we'd known some good ones. Now I found myself wondering what happened to those secrets, if the only other person who knows them beside yourself ceases to exist? Or he's still there, but with his memory fading.

Here we were, those same two lovers who lay naked in a Budapest hotel room sixteen months earlier, a little drunk on Hungarian wine, snapping pictures of their reflections in a ceiling mirror over the bed. I was sixty-two years old now, wearing a hospital gown over the same T-shirt I'd had on for three days in a row and a pair of Jim's sweatpants from the days when he'd belonged to the Olympic Club. There was an inch of gray at my roots, it had been so long since I'd seen a hairdresser.

"You are the most beautiful woman," Jim said to me, cleaning crumbs off the front of me as I could always count on him to do.

Beautiful to him, anyway.

He was so thin now I could see the outline of his skeleton.

Sometime over the course of the last few days his wedding ring had fallen off his finger. We had torn the bed apart but couldn't find it.

"Now the nurses might think they have a chance with you," I told him. But that kind of joke never amused Jim.

"I need to get a new one," Jim said.

"Ring or no ring, doesn't matter," I told him. "You are the best husband I ever had."

85.

*M*utation. *Change of antibiotic. Mutation again. Revision of antibi-otic. (Followed by insurance application. The wait for approval of some new and no doubt wildly expensive new drug.)*

In between mutations came drain insertions. Drain revisions. Endoscopy surgery. Three surgeries in a single week one time: endoscopy, drain adjustment, endoscopy.

And here were the stakes: Until the infection was cured, we could not get a scan to check for a recurrence of the cancer. If there were a recurrence, this would be bad news (terrible news, actually; the worst) but we'd be ready then with our next phase of attack. I'd get to work on filling out applications for clinical trials. Never mind in what city they might be taking place, we'd go there.

No one had told us the cancer was back. But I knew the doctors were worried. And already, I was preparing for it.

Jim would get more chemotherapy, of course—no longer with the same goal we'd had when we embarked on adjuvant chemotherapy after the surgery: to prevent recurrence. Now the goal would be simply to keep the cancer at bay for as long as possible.

"How long before we can get the infection under control?" I asked Dr. Kelley.

She looked at me a long time before answering this one. "I hope we can get the infection under control. But it's not always possible to do that."

Actually, she told me later, out in the hall, she had never known an infection as extensive as Jim's to be successfully eradicated. Not to say that this couldn't happen. She just hadn't seen it.

THE GREAT SURGEON for endoscopies was Dr. James Ostroff. Like Jim, he was an amateur photographer. The corridor leading to the room where he operated was lined with photographs he'd taken, mostly on safari in Africa. Pacing the hallway as I did so often now, I'd study Jim Ostroff's photographs and imagine another way things might have gone: that this hallway would have led to Jim's law office in San Francisco and the photographs might have been those taken by my Jim, not this other one. They were both Nikon men of roughly the same generation. One performing endoscopies. The other undergoing them.

Jim—my Jim—kept his Kindle at his bedside at all times, but he was starting to have a hard time reading. He always seemed to be looking at the same one page.

"I feel so diminished," he said. Even the Politico.com articles he was always reading—featuring Donald Trump more than either of us had anticipated—no longer seemed to interest him as they once did. When the doctors asked questions now, they addressed these questions to me, though when this happened I stopped them. "Talk to my husband," I said.

"I'm becoming stupid," Jim said. "Besides all the rest of it, having cancer is just so damn humiliating."

MOSTLY, OVER THOSE weeks, I slept at the hospital—for days on end, often—but other times I got up at two thirty or three A.M., around the hour the night nurse came to check his vital signs. I had figured out a trick about parking fees at the hospital. The lot across from Parnassus cost thirty dollars a day, and sometimes I'd leave the car there for three or four days at a stretch without exiting the lot, which would have left me with a bill of well over a hundred dollars. There were discounts available for families of patients, but who had time to make a trip to the DMV?

So you told the man at the gate you couldn't find your ticket. That way the most they ever charged you was for one twenty-four-hour period. Every time I pulled that one off, I allowed myself a small sense of triumph. A minor victory in an avalanche of losses.

Even in San Francisco, there were almost no cars out at three A.M.—a few Uber drivers, a few policemen. This made it possible to make the trip from the hospital across the bridge in half an hour instead of the hour and a half it took in the daytime. Or longer.

Home again, I climbed into our bed for a few hours' worth of the kind of sleep a person never experiences in a hospital, where a computer monitor glows through the night, and you can always count on some nurse or orderly coming in the room every hour or two, and voices calling out in the night, "Help me!" or sometimes just moaning.

Next morning I woke up early, took my shower, changed my clothes, picked up our mail. Sometimes, before heading back over the bridge, I stopped at my friend Karen's house first. I always knew I could walk in the door and fall into her arms, and for a solid five minutes, I might just stay there, crying. No need to say anything.

When I could, I got back to Parnassus Hospital in time to bring Jim a cup of good Peet's coffee to have with his breakfast, though when I didn't, our friend Bridget—a palliative care counselor working on the same floor where Jim was, who had been in our lives as my son Willy's best friend since she was thirteen—stopped by to check on Jim and bring him the good coffee. Long ago, during that hard year I spent trying to be a good mother to my two adopted Ethiopian daughters, it had been Bridget, more than anyone else, who had helped get us through the days. At the time, I had called that experience the most painful of my life. Now here she was to help get me through a harder one.

Bridget's job was working with dying patients, but Jim had not been identified as one of her clients, and did not see himself that way. In the hallway outside his room, on her breaks, Bridget and I talked a lot about that.

Jim needed to believe he would survive, and because of this, I needed to be, for him, the partner who supported that dream. I wanted him to have hope, but as my own hope faded, a sense of loneliness overtook me. Jim was the person I always talked to about the hardest things. But how could I talk to Jim about this one?

He was not getting better. The virus kept mutating. Every day or two, when the doctors made their rounds, they'd erase the name of the previous bacterium from the white board and write down the name of the new one: another organism onto which I projected the malevolent personality of some supervillain constructed by Hollywood, to wage war against my husband from within his own body.

This called for different antibiotics every day or two. New applications for insurance approval. New lab cultures. New visits from the infectious disease team and the medical students who followed after them, fascinated with Jim's case. Once, over a space of thirty-six hours, the bacterium mutated twice—so fast that by the time one culture came back from the lab, and we got insurance approval for the new drug to treat it, we were on to the next.

For a while it was difficult to understand why it was that nobody seemed concerned with cancer anymore. All they talked about now was the infection. Jim had been due for another CT scan back in February, but because of the infection, it had been postponed twice.

None of the doctors seemed to view the scan issue with particular urgency.

Then I came to understand why. The only reason we weren't discussing cancer now was because an even greater threat existed. If the doctors could not eradicate the infection, it didn't even matter about the cancer. The Pseudomonas would get him first.

There was no way to identify the presence of cancer while Jim's abdomen was filled with infection. Those abscesses in his liver would have concealed whatever else might be present. And gradually I came to understand what the most likely reason was for why the infection had taken hold in the first place, the knowledge each of our doctors carried, walking into Jim's room, but never spoke of. More likely than not, a tumor was growing—or many of them— and it was blocking Jim's biliary ducts.

We weren't dealing with two separate problems. Everything came down to those cancer cells, the ones the Whipple surgery had left behind. If so, this would be Stage 4 cancer, metastatic cancer— the kind that can no longer be cured.

86.

One day, sometime in the fourth or fifth week of our time at the hospital, an e-mail arrived from the editor of the travel magazine for whom I'd written my Chile story. He had an assignment to run by me.

He was writing to tell me that *Travel + Leisure* had instituted a program of luxury trips, personally tailored to each individual traveler. He wanted to know if I might consider going on one of these trips and writing about it for the magazine.

An all-expense-paid luxury trip for two people who'd spent their last forty days in a hospital? If you were paying for a trip like the ones my editor had suggested to me, the price tag would run somewhere between eight to twelve thousand dollars per person, but of course the magazine would pick up the tab and pay my fee on top of that. And one more thing: My editor was familiar with Jim's photography from images I'd sent him of our Chile trip and the New England road trip story Jim and I had worked on together back when he'd edited a section of the *New York Times* three years before.

"We'd like your husband to shoot the photographs," he wrote. "Why don't you take a look at our offerings and see if any of these interest you?"

For a moment I just sat there on the bed, Jim beside me, half asleep—two drains coming out of his abdomen and the ever-present IV in his arm, his arm draped across the sheet, thin as a child's, his feet elevated to help bring the swelling down.

I clicked on the link to the trip offerings.

There was the world, laid out on my computer screen: hiking in the Dordogne, horseback riding in Mongolia. A luxury train ride across India—two full weeks. Diving in the Grenadines, sailing in Greece. Kyoto cherry blossoms. The Great Barrier Reef. Bhutan.

The day nurse was just finishing up with her blood work when the letter from the travel editor arrived. I set my laptop between us and touched his cheek.

"Look at this, Jimmy," I said. "You've got a photography assignment." His dream.

We spent the whole morning side by side in that hospital bed deciding where we should go. We liked the Grenadines a lot, and Bhutan. Then there was Croatia. But all things considered, we chose Italy.

I look back on that day now—the hours we spent, considering our next expedition—and wonder if Jim ever believed we'd make it to one of those places. Or to anywhere outside the state of California together, ever again. If so, we had engaged in a mutual pact, to allow for the dream that we would board a plane one more time, for one more magnificent adventure.

87.

Two more weeks passed. Jim never spoke about leaving the fourteenth floor anymore. Highlight of the day now: hospital rounds, when the resident and a group of interns and medical students stopped by. They all carried cards with their photograph on the front. I had accumulated a collection of a couple of dozen by this point, laid out on the bedside table like baseball cards.

Mostly now, the doctors we saw were infectious disease specialists and internists, but Dr. Katie Kelley, Jim's oncologist, checked in too—by telephone generally. Then one day she showed up in person.

In the hallway after—where I had walked out with her after she finished her visit with Jim—she explained to me what she had not said in the room. She herself had recognized that there was information Jim wanted to hear and other information he'd just as soon not get into. What she had to tell me that day fell into this category.

"Back when I first met him, Jim told me if there was ever news like this, he'd prefer that I just tell you," she said.

The cancer was back. We had lived through a scare the summer before that had turned out to be a false alarm, but this time it was clear, and Jim's CA19-9 numbers supported Dr. Kelley's conclusion. The infection still made it impossible to perform the scan, but she knew now what the scan would tell her, if it were possible to perform one accurately. It was cancer that accounted for the bile duct obstructions, the liver abscesses, the weight loss so relentless that it no longer mattered anymore how many calories Jim consumed, how many shot glasses I filled with MCT oil. Trying to put weight on Jim was like pouring water into a bathtub whose drain is open.

This was what Stage 4 cancer looked like: the swollen belly, the sunken eyes, the muscles eaten away regardless of whether, like Jim, the patient somehow managed to get himself up off the bed to perform his four pushups. (His three. His two . . .)

Stage 4. There is no Stage 5. Dr. Ostroff could open up a duct for a week or two, but sooner or later—and probably not much later—that duct would close up again and the reason it would was because there were cancer cells inside and they were multiplying. The abscesses would not dry up because there was cancer there too. Cancer everywhere.

More than the cancer, Dr. Kelley was telling me now, out in the hallway, it was likely that the infection would be the thing to kill Jim. But cancer, same as always, was at the root of it all: those microscopic cells they didn't get with the Whipple the previous June, or with adjuvant chemo, after, with their hard little shells and their ready ability to size up whatever form of chemotherapy you threw at them. In my mind's eye I could actually picture those cells; I could even hear them. *"You already played your Folfox card,"* they were shrieking. *"We've got that one nailed. What do think you can pull on us next that we don't have figured out already? Do you actually believe, you fools, that there is anything you can throw at us as powerful as we are?"*

There wasn't. No drug left to try.

Katie was probably the age of my daughter, and a very kind person. We called her Katie, not Dr. Kelley. She sounded very sad as she spoke to me.

As for me: I had known this news already, really. It was almost a relief to hear someone say, out loud, the words you have most dreaded. To get it over with.

I stood there in that fluorescent-lit hallway I had come to know as well as my own home, in possession of more information about my husband's body—his future, or lack of future—than he possessed himself. It seemed unfair to be talking about Jim this way, without Jim getting to be part of the discussion. But Jim held onto the belief that he could get better, and he counted on me to be the source of his optimism. Every time another hard thing happened, he looked to me now to say what we were going to do about it—and I always had something up my sleeve. You could call this denial, and so would I, but it was the one thing that got him through the day.

Jim and I did not discuss his death. I had made the decision, based on everything he had said and done up to then, that no matter what, I needed to offer him some small measure of hope. Smaller all the time, but he needed that.

Outside our hospital room now—Jim on the other side of the door, waiting for me to climb back into the bed with him—I ran through our options.

Months ago, back when I prayed we'd never get to this place but knew we might, I had prepared for this conversation by talking with pancreatic cancer patients we knew who were holding the recurrence of their cancer at bay with infusions. Back home on my desk I kept a file of clinical trials for Stage 4 pancreatic cancer. I never wanted to be caught short. If it came back, I had told Jim, I'd have Plan B in my back pocket. Or Plan W, more like it. Plan Z.

There was a clinic in Arizona one of the men from the pancreatic cancer breakfast club had visited recently. A place in Texas where they had an experimental treatment my friend Barbara was undergoing.

"We'll start chemotherapy soon, right?" I asked Dr. Kelley. "Gemcitabine maybe?" For eighteen months, I'd been a student of pancreatic cancer and its treatment. Jim and I both knew the story with Stage 4—that once cancer came back, there the prospect of a cure was off the table. All we could do now was buy some time.

She shook her head. A cancer patient with an active infection did not qualify for chemotherapy. For a patient in Jim's situation, with an immune system compromised by antibiotics, one dose of chemotherapy could be fatal—not that his cancer was anything less.

Katie stood with me in the hallway as I ran through the list I'd kept of things we hadn't tried yet. Except we'd tried all of them now. No, no, and no. *I'm sorry.*

The next question was the hardest, but I asked her. How much time did she think Jim had left?

A couple of months maybe, she said. Maybe a little longer. She'd be surprised if Jim could hold on until the fall.

Dr. Kelley must have delivered news like this more times than she could count, but it appeared to me, watching her face, that it was still hard for her to say these words. However many times she'd had to tell a patient she had nothing more for him, she had not succeeded in sealing off her heart, and I doubt she wanted to.

She was a mother of three young children. One time in her office she'd told us about her father, who had tended the bears in state parks of the Sierra all through her growing-up years. When Jim spoke of the Owens Valley, Katie told us she knew it well. Sometimes, when she called us from home on a weekend, or an evening, I could hear a baby's voice in the background.

"I'm just so sorry," she said again, tears in her eyes.

When I went back in the room after Katie left, I did not tell Jim about our conversation, but a little later, back out in the hallway where I could be alone, I called Jim's children, and mine, and then Bridget, who had become for me—though she was younger than my daughter—like a wise parent. With Bridget, I allowed myself to have the conversations I could not engage in with anyone else, about death, and dying, and after. With rare exceptions, I had virtually not allowed myself to imagine a life without Jim, but now—in the quiet of those conversations, with Bridget—I did.

Another person I called, in the aftermath of my conversation with Katie Kelley was our attorney friend Robert in Miami—part of the self-created network of pancreatic cancer survivors I had sought out early on. Robert was a virtual anomaly—the only Stage 4 patient I knew of, now that our Stage 4 friend from the breakfast group had died, who had hung on so long and well. We had never met, but his was the voice I wanted to hear on the other end of the line that night.

He was heading to a Seder, he told me, but he always made time for me. I told him about Dr. Kelley's visit. The no-chemotherapy verdict. We'd hit the wall, I said. Or at least it was looking that way. But he was the man for whom a miracle seemed to have occurred, and some incorrigible part of me still held out for the possibility that Jim might find one too.

Robert had recently returned from a conference on advances in the treatment of late-stage pancreatic cancer. I was hoping he might have something to suggest that nobody else had come up with yet.

"Do you have anything for me?" I asked him—this man who had become, for me that year, the friend to whom I turned in my darkest hour.

He drew in his breath. Silence on the other end of the line.

"So, what are the words you'll speak tonight at the Passover table?" I asked Robert.

Later, I would ask another Jewish friend to explain to me the meaning of what my friend told me over the phone that day. I would learn that it was a metaphor, and a statement of hope. His words expressed a wish to be in Israel, my friend explained. But Israel as a symbol for whatever it is in each of our lives that represents the promised land. Somewhere between heaven and earth, body and soul. A peaceful resting place.

"Next year in Jerusalem," Robert said.

88.

It was the first week in March when Jim entered the hospital. It was late April when he came home. Wisteria time.

I had driven the BMW to pick him up—careful not to get the car dirty, with the knowledge that I'd be selling it at some point not so long from now. A nurse brought Jim to the curb in a wheelchair—hospital policy—while I came around with the car. When I pulled up, Jim wanted to take the wheel.

He drove more cautiously than usual, and without his usual finesse. One time on the bridge it seemed to me that he was weaving a little outside of our lane, and he almost missed our exit.

"I've got it, baby," he said, observing me gripping the seat. When we reached our driveway in Hunsaker Canyon, he took it slow, just as we had the first day we'd made our way to this spot, on Jim's motorcycle.

"We're home," I said. The live oaks. The fruit trees behind the house where deer liked to graze with their fawns. The hot tub where we used to sit—before the presence of those drains made this impossible—to watch the stars, or the sun coming up.

Like an astronaut emerging from the landing module after a long space flight, Jim climbed with exquisite deliberation out of the driver's seat. He stood a moment outside the house before going in. After years of drought, the winter had brought rain, and now the field behind the house was green all the way out to the oak trees. For the first time since we moved here, the brook was running again. You could smell the jasmine, and the wisteria was in bloom, same as it had been the first time we pulled up here just two years earlier.

We made our way along the path to our front door—Jim's gait slow but steady, mine matching his. As he placed his hand on the doorknob, Jim turned around again, his gaze taking it all in.

"This would be a good place to die," he said. We stepped inside.

89.

Though we had not spoken of it, life at home felt different now. A team of home care nurses had set us up with a schedule—weekly deliveries of the antibiotic Jim had been receiving at the hospital that we'd infuse at home now through a PICC line in his arm at eight-hour intervals, along with all the usual drugs. This was a demanding schedule, but it allowed Jim to be home in our own bed—with Willy's dog, Tuck, still on extended loan to us, under the covers by our feet, or in side-by-side chairs on our balcony at the end of the day, looking out over the trees of Hunsaker Canyon and listening to the birds.

The chief condition for Jim's release from the hospital was that I administer Jim's antibiotic infusions three times a day. The nurse had instructed me on the procedure for carrying out the infusions, and though at first the whole thing had seemed impossibly complicated and risky—particularly for a person like me who had never maintained anything close to a sanitized environment, (a person who could be counted on to have crumbs on her clothes and garden dirt under her fingernails), I knew that for Jim to stay out of the hospital, I had to get this right, with no margin for error.

I located an RN—a neighbor whose father had died of pancreatic cancer—who offered to oversee the infusions until I felt more confident about delivering them myself. I had never met Lori before, but now she arrived at our house at five in the morning for the first infusion of the day.

We performed the infusions at Jim's precious glass table—a piece of furniture that I had once disparaged for looking too cold and sterile. Now I laid out the components for each infusion as a priest might the sacrament: Clean white towel. Saline syringe. Sterile wipes. Another saline syringe. Tubing. Tubing cap. Bolus of antibiotic (warmed to room temperature the hour before). Another syringe of saline. Syringe of antibiotic. More sterile wipes. I set the containers of medicine and saline in a row, in the order I'd administer them. First I washed my hands three times with the hottest water. If the tip of the syringe touched my hand before I got it into the PICC line, I started over with another sterile swab.

Jim, in the chair beside me, always told me what a good job I did. "You could have been a great nurse," he told me.

Well, only to him.

He told me he wanted to play golf again. Maybe a nine-hole course. Next winter, he said, maybe we could go skiing, but gentler slopes than in the old days.

"There's always ping-pong," I said. No question, he could beat me at that.

ONE OF JIM'S classmates from law school who knew about the cancer suggested a gathering in the city—nothing too elaborate, just the members of their class meeting up for drinks in the city. "It's been too long since we all got together," he wrote to Jim, though there was a little more to this get-together than that, as we all knew.

It had been months since Jim put on a suit, and none of them fit anymore. We cinched in his pants and kept the jacket buttoned, though that hardly concealed the truth of what had become of his body over the last year and a half. He laced his shoes, spent time considering the tie. He stood at the mirror a long time then, taking in the sight of himself in the beautiful Calvin Klein suit. Looking at him studying his reflection, I tried to imagine what it must be like to see, in the mirror, a person who no longer resembles you. More than once over the past year, on the rare occasions when we'd gone out in the city—to the symphony one time, and once to the ballet—we had run into some old friend who no longer recognized Jim. His physical appearance had altered that much.

Now, as he suited up for the law school reunion like a knight preparing for battle, I studied his thin, pale body with a rush of protectiveness as well as love.

"You are such a handsome man," I told him. In spite of everything, this was still true, though he looked like David Byrne in his big suit in that Talking Heads video of our youth.

Jim drove us into the city, and—slowly, as we did everything now—we made our way from the parking garage to the lobby of the high-rise where Jim's old friend Phil had his offices, and up the elevator to the swank conference room where the evening's gathering was taking place. Platters of fruit and cheese had been laid out for us, along with drinks.

This was a good-bye, of course, a send-off. But the Hastings Law School Class of '77 greeted each other with lawyerly restraint. Most of them were still practicing law, many having come straight from work to attend the gathering. Their talk was of cases, the Warriors basketball team heading into the playoffs. The California primary.

Everyone seemed to have a trip coming up: One of them was marking his upcoming retirement by embarking on a yearlong sailing adventure; someone else had recently walked the Camino de Santiago. One woman had taken up dressage riding.

Mostly they reminisced about the old days: Jim, a law review editor back in the day, was always the one you could count on for the wittiest comeback, the most fun, the biggest laugh. One of the group—who evidently hadn't heard the news and seemed not to have noticed that Jim had probably dropped forty pounds since the last time they'd had drinks—inquired where Jim was practicing these days.

"I've had to scale back for the moment," Jim said. "I've got some chemotherapy coming up."

The conversation shifted swiftly then, back to other topics. Grandchildren. Wine.

In the car on the way home I kept my arm around Jim's shoulders as he drove. We were giving one of his old colleagues a ride home, so the banter continued. After we dropped her off, we didn't say much for a while.

"You were my favorite lawyer tonight," I told him. "You are always my favorite."

He didn't look the part of the Super Lawyer anymore, that guy with the number 10 Avvo-rating score, one of those debonair man-about-town types—*the swinging dicks,* he called them—who played golf at the Olympic Club and drank whiskey shots at Tadich's. The man who used to take curves fast on the Pacific Coast Highway had taken his leave. The closet full of good shirts, miles too big for him now, had been donated to Goodwill. No more small talk over cigars, discussions of some six-figure settlement fee. At heart, Jim was never really the high-roller super-lawyer type, but he had played that game well enough, for all that it mattered, which no longer seemed like much.

It came to me, driving home over the bridge that night after the gathering of lawyers, that something had shifted over the course of these terrible months.

I had admired Jim as he was the day we met, and came to love him not so long after that. I had loved dressing up for nights on the town, speeding up the highway with the top down, sitting at some bar watching my fine, handsome husband coming in the door, brief-case in hand, and knowing he was headed for my table. But the man I lived with now, as diminished as he believed himself to be—a scarecrow in a suit with enough room left over inside for another whole person—was a man in possession of more compassion and humility than the one he'd been when times were good. He had become his finest self over the course of his ordeal. Not always, but on my better days, I like to think the same was true of me.

90.

It was one of his last pleasures, having a glass of wine, and what he liked best was sitting out on our patio, wrapped in blankets now, and having one with me.

At this point over three months had passed since I'd had a drink, and I didn't even find it so difficult anymore, doing without. But after our return from the hospital—in this new world of Stage 4 cancer, where the horizon line lay starkly in front of us, the glittering distant vistas we used to contemplate no longer within sight—I wanted to have a drink of wine at the end of the day with my husband. I also just plain wanted a drink. More vigilant than before—when we'd polished off a bottle over a single dinner—I allowed myself to do this. "I'll probably have to give it up later," I told myself. I did not allow myself to form a picture of what later would look like, or where I would be then.

One night over the dinner Jim could no longer eat much of— dinner, and red wine—something possessed me to lay out for us a fantasy. In the absence of real travel, I wanted to take us someplace, if only for the space of that one meal.

"Suppose there was this clinical trial," I said. "And they accepted you."

More than once over the four and a half years of our time together, Jim had told me he possessed no imagination. He said this as a person (me, for instance) might admit to being a bad driver, or to having no aptitude for tennis. Maybe it was more along the lines of acknowledging color blindness, this lack he admitted to—but what he had spoken of was a deficit of something so basic and crucial, in my world at least, that his words had stunned me. I could no more picture life without imagination than I could picture life without breath.

But there was a truth to what Jim said about himself. He could come up with elegant legal strategies or hundred-point Scrabble plays, but he could not dream up scenarios that differed from life as we lived it. Maybe his father had terrorized all fantasies out of him years ago.

So now I laid out a story for him—much as, long ago, I had told my children tall tales around a campfire, or sitting by their beds at night.

The story I spun out that evening was meant for me as well as for Jim—a few minutes' reprieve from the unbearable hopelessness of his situation.

"Suppose they put you on this new drug," I went on. Slow and quiet, my voice not so different from the one in which I had read to my children. "Some brilliant young scientist came up with this, and nobody ever tried it before, but they chose you to be the first.

"And the cancer . . . went away."

I watched Jim's face as I filled in the details—the trip to some new city for treatment (Houston maybe? Berlin? Philadelphia? Why not make it Paris?). It was as if I had offered him a ticket for the most wonderful thrill ride anywhere, the most spectacular show. *Come watch this with me. I'll buy the popcorn.*

He was there.

"You'd start to feel so much stronger then," I said. There would still be all the mess left by the Whipple procedure, of course, but I had a scenario to deal with that one too.

"And your pancreas grew back. Not all of it, but enough that you wouldn't even need Creon anymore.

"You could eat regular meals again," I said. "No more drains in your belly. And you wouldn't need all those Dilaudid pills, messing up your brain.

"I'm with you," Jim said. His voice was low, and he had set down his fork.

What then? Where would I go with my fantasy, now that I'd started to construct it? Would I put Jim in some big law office in the city with views of the bridge and giant estate battles to litigate? Would we rent a house in Provence? I could sell a book to some big movie studio and make a pile of money. Jim could have his Tesla.

I had the imagination for this. No problem there. But I felt no need for further embellishment of the dream. For us that night, it was enough to savor the picture I'd already laid out. *Cancer eradicated. Pain gone. Us together in our bed. End of story.*

We ate our meal in loving silence then, as we often did. As little basis in reality as my words possessed—none, actually—it had felt good just letting ourselves go to that place for the space of a few minutes (the one trip we could still take, since Italy and Croatia were out now) and to realize, as we did, that there was nothing more we would ask for beyond the restoration of Jim's health. That alone represented the dream. All the things we'd hungered for at other stages in our lives—success, money, beauty, passion, adventure, cars, houses, guitars—were immaterial. Breathing would be enough. Getting to walk down our road together, and come in after to share a meal. That, and ending up in the same bed every night with our arms around each other. What more did two people need?

91.

Even though she'd told me that day in the hallway outside Jim's hospital room that she could tell the cancer was back, Dr. Kelley scheduled one more scan. I had come to accept the part about the recurrence, but I allowed myself the slim hope that maybe this new scan would reveal the abscesses in Jim's liver sufficiently diminished that he'd qualify for chemotherapy after all. No longer lifesaving, only life-extending. From where we stood now, this would have qualified as great good luck.

Sitting in Dr. Kelley's office that afternoon awaiting Jim's results, we took our familiar positions. For months it had been the way things worked at doctor visits, that I'd answer the questions about Jim's medical history, starting with his birthdate that I had recited so many times that I knew it better than my social security number. *061252.* Moving on to his medications. I could run down the list a lot faster than Jim.

Date of diagnosis. First symptoms. Allergy to medications. Date of Whipple. Most recent bowel movement.

Then Katie asked Jim how he was feeling. I left it for him to answer that one.

"Pretty good," he told her, though I knew he wasn't. "I'm doing great, actually."

I did not correct him. I knew what he was doing here: trying to put on a good enough show that his doctor would give him a shot at more chemotherapy. Maybe even—if we were really lucky—recommend him for a clinical trial.

To this it had come: concealing how rotten you felt, so you

might get to have a drug that would make you feel ten times more rotten. Putting on a brave front to your own doctor. As much of his pain as I witnessed, he was probably working hard at looking strong for me, too. (Those pushups he still did every night before bed. *Pushup*, singular. He was down to just one.)

And still he was chasing after chemotherapy. My Eagle Scout husband had become a supplicant, lying to his own doctor in the hopes she'd agree to infuse him with the most deadly chemicals, even though as we well knew, they could no longer prevent—only postpone—his death from pancreatic cancer.

Dr. Kelley looked at Jim squarely, her voice level, with a look of deep regret. "For you to receive chemo, Jim," she said, "we'd need to see evidence of major reduction in the infection." This was familiar ground we were treading. We'd been here before.

Just as she spoke the words, Jim's scan results came through on Dr. Kelley's computer. I studied her face as she examined the images of Jim's abdomen—the dark circles that I had come to recognize as the liver abscesses.

No change in those. If anything, there were more of them. One way or another there would be no chemo for Jim.

I didn't have to reach for his hand then. I was holding it already.

ON THE DRIVE home, I raised the topic carefully. "Maybe it's not so terrible that you're not getting more chemo," I said.

Jim looked baffled.

I hated doing this. I reminded him of the facts that had been laid out for us.

"It is possible," I said, "that we might have decided ourselves that we didn't want more treatment. Even if it was an option."

"I don't understand."

I had recently reread an essay in the *New Yorker* on this topic by Atul Gawande, called "Letting Go." The essay, which I'd printed and given to Jim, was about recognizing when to surrender. Our friend Bridget had been talking with me about this too.

"Chemo would have made you very sick," I said. (*Very sick.* What did that mean now?) "And we already know the story on chemo for Stage 4."

A look of incomprehension came over Jim then. If he didn't love me as he did, this might even have been a moment in which he'd have expressed impatience and irritation. *Not want chemo? What was I talking about? Getting chemo again was everything we'd been working for.*

"Chemotherapy won't cure a recurrence, sweetheart." I told him. "Once the cancer comes back, there is no cure."

It was a fact we'd known since the beginning, but now Jim looked at me less with grief than with astonishment.

"Nobody told me that."

I had, of course. And he had read it. The doctors had said it. The men in the pancreatic cancer support group. The wives and the widows. It was a part of the landscape we'd inhabited from that first day at the doctor's office in Walnut Creek, eighteen months and a million years ago, when they delivered the news.

"I guess I didn't understand," he said quietly. "I though I'd be getting more chemo soon."

Oh, Jimmy.

He was driving. Not as well as he used to, but holding on to the wheel, ten o'clock and two, tighter than usual maybe. He, the man with plans to accompany me on the *Travel + Leisure* trip to Lake Como and the Amalfi coast. The man who had said to me, the week before, when I planted tomatoes in the garden: "We have tomatoes in our future." How resolutely he had held on to that.

The idea of a future. The man who had told our friend Bob, back when he went in for the Whipple procedure, "If I can just get a few more years with Joyce."

It is hard enough delivering terrible news once. But I had to deliver it multiple times. He kept forgetting he was going to die, and who wants to be the one to remind a person she loves that this is so?

92.

One Thursday, trash day, he said he wanted to push the bins to the road with me, but they were very heavy. I ran out before him, to dump half the contents of his bin into mine. Still, it took twenty minutes for the two of us to get the two containers down our driveway.

"We have to go into the city," he said. Not for a doctor's visit this time. He needed to replace his wedding ring. The one that fell off his finger.

"Maybe we'll get the ring tomorrow," he told me, a half hour later, suddenly exhausted. We spent the afternoon on our bed—I, still scouring the globe for experimental treatments. Jim asleep. Outside our window, a bird had somehow gotten his wiring mixed up. All day, and all the next, and for a solid week after that, he kept crashing into the glass at one-minute intervals. *Smash, smash, smash,* he flung his small feathered body against the same window.

Then one day he was gone. We never knew what that was about, though the marks he made remained on the glass, and I never wanted to clean them off.

I CALLED BOSTON, the office of the great Beth Israel pancreatic cancer team. I thought they should be made aware of where things stood. Someone must be keeping records there. After all those months of monitoring Jim's scans, not to mention that fourteen-hour surgery, they'd want to know how the story turned out.

It was a naive idea. Dr. Moser was a busy man, of course,

performing Whipple procedures four days a week. Two Whipples a day sometimes. There was a whole new group of patients now, sitting anxiously in the waiting room, no doubt, awaiting word on whether the Folfirinox was succeeding in shrinking the tumor enough to make possible the longed-for surgery. A whole new group of husbands with wives at their side, wives with their husbands, filing in two by two.

I left a message asking that Dr. Moser call, because it seemed to me he'd want to know, if only to keep the statistics up to date. I never heard back. Maybe if I'd kept trying long enough, someone would have returned my call, but I let it go.

93.

After all those years of construction, the San Francisco Museum of Modern Art was about to reopen. Jim had been carrying his new membership card in his wallet for months. "We'll wait a couple of days for the crowds to die down," he said. "So we can see everything better."

We made another trip to Parnassus hospital. Another procedure— no more endoscopies for us, but they were still trying to drain those abscesses.

From my familiar seat in that room, checking my watch for the time I knew they'd be bringing Jim back to the recovery room, I spotted Dr. Nakakura, the great Whipple surgeon at UCSF, standing in the hallway in his scrubs, speaking to an anxious-looking woman and a couple of young adults who appeared to be her children.

I recognized this moment. I knew the look. Someone these people loved—mother, father, wife, husband, daughter, son—had just undergone the Whipple procedure. I could barely look at their faces, they were so full of gratitude and hopefulness.

"We got twenty-five lymph nodes," he was saying. I knew that story, too.

I BOUGHT US three tickets to a Giants game. For me, for Jim, and for his son Kenny. Jim put on his orange shirt and his Giants cap— so did I—and the vintage Giants jacket my son Willy had given Jim the Christmas before. I took a picture of father and son together in the stands—Kenny looking heartbroken, Jim giving the thumbs up. He got a hot dog, not that he could manage more than a couple of bites.

It was a day game—chosen because the ballpark wouldn't be so chilly then—and the Giants won. We had ridden the ferry to the city, leaving the BMW at a parking lot in Jack London Square, but when we got there, Jim couldn't locate the keys.

We took out everything in his backpack. No keys. Finally we called Kenny's girlfriend to pick us up. We'd leave the car overnight and come back for it the next day.

In the old days, I would have made some sharp remark. *How could he?* I didn't do those things anymore.

"If only," I often said, "you could learn the lessons of cancer without having cancer."

94.

My novel came out. There was a book tour scheduled. Twelve cities across the country, finishing up with a party in New York, a hundred friends invited.

But I couldn't leave Jim anymore. Not all at once, but one by one, I canceled the stops. First Seattle, then Chicago, then Kansas City, then Philadelphia.

"I've ruined your career," Jim said, the day I pulled the plug on the party.

There had been times, in months gone by—as first one deadline passed to deliver the first of the two novels I'd contracted to write, then the second, and the money from my advance disappeared with no new novel under way—when I had registered my own level of bitterness over what Jim's illness had done to my own life and work, not to mention my finances. I had not always done a good job of protecting my husband from my sorrow and frustration. One time—a rare occasion when he'd been short with me—I had snapped at him, "I've given up my life for you." When I said that, he'd put his head in his hands, and a look of as much sorrow as I'd ever seen came over his face.

"You think I don't know?" he said, the closest he ever came to tears. "All I ever wanted to do was to be a good husband for you."

I didn't care about any of that anymore: book tours, publication parties, the Facebook posts I read while on the bed in Jim's hospital room that made a person feel as though everybody else she knew was having this amazing, glamorous, wonderful life, celebrating anniversaries on Kauai and the births of grandchildren. Writers whose books were being made into miniseries. Couples we'd pass as we drove down Mt. Diablo Boulevard on our way to or from the drugstore for prescriptions, sharing six-dollar ice cream cones, running off to play tennis.

Were they loved as I was?

"I'm glad I'm staying home," I told Jim. "Hardly anybody even goes to book readings anymore anyway."

95.

Jim had been home from the hospital a few weeks, but the infection hung on. Three times a day, I lined up the syringes on the glass table next to the box of sterile gauze wipes and rubber tubing and the IV infusion pole. I removed one of the boluses of antibiotic from the refrigerator (warmed it up first) and, after a series of flushes, connected the tubing with the bag of antibiotic. For the next hour then, we sat together while the antibiotic dripped into Jim's arm. Then I disconnected the bolus from the tube and sterilized again. We did this at six A.M., at two in the afternoon, and again at ten, just before bed. His body had become a site for procedures. Mine I no longer considered.

One night Jim woke me up sometime after midnight.

"I want to give you a massage," he said.

Not without some effort—everything required effort now—he lit three candles. He must have planned this, because the massage oil was there on his night table: I lay back on the bed with the moonlight coming through the window.

He knelt over my body. I have to believe every inch of him hurt. Slowly . . . everything was slow . . . he poured the oil onto his hands. He began to touch me. I lay there on my back, looking up at him in the moonlight—his face, so deeply lined, his hands, familiar to me as my own.

The thought came again, as it often did now. *Remember this moment.*

★ ★ ★

JIM'S FRIEND JAY came from Cleveland. His cousin Helen from Ohio, the only child of Jim's beloved Uncle Al. We ate lunch on the patio under the last of the wisteria, Jim wearing a sweater with a fleece over it, and his Patagonia jacket over that; also a hat. The thermometer read sixty, but he was cold all the time.

He had told me the stories, many times, of fishing trips in Minnesota with Uncle Al, times the two of them rode around in Al's Ford Falcon convertible. At age eighty-one, following a minor elective surgery, Al contracted mad cow disease from a blood transfusion. Jim had visited him in the hospital. It had been a terrible death.

"Don't let that happen to me," he said.

IT HAD BEEN months now since we'd taken the walk we used to go on, just down the road from our house, that required us to climb over a metal gate—miles of open trail up into the hills, with views of Mt. Diablo and hawks circling. It was a good day now when we made it out into the yard and sat in our chairs with our glass of wine, watching the deer graze.

One day our neighbors stopped by to tell us there'd been a rattlesnake sighting on the trail. Next week, the dirt was dug up under a stand of aspen, the work of feral pigs. The week after that, another neighbor's dog was attacked by a mountain lion. It felt as if the animals were winning here.

THE WARRIORS WERE in the playoffs and our friends Karen and Tom, who were season-ticket holders, gave us two tickets courtside. I gave mine to Kenny, texting him three times during the game to see if Jim was doing OK. Kenny texted me a picture of the two of them—father and son—in their matching yellow Warriors shirts and Warriors caps.

"You cannot imagine how great it was to be sitting there with my son, right down on the floor," Jim told me after. Steph Curry, the star forward for the Warriors, was a particular hero—master of the three-point shot, dropped in the basket in the last seconds of a game. Steph Curry was six foot three, but because the other players on the team were so much taller, Jim called him a little guy, like himself.

"Next time I'll bring you, baby," he told me.

A TEXT MESSAGE reached me. For a moment I could not recognize the name of the sender, Billy, but then I remembered: He was the young parking valet to whom Jim and I had given the keys and title to our red Plymouth LeBaron. The car that had transported us across Maine, New Hampshire, and Vermont—with the wind in our hair—over the happiest summer of our lives.

He still had the LeBaron, he wrote. He had rebuilt the engine, fixed the dents in the body. That winter, Billy and his buddies had driven the car all the way to Florida with their golf clubs in the back.

With no idea of the cancer, or anything else, he just wanted Jim and me to know that out on the eighteenth hole, he had been thinking about us.

I called up a woman I'd met at a party one time, who'd told me if I ever wanted olive trees to let her know. She had some to give away.

A week later I planted them. Thirteen trees, out on the hillside where we'd always planned to put them. The day we set them in the soil, Jim said he wanted to walk out to see them.

"How long again, till the first crop?" he asked me.

Five years.

THEN THERE WAS the matter of the fifth season of *House of Cards*. Over recent weeks we'd gotten through every episode of season four—me, with a sense of dread, as if the conclusion of every episode served as another step in some unnamed but ever-present countdown.

"When does season five start?" Jim asked, as the credits rolled for the final episode of season four.

Next fall.

ONE SUNDAY, HE wanted to go to church. When it was time for Communion, he got up from his seat on the pew. Later in the service, the priest asked if there was anybody the congregation in need of special prayers that day. I knew Jim would not want to be singled out, and so said nothing. I had been saying special prayers for quite some time by this point. But the only time I said them out loud was when I drove alone into town. Usually to fill prescriptions. Or to call Pam or Deborah—the two friends who understood better than anyone else what it was to watch the man you loved eaten away by pancreatic cancer.

96.

On his desk one day, I found a list. It was written on a scrap of notepaper. The heading: *Places I Want to Go with Joyce.*

Idaho—all the national parks.
Hiking in the Dordogne.
Hiking in Scotland.
A bike ride. Flatter trails. Cambodia?
Prague of course.
Greece. An island.
A barge in France.
Italy, anywhere.
India. Same.
The Galapagos. Turtles!
The Owens Valley. Stars.

97.

I had exhausted all reasonable options, and all the farfetched ones too. We were looking for magic now.

Not even that. I no longer believed I could find a way to save Jim's life. But living as we did by this point—with no remaining prospect of chemotherapy—was harder than any surgical procedure, more brutal than the effects of any chemotherapy infusion. Nothing else had been too much to bear, but this was.

Over the eighteen months that had passed since the diagnosis—hard as they'd been—we had been able to hold on to some crumb of hope. And even now I wanted there to be something we could do beyond waiting for Jim to die. It seemed clear that whatever it was would not save Jim's life, but I wanted him to feel, at least, that we were doing something about this.

A dead duck, he had said. *Am I a dead duck?*

If there had been a website for ordering magic potions I would have logged in there. As it was, I put a note on my Facebook page—a community that had grown to many thousands of readers over the months I'd been writing about Jim and me. I asked if anyone might be acquainted with a woman who had delivered a baby within the past seventy-two hours who might be willing to send us a very small amount of colostrum—the first thing that comes out of a woman's breasts, before breast milk, when she begins nursing a newborn.

I had not read any research or articles about this. There were no outlier healers suggesting that colostrum might cure cancer or even infection. It just seemed to me, when I considered what might best constitute a truly miraculous elixir, that colostrum would come the closest to filling the bill.

A dozen women wrote back offering to express mail us their frozen breast milk. One of these women still had colostrum.

The package arrived by FedEx two days later, packed in dry ice. Jim took a picture of me holding the precious vial, and then I took a picture of him doing the same. The quantity no more than what might fill a shot glass.

And what purpose did this vial serve? Almost certainly, none. But if the colostrum served to do nothing more than to offer us a little dream for a moment there, that was reason enough to down the contents. In a single gulp he did.

WE RETURNED TO Michael Broffman—to the beautiful office with the wall of wooden drawers containing mysterious herbs and dried Chinese mushrooms, the Tibetan prayer flags, the sound of water running over stones.

He had prepared a list of options we might try—the focus no longer on eradicating cancer, only beating back the infection as much as possible.

It had been over a year since we last visited the Pine Street Clinic. Jim had probably weighed twenty pounds more than he did now. But there was more to the change than his weight: His gums were pulling away from his teeth; his eyes had taken on a deep, penetrating gaze—a look I remembered from that *National Enquirer* photograph of Patrick Swayze in the final days of his struggle with pancreatic cancer, as if his vision now allowed him to see things none of the rest of us did.

No doubt this was not the first time Michael Broffman had sat across from a person with this look. This room had been one of our first stops on our quest to save Jim's life. Now it would be among our last.

He gave us a list of liquid vitamin supplements—C, D, Gluta-thione, B12. He told us about something called ProBoost formula to put in Jim's drinks. We should order organic cannabis-leaf juice in frozen shots. One daily. Buy bone broth.

"There's one other thing that sometimes provides impressive results in combating infection," he said. "You might think about a hyperbaric chamber."

Two days later, we were there. It was an hour's drive from home (operators of the closer chamber having turned us down), and the cost, after the first consultation, was $425 a session. For a person with Jim's level of infection, the visits should take place daily, for twelve weeks straight, minimum.

Never mind the money. Never mind that the chamber Jim would lie in for treatment—with its state-of-the-art sound system and overhead DVD player—was smaller than the MRI machine that had led to a major attack of claustrophobia. Still, Jim was game to try.

We paid just three visits to the hyperbaric chamber—each of them, because of the drive and the traffic, occupying most of a day. Each time Jim emerged from the chamber I asked him if he'd felt anything. He shook his head. Other than claustrophobia, nothing.

Maybe it was too soon for results, we said. They'd told us Jim needed twelve weeks. In Jim's calendar now, this was a lifetime, or what was left of one.

The cost of the chamber would not have stopped me, but the cost of our days did.

The third time Jim emerged from his ninety minutes in the chamber, he did not stop at the desk to sign up for the next round of treatments. Out in the car, he took my hand, or I took his.

"Let's just go home," he said. "I want to take you to the Owens Valley."

98.

Jim's doctors all advised against this. The abscesses in Jim's liver left him highly vulnerable to sepsis. It could happen at any moment, and when it did the effect would be like a wildfire in a drought-stricken forest.

"You haven't seen what happens when a person in Jim's condition spikes a fever," Dr. Kelley told us—though that day at the airport in Guatemala City, standing outside the men's room when Jim wandered out in a daze, had provided a glimpse. "It can be terrifying, more for you maybe than for him. If it happens, you will have very little time to get him to a hospital."

There were hospitals in the Eastern Sierra, I pointed out. The BMW went fast. Then came another idea, wilder even. Among Jim's friends at The Family club was one—a former fighter pilot in Vietnam—who owned a helicopter company. I wrote to Jim's friend, Steve, to ask if there might be a way, in an emergency, for him to pick us up. He wrote back, *yes*.

Jim's son Kenny asked if he could come with us, and though this wasn't how I'd pictured the trip, I asked Jim what he thought, and Jim said OK.

"Just so long as my dad doesn't do the driving," Kenny said. "I don't want to die on the highway."

Hearing this, Jim shook his head. Driving that car was part of the point of the trip, and how much traffic would there be anyway in the Sierra?

In the end, Kenny chose not to join us. I was OK with Jim taking the wheel as long as he said he could. He would never let anything happen to me in the desert or anyplace else.

We had taken many road trips in our days together. None like this, though. I doubt many people have.

This time there would be no hiking. We would take in the mountains through the windows of the car, mostly, but through the window was good enough. In the back seat, I set up a special cooler I'd ordered online, connected to the cigarette lighter, to keep a four-day supply of antibiotic boluses chilled. Farther back, we set the IV pole. In the glove compartment, a full supply of Creon and Dilaudid, and a little marijuana, though Jim would go easy on those when he was driving.

In those first days after he bought the BMW, Jim had loaded the sound system with hundreds of songs—a vast collection with all kinds of music. But for this trip he only wanted to play the Beatles. Early Beatles mostly. As we made our way south to Tracy, then east toward the desert, we listened to their young, joyful voices: the Beatles as they were before the Maharishi, before Yoko, before the breakup, before Mark David Chapman and George's cancer— the old uncomplicated songs sung by those four glorious boys, younger than any of our sons were now.

"She Loves You." "Help!" "You're Gonna Lose That Girl." "Norwegian Wood." "Michelle."

Somewhere around Bakersfield, we switched briefly to the Rolling Stones—early Stones—and a couple of times he clicked over to some other artist from our youth. Simon and Garfunkel took us onto Highway 317. "Stairway to Heaven"—one of the first songs Jim had learned on his bass—was playing when we entered Tehachapi.

But we kept coming back to the Beatles, and there was no need to ask why they were the ones Jim wanted to hear that day. The Beatles were our youth. They provided the soundtrack to our biggest romantic hopes, our first and most enduring ideas about love: that love was all you needed. And in the end it seemed to me that this was so.

Sometime around Visalia, we shifted over to the Beatles' middle period. *The White Album.* By the time we reached Bishop we were ready for John on his own. *Imagine.* I sang along.

In the town of Lone Pine, we checked into the Dow Villa Motel, with its sign out front telling us the names of all the movie stars who used to stay there when they came to film Westerns. John Wayne. Robert Mitchum, Jimmy Stewart. All dead now. We climbed into bed and Jim took out his Edward Abbey book, reading out loud to me about desert flowers and trees until we fell asleep.

In our old road-trip days, we would have risen early to get out on the trail. Now there was an infusion to take care of first—an hour and a half to sit and watch the antibiotics drip into the PICC line. Jim moved so slowly these days that even after the infusion was finished, it was ten thirty before we got out to the parking lot.

"I'm going to show you a good time, baby," he said. We drove to a diner where we ordered pancakes—the gluten-free plan abandoned now that every food seemed equally difficult for Jim to digest—augmented with New Hampshire maple syrup I'd brought from home and carried in my purse. From there we drove to a place called the Alabama Hills and then to the abandoned internment camp at Manzanar, where we got out of the car and—slowly, slowly—made our way down the path the interned Japanese must have walked seventy years earlier, building their Zen gardens in the desert, playing baseball among the cactus and scrub pine. Manzanar was empty of all human habitation now, but ten thousand people had lived here once. Nothing remained but the remnants of a few gardens and a few graves and a string of paper cranes left by a recent visitor.

On the road again. We had always been good at that. There was a huge, powerful telescope set up in the desert that Jim wanted to see, though it turned out that only authorized personnel could get in to visit there. We went to the ghost town of Bodie, but not to the Ancient Bristlecone Pine Forest where Jim had taken some of his favorite photographs. Too far. We had only four days' worth of antibiotics with us and we had to get home before we ran out. The clock was ticking.

On the edge of Mono Lake—that other-worldly landscape—after his late-afternoon infusion, Jim set up his tripod to catch the golden hour over the water. Next day we drove to Mt. Whitney one last time, the place where Jim had set out on his epic one-day climb back in 1989 to mark the end of his marriage to his children's mother. He had wanted to put himself through something very painful that day, endure punishment. Twenty-five years later he had yet to absolve himself.

He told me a story. When his children were little, Jim brought them to this place—a rare and brave choice for a single father of three, the youngest of whom had yet to reach her fourth birthday. These camping trips would have born little resemblance to the ones his parents took him on during his own lonely childhood years, and that was the point, probably. For Jim, it would have been important to get out onto the trails. To show his children not simply a campground, but the Sierra.

On one of these trips, when Jane was only three, she'd fallen on a rock and cut her head. The blood was pouring out of her—cuts to the head always the worst for bleeding. Jim had picked her up and ran with her, over two miles—her two older brothers following—all the way back to the car, and from there to the hospital at top speed. He told me he would never forget holding his daughter as he raced down the trail, her body pressed against his chest so tight he could feel her heart pounding, as his was too, no doubt. She was all right—needed only a few stitches—but the memory of his terror that she might not be OK had never left him.

There was one more stop on our road trip, and Jim had saved it for our last day.

Back in the sixties, his father had bought a piece of property in a place called the Olancha wilderness. There was no water on this land, no electricity, and though there were eighty acres, the shape of the tract—a long, narrow strip—rendered it nearly useless for anything but one activity: target shooting.

When Jim came here with his own children, he'd set up tin-can targets as his father had done with him, when he first taught Jim how to use a gun. Now, more than fifty years since the first time he'd fired a shot, he was going to teach me.

Back at home, he had taken out his old Beretta in its case and set it in the back of the BMW next to the IV pole. We had stopped at a sporting goods store to buy earplugs. Now, after pulling the car over along a deserted stretch of highway, he lifted the case from the back and took out the gun.

I had wondered, when we reached this spot, if Jim could make it to his land. It was set back from the road, accessible only by foot. Slow and steady, we got there, though I had no idea how Jim could tell that it was this particular patch of dirt that belonged to him—this spot, amid the vast expanse, with its scrubby outgrowths of dry grass and rock outcroppings as far as you could see.

I had never once fired a gun, but he showed me how. He had set up a row of old cans we'd found—a tin plate, a piece of cardboard—and told me how to aim, and to hold my breath as I squeezed the trigger to keep my arm steady, but my bullets never touched the target.

Then it was Jim's turn to shoot.

When we set out on our long-awaited Owens Valley pilgrimage,

I had considered the possibility that Jim might die in this place. When the doctors spoke of the risks of our making the journey—the infection suddenly going septic—I had privately concluded we had nothing to lose. There were worse places for a person to die—particularly Jim—than in the shadow of Mt. Whitney.

As I handed him the gun, I considered a second possibility. As bad as things had become for Jim, it seemed pretty clear now that they were only going to get worse. He could still stand up, still walk, still drive, still kiss me, still make me laugh. Better maybe to call it quits while this was so. He could end it here, if he chose. The whole sorry mess.

Already, one time—during one of the rough bouts I could no longer distinguish from all the other rough bouts—he had said to me, "Maybe it's time to go to Oregon." He was talking about assisted suicide. But if you're holding a shotgun in the Eastern Sierra desert, you don't need a trip to Oregon. As terrible as it would have been to watch him fall to the ground in that patch of dirt and scrub, it would not have been the worst thing.

Except that Jim would not have wanted that for me, or for his children. When he took aim, it was for the target. Five shots only, every one straight into the center of each tin can.

"That's enough," he told me. Then we drove home.

99.

It was May now and we were sharing our nightly dinner together, the ritual I had held on to as so much else had fallen away. By this point I had lost much of my enthusiasm for cooking. Jim so seldom was able to eat more than a few bites of whatever dish I prepared, and all the months of FODMAP diet, macrobiotic diet, gluten-free diet, ketogenic diet, had taken out most of the joy of eating for me. I had grown weary of all the shopping for food I'd mostly end up throwing out.

Still, we sat kitty-corner from each other every night at the glass table, with the candles lit, and held hands to say grace before the meal. If I wasn't too exhausted, I still tried to put on one of my dress-up outfits. Jim had lost the taste for wine but still liked sharing a drink with me. Ever since I'd started drinking again, after my three month hiatus, I'd generally limited myself to a single glass a night, but that evening after I finished my first drink I poured myself another. A generous one.

"I'm feeling a little strange," Jim told me, somewhere around ten o'clock, just as the two of us were climbing into bed. Stranger than the normal amount of strange.

I put my hand on his forehead. I took his temperature. 99.4.

A half hour later, when I checked again, his fever was up to a 99.8. Twenty minutes after that, 100.

I texted a friend of ours, an ER doctor, hoping for reassurance.

"Watch him closely," Pat texted back.

Tylenol would help. Cold compresses. But for a person in Jim's situation—a person suffering from chronic infection—we understood the risk of sepsis and that if it happened to Jim, things could get very bad very fast.

At ten thirty Jim's temperature was up to 101. At ten forty-five it was 102. He was behaving strangely now, saying things that no longer made sense. I was texting Pat while putting my shoes on, and thinking about the two glasses of wine I'd had, the long drive over the bridge into San Francisco.

The memory came to me, of that blue police car light that night in New Hampshire. The handcuffs and the Breathalyzer. Weirdly, the novel I had published that spring concerned the situation of a woman making a middle-of-the-night drive to the emergency room when her son comes down with appendicitis. In that book, the woman gets pulled over and loses her license. Now the woman with the wine in her, needing to make it to the hospital, was me. I could call an ambulance, but it would take twenty minutes to get here.

"Get him to a hospital right now," Pat told me, when I called again. Jim's temperature was up to 103.5.

"We're getting you dressed," I said to Jim, gulping down cold morning coffee.

I had to help him down the stairs. Once he got there he could not move. I was pulling out drawers, looking for socks. Throwing a sweater over my T-shirt. On the floor, lacing his shoes.

Suddenly, Jim was a different person. No one I knew. He was yelling at me to get away, to stop touching him. Leave him alone. He was talking about planets, talking about clients, cases, motions, Republicans.

"We need to get to the car," I told him. But he wasn't moving.

"We have to go to the hospital now, Jimmy."

He stood there in our front hall, staring at the Guatemalan masks on the wall, saying nothing. When he looked at me it was as if I were a stranger.

"Get your hands off me," he said. "Or I'll sue you."

But I was stronger than he was now, and I got him in the car, gulping more coffee down as I threw on my coat.

At eleven o'clock at night a person could make it from Hunsaker Canyon to UCSF Parnassus hospital in thirty-five minutes, and I did, more or less. When we pulled up to the emergency room I left Jim in the front seat and raced inside for help.

His fever was up to 104 by now. They carried him in on a gurney.

The nurses hooked him up to IV antibiotics and the fever went down, and after a night in the ER—with all the usual exchange of details that I could by now recite in my sleep—he was admitted to the hospital. By the next afternoon he was looking all right and wanting to go home.

"We could keep him here," one of the doctors said. "But if we do, he might not ever make it home again."

The infection had taken hold of him, the doctors told us, and it was just a matter of time before the same scenario occurred again. The spiking fever. The delirium.

"What if I hadn't driven him in when I did," I asked.

The fever might have gone down on its own. Or Jim might have died. That was how things were. That's how they would be from now on.

We wanted to go home. But the decision had to be made: What we were going to do if it happened again? Drive back to the hospital? Replay the same awful ride, with the same unresolvable situation in the end? Or stay home and let things play out as they were going to sooner or later. With the comfort of knowing we'd be home when they did?

We chose home.

100.

This was not the first time anyone had mentioned the word *hospice* to us. But always before, when they did, we had shaken our heads. Signing up for hospice meant that you'd always have access to nurses who would come to your house at any hour of day or night, that you would no longer need to make all those trips to CVS, because your drugs would be brought to you. There were volunteers ready to help with grocery shopping, if you wanted that. You wouldn't dread holidays and three-day weekends as I had come to do—dreaded them because you could never reach a doctor over that endless stretch of hours that constituted a three-day weekend. In hospice, you could always reach a doctor.

But when you did, the doctor would not be offering a chance of a cure. This would be palliative care only. You could have counselors and volunteers to go shopping for you, a hospital bed if you wanted, though we never would.

But you agreed, when you signed up for hospice, that no more extraordinary measures would be undertaken to forestall the inevitable. There would be no more trips to the hospital, no more antibiotic infusions. No more surgeries to correct obstructions. No further dream of chemotherapy or clinical trials. When you signed up for hospice you acknowledged that you were not going to survive this illness. You would not have to fear some late-night ride to the hospital and all those hours of waiting while they searched for a room. You could stay in your own home. But you knew now you were going to die there.

101.

Finally, then, we named it. That Jim was dying. Together, we talked about that last trip to the hospital—the fever, the delirium, the terrifying rage, those hours in the emergency room while we waited for Jim to get admitted—and though I would have been willing to deal with any of that, what I did not want for him was that he spend his last days in a hospital room, with that never-ending parade of well-meaning nurses and doctors coming in and out, along with the medical students—the trays of bad food, bad coffee, the noises in the night, the smell of ammonia, and never a quiet moment for the two of us to lie together in the dark.

No music. No breeze through the windows. No Boston terrier on the bed.

When we left Parnassus that day we knew we would not be back.

Home again, I filled the house with every good thing I could think of. Changed the sheets on the bed, set a vase of Stargazer lilies on the table on Jim's side. Lit candles. Put on music. No need to bring in the dog. He was already there.

"I don't see any reason why I can't eat pie now," Jim said, so I baked him one—apple—though he could eat only a few bites.

The weather was warm enough that Jim could actually sit outside sometimes, with a blanket over his knees and a cigar in hand. We had a dozen of the good Cubans left. Those would probably last him.

With no more *House of Cards* to watch, we switched over to

Bloodline, but it had become almost impossible for Jim to follow the storyline of a show. One day, after we ended up watching the same episode three times in a row, I recognized that he was done with this.

Afternoons, we sat on the patio, looking out over the property we'd planned to grow old in together. We could no longer envision our future as a couple, and the knowledge that Jim would not be part of mine made it terrible to contemplate.

I allowed myself one image only: the house on the lake in New Hampshire that I'd bought that winter, sight unseen. The boathouse where I'd write. Though in the past, we had talked about everything, I did not speak of this to Jim. Having spent our days on the same path for close to two years, we were coming to a fork in the road. He'd turn one way, I the other.

"You are swimming now across this vast lake," my friend Graf wrote to me. (Graf, the friend with whom I had swum since we were teenagers.) "And you know now that only one of you will make it. What can you do but keep moving toward the shore?"

Sometimes now, during those afternoons on the patio with Jim, I took out my pencils and an old box of oil pastels, and I drew him. The image created by a camera would seem too harsh now.

It had been years since I'd done much drawing, but now I did this almost daily—Jim in his yellow Warriors shirt, his battered chest and his bone-thin legs sticking out from his shorts, standing in the middle of our bedroom. Jim in his chair, with his Kindle in his lap and a cigar in his hand. Jim in his baseball cap. In the pictures I made of him, I colored his face blue. It seemed better than the pale shade of yellowish beige that was his real color now.

It was not difficult for Jim to sit still for me.

102.

Our friend Jason from Boston—in San Francisco for a conference—drove out to see us. As the visit drew to a close, he challenged Jim to a game of ping-pong.

This seemed wildly improbable. At the point Jason arrived, Jim was lying on the couch, drifting in and out of consciousness. He had recognized Jason, but he seemed to inhabit a cloud.

But the mention of ping-pong had the effect of bringing Jim to life. Now he bent to put on his shoes—also another layer of fleece to ward off the cold—and the two of them headed down the stairs, one slow step at a time, and outside to the ping-pong table.

Something happened when Jim picked up his paddle. A look of focus and intensity came over him that I had not observed in many days. He moved, in slow motion, with obvious effort, but he still had his serve.

Jason got a bunch of points off of him. Then Jim rallied and got a bunch of points off of Jason. Maybe there was some generosity involved on the part of Jim's opponent, but the two of them appeared to stay evenly matched to the end. When it was over—a tiebreaker taken by Jim—they put their arms around each other's shoulders and walked back to the house.

"I'm not dead yet," Jim said.

103.

One good thing about going on hospice (there's the opening of a sentence for you) was that you qualified for stronger drugs. Before, the most he could have was Dilaudid, but once Jim went on hospice care, we had a store of methadone syringes at our disposal, and if we needed it, morphine.

Jim stayed away from the morphine at first. But the methadone was a revelation. It dulled the pain without making his brain so stupid, he said.

"If I'd only known about methadone sooner," he told me—and for once, Jim was not making a joke—"I could have kept practicing law."

104.

I sent an e-mail to Liza, the wife of the pancreatic cancer patient in Marin County with whom I'd made a connection back in the early days after Jim's diagnosis. Like us, she and her husband had also made the choice to travel to Los Angeles every week for the controversial treatment protocol of Dr. Miracle, including the six-thousand-dollar infusions of Avastin, a chapter that now seemed to have taken place a hundred years ago, though it had been less than a year and a half. Unlike Jim and me, Liza and her husband had continued to seek treatment with Dr. Miracle.

It was always hard, checking in with a friend from the pancreatic cancer world after a space of months or even weeks out of communication. You might discover your friend's CA19-9 level had suddenly spiked from 300 to 14,000. You might discover he was dead.

But when Liza wrote back, the news was good. "I know Dr. Miracle's a pretty unpleasant human being," she wrote. "And the bills are killing us. But Art's riding his road bike a hundred miles a week now. Next month we're heading to Italy."

So was Liza's husband just luckier than mine? Or had we made a terrible, wrong choice abandoning Dr. Miracle when we did? Maybe if we'd gone with one of those other surgeons, if we hadn't traveled to Chile, if we'd waited twelve weeks for the adjuvant chemo instead of starting at eight.

A person could drive herself crazy trying to figure out the answer to those questions. When the truth was, we'd never know.

105.

Putting away clothes one day, I came upon a small black notebook belonging to Jim, and I opened it. This was not a diary—just notes about errands he needed to run, things to pick up on his way home (*Good olives. Smog certificate. FLOWERS FOR JOYCE!*)

Then came this page covered with small black lines—row after row of them, in groups of five, four parallel lines with a fifth slashing through them on the diagonal. In the margin Jim had written the total count: 118. The number of days I'd been away over the first two and a half years of our relationship. What would I have given then, to have those hundred and eighteen days back.

106.

He voted. Because we had never gotten around to mailing in our absentee ballots or reregistering in our new town of Lafayette, this required us to drive to the polling place in Oakland to vote in the Democratic primary. Jim walked in on his own steam and cast his ballot.

"I don't suppose I'll ever know how this election turns out," he said.

107.

The Warriors were in the NBA finals now. Because we didn't get cable service, we went to our friends Karen and Tom's house to watch the games, when Jim was well enough. Each time we did, he put on his Warriors hat with the number 73 on the front—for the number of victories that season—and the bright yellow Warriors shirt he'd gotten that day he and Kenny went to see the game at Oracle arena in those amazing courtside seats. I put on a yellow shirt too. Before driving over to Tom and Karen's house, we attached a Warriors flag on either side of the BMW. As we made our way down the road, they fluttered in the wind, giving us the appearance of a couple of fun-loving revelers.

Our team was four games into the playoffs, having won the first two, only to lose the next three to Cleveland. Jim was in such rough shape that night I didn't think he'd be up for the next game but he said he was, though once we got to Karen and Tom's house, he had fallen asleep on the couch and stayed there that way through most of the game.

He woke up in the fourth quarter to see the score: the Warriors losing badly. The team's star—Steph Curry—couldn't seem to get one ball in the hoop.

Jim opened his eyes just for a moment, looked at the screen, and shook his head. He looked delirious, though I had checked his temperature, of course—I checked it constantly—and knew it was normal.

"Steph Curry's gone septic," he said.

Septic. The thing we most feared for Jim. Its implications greater than a lost playoff game.

By the time the game was over, Jim had fallen asleep again. He did not ask, on the drive home, whether our team had won or lost.

108.

I don't want to leave you," he told me. It was nighttime and we were lying in our bed, as close as the drain tubes allowed.

I knew what he meant here. He was not talking about fearing death. He was talking about his sorrow at leaving me on my own again. He, my guard dog. Going off duty.

If he had been a soldier—if there had been a war on that he believed in, or if, more simply, he had seen me in danger—he would have been there to rescue me, and never mind the bullets whistling past his head. He was the man who'd scaled a fourteen-thousand-foot peak in the Andes on seven rounds of chemo; the father who'd run two miles with his bleeding three-year-old pressed to his chest, to get her to the hospital; the quiet, sober attorney who'd written the letter that got my daughter her house. He was the one you wanted to have next to you in the trenches, the one you'd count on in a terrible calamity to get you through.

We were in one now. The problem being that when the terrible calamity came, Jim could no longer be the one protecting me, because it was the fact that I'd be losing him that was the terrible calamity, and when it happened, he wouldn't be there to offer comfort anymore.

109.

Driving into town with me, Jim hit a post in the parking lot and dented the BMW—virtually the only time in his forty-eight years of driving that he'd done something like that.

A few days later, on a stop at the hardware store to buy more electronic rattraps, he did it again.

The third time, backing out of a parking lot, he knocked out the special sensors that tell you if you're getting too close to another car. The repair ran a thousand dollars.

After that one, Jim laid his head on the steering wheel. He handed me the keys.

"I'm done," he told me.

110.

Three other times in my life, I had lived through a terminal situation. Only one of those times had been literally terminal, though each was brutal, each a situation for which there would be no hopeful resolution. Nowhere to go. A tunnel with nothing at the other end but darkness.

The first time it was my mother's glioblastoma. I was thirty-five when she died, and at that point—though I'd lost my father seven years before—nothing more terrible had ever happened in my life.

I encountered the second terminal situation at precisely the same moment in my life that I lost my mother, when—for all sorts of reasons that went well beyond the fact that he'd fallen in love with someone else—my first husband had said he didn't want to be married to me anymore.

We had continued to live in the same house for a solid month after he'd made this determination. We'd shared the same bed—made love, even, though we did so with full knowledge that we had no future together. We built a fire and lit the match. Nothing but ashes remaining when it burned out.

The third terminal situation came in those excruciating weeks—six of them—after I knew my Ethiopian daughters would be leaving to live with a different family.

Then, even more painfully than was true in my marriage, I had known the experience of making my way through the days with the terrible, sick knowledge—sitting like a stone in my stomach—that when I said good-bye I might never again lay eyes on or put my arms around two girls I had once believed would be part of my family forever.

When Jim went on hospice there was nothing metaphoric about the terminal situation he and I inhabited. We were going our separate ways soon and we knew it, but this one wasn't a divorce or voluntary relinquishment. After months of rejecting the idea—months we'd spent grasping for every increasingly far-fetched prospect of a cure—we woke every morning now with the full awareness that Jim was going to die. Maybe today, maybe tomorrow, maybe next week, but soon. As much as we might have anticipated this, and might have known this as early as that first day we received the diagnosis, a profound shift occurred once we went on hospice. For eighteen months my focus remained lasered onto a single objective: saving Jim's life. Now I could do nothing but shepherd him in the gentlest and most loving way to the moment of his death.

We had lived on hope for eighteen months, and when that was gone, there seemed to be nothing. No doubt some people locate comfort in the form of God at such a point, and I want to believe Jim found some solace there, though his relationship with faith had been a complicated one. Only a handful of days before, I had watched him take the communion wafer. But in the night, when I turned to him, he told me he was afraid. In all our time, it was the first time I'd heard him say this.

The worst wasn't dying, he said. The worst was the thought of not living anymore. Not getting to have our life together.

Over those last weeks in the hospital, when Katie Kelley told me the cancer was back and there was no more to be done about it and I was standing in the hallway outside Jim's room, taking counsel from Bridget, I had talked with her about how much I wished that Jim and I could acknowledge the truth of what was happening to him.

Now that he had done this, I wondered why I ever supposed that it would make anything easier. Denial—if that's what Jim had engaged in—was viewed in many quarters as indicative of some less spiritually elevated, less enlightened way of living. But denial had allowed him to get out of bed every morning and perform his pushup. Denial had inspired him to call his friend Woody and suggest they meet up for golf. Now in addition to everything else that was gone, he had lost that last shred of hope, and the fact that this was so had left him in a landscape of desolation more vast than all of the Olancha wilderness.

111.

Looking for some place we might locate a little joy—or failing that, a pleasurable distraction—I sent an e-mail to the men with whom Jim played music, suggesting that we gather for a jam session.

The day was set, this time not at our house in the canyon, but at the house of a guitarist friend from The Family, Rich. Other friends from the Storkzilla group would join us too: Allan on drums, Tony on accordion, Dave on keyboards, Mike on guitar. And Jim on bass.

There was a long run of stairs leading up to Rich's house, and for the first time, Jim did not argue when I took the amp, but he made it to the top of them on his own.

How many times over the fifty years since he'd bought his first bass had he lifted his instrument out of its case? In slow motion now, he swung the strap over his head and placed his left hand on the neck of his Fender. Left hand checking the tuning, right hand on the strings.

I was never a musician. So it is hard for me to say what it was about how Jim played the bass that distinguished the way he played, except to say that he did it in the way Jim did many things. Unconventionally. For starters, he had a very good ear—could always tell when an instrument in some band was out of tune. Even when there were a dozen musicians onstage he'd know which one it was. Sometimes, when we'd be listening to a band, he'd mention, quietly, that the bass player, workmanlike, had chosen to follow a predictable series of notes. Jim liked to take the bass line off the beaten path. He was not a man to easily display emotion. But when he played on those four strings, he did.

I can still see Jim as he was in our friend's living room that day, standing up as he always did when he played, and a little off to one side. Never the center of attention or the lead, but just see what happens to a piece of music when you take the bass line out of it.

He probably weighed less than ninety-five pounds by this point, though we had stopped checking. He had on his black jeans as always and his black fleece, and his Patagonia parka and his Maine Woods hat. His ring finger, on the neck of his guitar, was missing its gold band—a source of distraction at the time. Every morning he told me were going shopping for a new one, first chance we got.

As much pain as he must have been enduring at the time, Jim did not choose to sit. His back remained straight as he was playing, and his head was raised upward in the manner of all rock and rollers when they play a stadium, and they want their music to reach the last, most distant row of fans. Here in Rich's living room, there were just the wives to listen. Aging groupies, I liked to think of us. I, Jim's number one fan.

The men played a few Rolling Stones songs that afternoon, and one by Creedence Clearwater: "Who'll Stop the Rain?" They played "Kansas City," and—at Jim's request—"She Loves You." Then "Sympathy for the Devil."

Ever since the terrifying night Jim's fever had spiked, when I'd driven over the bridge to bring him to the hospital as my ER doctor friend texted me messages about sepsis and asked me, at three-minute intervals, what his temperature was now—we had carried a thermometer with us wherever we went. Why we did this is hard to determine, since the decision to go into hospice had meant that in the event of a fever spike like the last one, we would not seek medical attention as we had that other time.

Having made the decision not to pursue extraordinary measures again, we would have nothing to do if Jim's temperature went up besides placing ice on his feet and giving him a Tylenol, and waiting. It was as if, like a suicide bomber, the man I loved now wore a package of explosives strapped to his chest that might at any moment of the day or night be detonated.

The guys came to the end of the song—the *woo woo woo* part. Then Jim set down his bass.

"I think something's happening here, baby," he said to me quietly. "*Fever.*"

I took the thermometer out of my bag.

Five minutes later we were out the door and in the car on the way back to Hunsaker Canyon, the bass and amp packed in the back with the help of our friends. Home again, Jim lay down on the couch. I lay down next to him.

"This might be it," he said. I set the ice beside him and went for the Tylenol. We stayed there like that for most of the evening.

His temperature climbed to 100 that night. But then, miraculously, it went down again. Eventually, when he seemed out of danger—meaning out of danger that night, or that hour anyway—we went to bed.

Lying there with him in the dark, we spoke of the music he'd played that afternoon. Four songs. "I hated letting them down," he said, of the other players.

"They were just happy we made it at all," I told him. "We were having so much fun. We can do it another day."

"I don't think so," he told me. "I've let go of all that."

I wanted to wrap myself around him, but I could no longer do that, there were so many places on his body that hurt now. I slept pressed alongside him, listening to the sound of his breathing, my hand in his hair. I would keep my diamond ring, but sometime in the night I slipped my own wedding band on his finger.

112.

There was a question I asked myself many times. I talked this over with the other pancreatic cancer wives too, on occasion.

If, tomorrow, one of us received the diagnosis our husbands had, would we choose to pursue the Whipple procedure?

Deborah said never. For Pam, the jury was out. "We had to try," she told me. "But I never dreamed it would be so hard."

Robert, the Miami lawyer who experienced complications that required a second operation, followed by a recurrence of cancer four months later, had approached his choice to undergo the Whipple with the sober realism of an attorney.

"If I knew how my story came out," he said, referring to his recurrence, "I certainly would not have undergone the Whipple. But I had a decision to make, and I don't regret it at all. There was only one way to beat the cancer, and it was to undergo the operation. I may have had only a twenty-five percent prospect of success, but that was my one chance."

Then there was Roger, the husband of a Facebook friend, who'd undergone the surgery months after Jim. Though we had never met, I followed his progress on the Caring Bridge website, and so far he was feeling strong and good. He had even gone skiing that winter. His story—however rare it might be—represented everything I'd longed for, for Jim.

As for me: I thought back often to that day at Fenway Park—the day before Jim checked himself into the hospital to undergo the Whipple procedure—when we'd eaten all those oysters, and Jim had felt so good. Like his old self, almost. We might have had a whole summer like that. More maybe, who knew? There would have been this too: a sword over Jim's head. The knowledge that all the while, the tumor was growing, and that one day it would do him in.

Meanwhile, though, we might have had our life for longer. Knowing what I knew now, I'd probably choose to leave my insides intact and let the cancer have its way with me.

Not Jim. He had been ready to try anything. He would fight to stay alive if it killed him.

113.

The newly expanded San Francisco Museum of Modern Art had opened—an event Jim had talked about since we met. On a Tuesday—when I hoped the crowds would be thinner—we drove into the city to take it all in. I was the one at the wheel.

We walked like a couple in their nineties through the museum—the kind of couple we would never be—and stopped often to sit. There was one painting Jim particularly loved—a Brice Marden that looked like tangled-up rope. We sat a long time in front of that one, because he loved the painting. And because he was tired.

In the British sculpture room, one work caught Jim's attention over all the others. It was the highly abstracted rendering, in metal, of a man, the image of him created not by solid forms but by floating metal rods. Depending on what angle you were viewing it from, the sculpture might look like nothing but a random assemblage of metal. When you walked around it, suddenly the man took shape. Five more steps to one side or the other and he was gone.

Slow as a minute hand, Jim made his way around the sculpture, front to back and back again. As he walked around the sculpture, I snapped his picture—first one, then a second, then a third, all the way around.

Later, when I looked at the pictures I'd taken of Jim that day, it seemed to me they were not pictures of a man at all. The images of the figure hidden in the sculpture remained clear, but Jim—standing a little ways off behind it, in the black fleece and black pants that were his uniform now, and the baseball cap—looked like an apparition.

"He reminds me of myself," Jim had said, of the stick figure man in the sculpture. "Disappearing."

114.

In early May Jim's children came to see him, and in June, one by one, mine came to say good-bye—first Audrey, flying in all the way from New Hampshire, then Charlie, then Willy. They had only known Jim four and a half years but they had loved him.

When Willy came, he had just recently returned from shooting a movie in Romania. We'd been taking care of his dog, Tuck, for several months and I knew he missed Tuck badly, but I asked if we could keep him with us a little longer. Tuck slept in the bed with us every night, and during the days, when Jim lay mostly on the couch now, Tuck stayed at his side.

Now came Willy, not to take Tuck home, but only to see Jim—Willy, the one whose wedding toast to the two of us had begun, "My mom has had a lot of boyfriends . . ."

"My mom's not the best driver around," he said. "So we all appreciate having Jim take over there."

What he really appreciated about Jim, more than anything else, I knew, was how Jim had made his mother happy.

There were no elaborate good-byes with the children. Jim had given his best guitar—the Martin—to his son Kenny, and also the twelve-string. But before each of my sons left on the weekend of their separate visits, he gave them each one of his bass guitars, and for my daughter, one of his old film cameras, because—an old-fashioned person—Audrey liked those more than digital, and because, she said, it would remind her of Jim. He gave her his simplest digital camera too—the simplest one, because Audrey avoided fancy things. After she got it home, she had found the SIM card inside, with photographs he'd taken years before, back when the two of us were first together. She called me up to tell me she would send me the images.

"You two must have just met," she said. "I never saw you look that happy."

115.

He was fading away—every day a little less of him, like an old negative exposed to too much light, so thin you could almost look through him.

I didn't want this to happen, but it started to now: Sometimes during our day together a picture would flash into my brain—an image of my life without Jim. My life after.

I looked at the Boxster out in the driveway, with its fabric cover over the top, so much time having passed now since the last time we'd gone anywhere in it together. Though I could operate a stick shift, I had never once driven that car, and never wanted to. For me the thrill lay in being the passenger. Sometimes when we were driving together and I was at the wheel, Jim had pointed out things that would improve my driving: the correct positioning of my hands at ten o'clock and two, the way to set my elbow on the arm rest, the concept of looking not at the road directly ahead, but beyond. I was the one driving the BMW now—I, a woman whose own car was a 1995 Honda Civic—but in all this time I had never taken the wheel of the Boxster.

"I should get him to teach me how to drive that car," I thought now. Then just as quickly. *How could I ever?*

116.

The long-delayed closing date came for the cottage on the lake in New Hampshire. Months had passed since that New Year's Eve day my offer had been accepted, but after those first few weeks Jim and I had ceased to talk about going there in summer, sitting on the porch with our wine and his cigar, our feet on the railings. I had still not laid eyes on the property, except in pictures online, but I'd sent the deposit check and now I signed the papers. When the day came that the property was put in my name, I didn't mention it to Jim.

Some time before, in the early days of our battle with the rat, Jim had laid out rat poison. When Tuck came to live with us, Jim made his way slowly around our property again, getting down on the ground in a way that could not have been easy for him in that post-Whipple life, to make sure not a crumb of the deadly stuff remained within reach.

Then one day in late May something surprising happened. We came home from a trip to town—the drugstore, our daily stop—and there was a dead rat on the patio. I liked to think this was not simply a rat, but *the* rat.

He was certainly enormous, for a rat. He was large as a cat, with a long thick tail and very long whiskers like the kind Jim had found on the glue trap that day when he'd almost caught the rat, only to be outwitted again.

The rat was dead. He lay there on the flagstone, eyes open, facing the pergola whose beams he would no longer tread. "I guess this is the end of an era," Jim said.

We picked him up with a shovel and threw his body in the woods, and that night there were no footsteps on the roof, or anyplace else. No sound but the owls somewhere out in the woods behind the house, and in our bed, the slow steady sigh of our own breath.

117.

Back in the winter, Jim had started ordering a lot of things online. Pants in particular, because none of his fit, and anyway, what he needed at this point were the loose-fitting drawstring kind, in the smallest size they had.

Now I'd catch myself thinking when he took another pair of pants out of the package, "I could wear those."

He ordered many books, though I don't think he read any of them. Reading was difficult now. He ordered remastered copies of the albums he'd loved: the Rolling Stones, the Kinks, Led Zeppelin, Cream, back to the Beatles. It was as if he was tracing back through his musical life. Pushing rewind all the way to the beginning.

A BMW mug arrived. A San Francisco Giants shirt. A PC computer, though he was a Mac guy, because sometimes when doing legal work a PC was needed. He ordered a robotic vacuum cleaner, and a hat, and a bar of French soap of the kind we'd encountered on our trips to Paris, at the wonderful little hotel we always stayed at in St. Germain. He ordered his special brand of razor blades. Many of them.

Every day the UPS man showed up with a package from Amazon, sometimes as many as three. Often they contained shoes, though no longer the soft leather shoes that filled Jim's closet from his lawyer days. Now he ordered sneakers, and more sneakers, and a pair of zippered black boots, and a pair of white bucks of the sort a person might wear, with a seersucker suit, to a garden party or a summer wedding. (Like the one we had, for instance, not even three years earlier.) First one pair of white bucks arrived, then a second identical pair. I even tried on some of the sneakers—because they were very good ones, and not cheap, and mine were old. But though my feet are large for a woman, and his small for a man, they were still a size too big.

Out by the trash cans the cardboard piled up but I made no comment. I had my own purchases arriving, though mine were generally medical supplements, elixirs someone told me about on Facebook, super protein powders, frozen breast milk, a kind of honey said to possess nearly magical immune boosting properties.

One day I found a stack of unopened bills in a corner of Jim's office. The insurance policy on the BMW was about to be canceled. So was his phone service. Months of payments were due on the conference room he'd rented in the city, that he hadn't used in six months.

Two of the men in the pancreatic cancer breakfast group died in a single week—leaving the membership to three. I wrote to their wives, but did not discuss the news with Jim.

I still lit the candles for our dinners together, still put on the streaming radio program we favored, *Folk Alley*. One night, as we sat there, a John Prine song came on and I got up from my chair. I reached out my arms.

Very slowly then, he stood up and we held each other. I knew as we danced—just a few steps in place next to the table—this was the last time.

118.

A note came from my friend Deborah, with a link to Bob's obituary.

"I never thought this day would come," she wrote. "But come it has. I sit up half the night, dreading to go to sleep, because when I wake up in the morning there is a wee tiny almost unmeasurable moment when I open my eyes and all is as it should be. And then SHAZZAM!!! I remember Bob is not here and I don't really know where he is. I just know he won't be back. And it's like living the heart-wrench over and over and over. Friggin' Ground Hogs Day.

"My heart has broken in a thousand pieces," she wrote.

119.

I was up late one night on Facebook—the place where I had found a surprising measure of comfort over the months of Jim's illness, from a large and growing community of readers who had never met me, never met Jim, but seemed to care about what happened to him. It was not uncommon now, when I posted some update about what we were going through, for a few hundred messages to scroll onto the screen in the space of an hour, and they would keep coming in all day and into the night.

This time, though, I heard the ping of a private message, and I went to my Facebook mail.

It was from Layla, the older of my Ethiopian daughters.

More than five years had passed since I'd seen her or heard anything from her or her family—though I had Googled her name a few times, which was how I learned about the medal she'd won for her running, and that she was on the honor roll at her school.

The last time I'd seen her, when I reached to stroke her head she'd turned her face away. Now she was writing to say hello.

It was not a long message. But her English was almost perfect.

"Many people think you were a bad person to let us go," she wrote. "But Adenach and I don't. You did the best thing for us. You got us to this country and you found us our parents. I wanted you to know we're doing great."

I reread Layla's note several times before writing back. There were a thousand things I would have liked to say to her, but I didn't want my words to overwhelm her, so I wrote only a few.

"I am so happy to hear from you," I said. I told her what was true, that I thought about her and her sister every day. "I want you to know that if the day ever comes when you'd like to talk to me," I wrote to her, "I will always be here for that. I have always hoped and believed that we'd get to see each other again."

I told her that Willy still kept her picture on his refrigerator—hers, and her sister's. I told her I was ready to hear whatever she would like to tell me.

I sat there watching the dot, dot, dot in the conversation box—the indication that the person you have written to is still there on the other end, writing her response.

"That sounds good," she wrote. "Adenach and I will come see you when we are all grown up."

I wrote back to say I'd love that. A small good thing in my world of sorrow.

120.

The first week in June, Jim brought me into the room where he kept his camera gear. He had laid everything out on the rug. One by one, he explained every camera and lens, and the person to whom it should go. The Nikon D-7000 for Kenny. A good lens for Audrey's boyfriend, Tod. His Nikon D-8000M, the best camera, was for me. "You might not know how to use this yet," he said. "But you can learn."

It was important for him to locate his merit badge sash; we spent a couple of hours searching for it, and we did—also his neckerchief and his cap and his Venice High track letter.

He made lists now, like the ones I used to prepare for some babysitter when my children were young and I went out of town on a trip—the kind of information a person needs to know about how to take care of things when the one who's generally in charge goes away. Jim wrote down his computer passwords for me, and his other passwords. He showed me which files of legal papers needed to be saved in case some former client needed them and which ones could be thrown out. He told me which of his possessions should go to his children, which painting to Patrice.

He was letting go of everything—not just camera gear, guitars, his best leather jacket, his Rolex watch.

No more oysters. No more martinis. No more checking up on Donald Trump's poll numbers.

No more driving. No more motorcycle. No more dancing. No more rock and roll.

One piece at a time, Jim was saying good-bye to the world.

The words that came to me harkened back to a time long ago, with one of my babies on my lap, and the well-loved book in my hands.

Goodnight moon. Goodnight cow jumping over the moon.

He wanted his friend Jay to have a particular hat and his fly fishing rod and reel. For his children: money to help with a down payment on a home.

Goodnight stars. Goodnight air.

He was going away, and at certain moments I almost wished I could be dying too. Except for the pain part, that might have felt less harsh than this: the knowledge that he was leaving, and, for the moment, I was not.

121.

I have known of people—people in couples—who, when they are dying, and they know this with certainty, say to the partner who will survive them, "I want you to find someone else. You need to marry again."

These were not words Jim could have spoken. Jim, who said to me once, as we lay in the dark, "You will never know how much I love you."

Except that I did. Jim, in whose eyes I was the most beautiful and desirable woman on the planet, and therefore desired by every other man in whatever room we entered, which had left him not jealous or controlling, but fierce in his intention to be such a good husband I'd never feel inclined to run away with one of them. Not that any of Jim's imagined competitors for my affection had shown the slightest indication of offering a threat. It was only in his imagination that this was so.

His imagination. He always said he had none. The idea that one day, Josh Brolin might spirit me away—or Dan Rather (another competitor, in Jim's eyes) may have been the scenarios he envisioned, but they haunted him.

Now, as our days together dwindled, we did not speak of what I would do with my life, After. It was not just the cottage in New Hampshire that went unmentioned, but the years ahead that I might have, and he would not—where I might spend them, and with whom.

He was, unfailingly, a man who sought nothing so much as my happiness. He would have wanted that. He simply couldn't bear to picture what it might one day look like, for me to find that again with someone other than him.

But I knew he thought about it. Pressed up against his withering body in the night, it sometimes seemed to me I could actually feel the thought passing through him, and when I did I held him tighter.

I did not say, "You are the only man for me." I did not say, "I'll never marry again." (I had just discovered, at age sixty-one, how much I liked to be married.)

What I said was, "*I will love you forever.*" It was a promise I would have no difficulty keeping.

122.

On one of these afternoons, a thought had come to me with searing clarity.

Always before, for as long as I'd had children, my children had remained at the center of my universe. Whatever man entered the picture—and many did, very good ones in some cases—this never changed, and I never questioned any other feeling but that one. Before I was anything else, I was my children's mother.

I remember saying once to David, the good and loving man who had wanted to make a life with me years before, that I could only consider this if my children liked him. For Jim too, as uneasy as things had remained with one or more of his children over the years, the fact of his being their parent had remained the central and life-shaping fact of his life. When, at the age of eight, his older son had laid down the edict that he would never accept Jim's new partner or be in the same room with her even, Jim had accepted those conditions and adapted to them. For nineteen years his relationship with Patrice endured, but he never lived with any other woman but his children's mother until he lived with me.

Even when we got together—and as much as I loved him—I continued to view my children's preeminence in my life as immutable. I maintained the view that they were the most important people in my universe, long after I ceased to be the most important in theirs. And of course, it was only natural and right for them that this would happen. They were doing what children are supposed to: making their own good lives, separate from their parents. I just never believed that I might do the same.

Even on the day I married Jim, I would have told anyone who asked that my children came first. When, with one of my sons holding each of my arms, I walked through the wildflower-filled field on that New Hampshire hillside to speak my wedding vows to Jim I did not say this, but I might have. "I love you more than anyone. Except my children."

Maybe Jim was doing the same thing when he made what had seemed to me at the time like a nearly unforgivable choice to walk away from the dance floor that day, just as the band started up, because his older son had chosen this moment to say he wanted to talk. What would we not do for our children?

I would still do just about anything for mine. But a shift had occurred sometime over the not quite three years that constituted my marriage to Jim. I don't know when it happened. I do know that the fact it did, and my willingness to say so, would cause no injury to my three very well-loved children. There is nothing I could say that would cause them to doubt how I feel about them.

Not on our wedding day, or for some time after that, but sometime in the space between that moment and this one, Jim came to occupy, for me, that place in the dead center of my heart.

One of those last days we spent on the patio, as we sat there in the late-afternoon sun watching the deer amble through the grass, I had set down my wineglass and reached over for Jim's hand.

"You are my favorite person," I told him.

All those years I spent envying the people with big, loving families surrounding them—people whose parents were still alive, people whose brothers and sisters lived down the road and stopped by for coffee on Sundays, people who had to put two leaves in the table at Thanksgiving because of all the relatives who came to join them that day, and most of all those who got to raise their children with their children's other parent—I had felt, even as the mother of three, like a woman short on family. All those years I'd been on the lookout for mine.

I'd carried around all those pictures: blessedly "intact" families I read about on Facebook; happily blended families; adoptions that worked; my old dream of that fourth baby I never had. And here it was, finally: the family I'd been looking for. My children would certainly be in this picture, as it now appeared Jim's would not. But Jim was my family. The one I counted on to be there when everyone else was gone.

123.

Suppose we get in the BMW," he said one morning, "and just start driving. Take a road trip. No telling where we'll end up."

Just keep on driving until we can't anymore.

124.

One afternoon—one of the last, and I knew it—I opened the door to let Tuck out and there was Jim, standing on the flagstone, holding the handles of our wheelbarrow. The wheelbarrow was full of wood. He must have hauled it all the way from the garage to the house, and because this wood had not yet been split, and the logs were large, these were not logs for our fireplace.

We had moved into June by this point. Warm weather now. Not the season for fires, but there was more wrong with the picture than that.

It was very heavy, this load of firewood. I had no idea how Jim had managed to push the wheelbarrow up the hill to the spot where he now stood on our doorstep. He looked like a man who had just walked a hundred miles in the desert without food or water. He looked like a dying man, and he was, of course.

And here comes the terrible truth: I was angry. All I could think, seeing this man I loved standing there, was that he had just about killed himself hauling this wood. All I could think: *He will be unable to do anything for the rest of the day.* And I would have lost out on the tiny window of minutes with him—narrowing all the time— when we might have sat together and talked on the couch, or shared our glass of wine, or maybe even walked out to look at the olive trees. He'd squandered a vast portion of what strength remained, on this one pointless mission to bring in the useless firewood.

"What were you thinking, Jimmy?" I said to him. "These logs aren't any good for burning."

If he could have looked any sadder than he had, before, now he did. Slowly, slowly, he turned around in the direction he'd come from. He bent to pick up the handles of the wheelbarrow, to return the wood to where it had been stacked behind the garage.

"Never mind," I told him. "I'll do it."

He did not argue. He went to bed.

125.

So it was June. Jim's birthday month. We were coming up on the day whose coordinates I had recited five hundred times over those last nineteen months, in one doctor's office or another. Jim's sixty-fourth birthday—the age Paul McCartney had written a song about, when it seemed so incredibly old. *Will you still need me? Will you still feed me?*

"*Only* sixty-four," I said.

Some months before this, when so much still seemed possible that no longer did, I had asked Jim to get us tickets to see Bob Dylan at the Greek Theater in Berkeley. They didn't come cheap, but remembering times past when he'd let assignments like this one slide, he bought us two great seats for his birthday weekend.

We were well over a year into cancer treatment, and with as much hopefulness as we still possessed, we had also learned that when there's something you really want to do, you shouldn't put it off.

Bob Dylan! I think I was about thirteen years old the first time I heard him (that would have been my sister's Columbia Record Club album, *The Freewheelin' Bob Dylan*). I fell in love with him then, studying that photograph of Dylan walking down a street in Greenwich Village holding the arm of a beautiful young woman, looking like two people who would be in love forever, though of course they wouldn't. I learned to play "Blowin' in the Wind" on my guitar. I memorized the lyrics of every song on that album, and the ones that came after.

Jim and I had loved a lot of music over our five decades of listening. But through all that time, one artist neither of us ever stopped following was Dylan. His music changed a lot, but he was always there in the mix, with new songs and old songs sung in totally new ways. Somewhere along the line, he turned into this old guy who even sang cabaret songs on occasion, as if he were Frank Sinatra—but more accurately, as if he were Bob Dylan paying homage to Frank Sinatra. My younger self would not have known what to make of this, but Jim and I were older too.

Now Dylan was seventy-five. (Thirteen years older than I was. Eleven years older than Jim.) And he was coming to a wonderful outdoor amphitheater in Berkeley, twenty minutes from Hunsaker Canyon. I'd seen Dylan many times over the years. Jim never had.

We'd actually bought tickets to see Dylan one other time a few years back, but that night Jim was called away on some legal work for a client that couldn't wait. Those were the days when we thought we had all the time in the world, and if a job came up that interfered with our plans to be together, we sometimes allowed the job to take precedence, as we would not now.

Five days before the Dylan concert—on hospice now, and methadone—Jim started slipping badly. Sleeping more. Remembering less. His gait, when he walked, was the slowest shuffle, the step of a man for whom lifting a foot off the floor represented an expenditure of strength no longer within his realm. He was barely eating; even the apple pie I'd made him sat untouched on the counter. His eyes had taken on a look I had not seen before. On the last occasion we'd gone out to a restaurant—lunch in Lafayette sharing a fish taco and a margarita—I recognized that the people in the restaurant had been staring at us uneasily, as if we no longer belonged in a place like this. You couldn't look at Jim anymore and fail to recognize he was a dying man.

As the date of the concert approached—June 9, a Thursday night—the idea of making a trip to a concert in Berkeley, the idea of making a trip anywhere, seemed impossible. I even went on Craigslist with the thought of selling our tickets, or trying to.

But I didn't list them for sale. Forgetful as he had become, Jim kept telling the hospice nurses and friends who came by that we were going to see Bob Dylan Thursday night.

"I'm taking Joyce on a date," he said, though I doubt they believed him.

The Greek Theatre is an outdoor venue. And even in the middle of the hottest summer days, my husband got so cold now he hardly ever wanted to be outdoors. Never mind at night.

That morning, though, we agreed we were going to this concert, and Jim rested up all day to be ready. The music wasn't going to start until eight—with an opening act—but knowing how slowly Jim was walking, I knew we'd need lots of time getting there.

He dressed up for this. He wore his black jeans with a belt that had a silver buckle, and a black turtleneck sweater and black boots, and a black hat a little like the one Walter White wore on *Breaking Bad*. He looked like some old rock star—a very old one. I wore my special leather jacket with fringe that made me feel like some rock-and-roll musician's girlfriend. Which I was, actually.

On the drive over, we talked about what songs we hoped Dylan would play. His choice was "Subterranean Homesick Blues." I said "Sad-Eyed Lady of the Lowlands," though we both agreed that on any given day we might have made totally different choices.

At the parking lot, we got a handicapped parking space, but there was still a significant walk to the amphitheater. With great slowness and some pain, no doubt, he made it, though making it along that three-block stretch of sidewalk took most of an hour.

We sat on the concrete then—but with Jim's inflatable pillow under him, and blankets—waiting for the show to begin. Only then Jim's eyes started to close, and he started rocking side to side in a way that had nothing to do with music, because the music hadn't started yet. If I hadn't held him up he would have flopped over.

I brought him to the medical tent. Except for the part about how it breaks your heart, it's not so difficult, holding up a ninety-pound man.

Here was one good thing about having a medical issue at a concert in the San Francisco Bay Area. If it's a rock concert, the people helping you out will be a team of great old hippie RNs—also a few young ones—from a group called Rock Medicine that grew out of a project the rock promoter Bill Graham started long ago, back in Janis Joplin days, back when the medical issue for people attending concerts was bad LSD trips. These nurses all work for no pay, just love of the music and a belief, as they explained to me that night in the tent, that if at all possible, a person experiencing medical difficulties at a rock concert should receive a little help so he could get back to enjoying the music.

Regular hospital nurses, looking at Jim as he was at that moment, would have told me I'd been crazy to bring him here in the first place, and instructed me to get him home right away. But the Rock Medicine nurses were there because they loved music, and they believed in the medicinal effects of rock and roll. They had no problem with letting Jim lie on a cot for an hour or so. There were no drugs to help him at this point, but I asked if anyone had a banana and one was delivered to us. Potassium.

By this point, the opening act was under way. It was Mavis Staples, another old-timer. From where Jim lay in the tent, and I on the floor beside him, I could hear her belting out her songs from the stage while the nurses talked about recent shows they'd seen and others that were coming up. Steve Winwood. Bonnie Raitt. Joan Baez.

One time Jim opened his eyes and seemed to come to for a

moment. "Bob Dylan?" he asked me, sounding even more baffled than the baffled state he inhabited most of the time now. Mavis Staples sounded nothing like Bob Dylan, of course, and even in his confused state Jim knew that much.

He lay there for close to an hour while Mavis performed. At one point he took a bite of the banana. A few times I had to put my ear to his chest to make sure he was still breathing. And then he opened his eyes and said he wanted to see the show.

"Let's do it," the nurses told us.

We brought him back out into the amphitheater in a wheelchair, which meant they put us in a really great spot reserved for the handicapped, and I wrapped him in all four of our blankets. His head was mostly flopped over, so all you saw of him was his hat sticking out from all the blankets in the wheelchair.

It was dark now, and the moon was out, a crescent. The lights on the stage came on. Then, there he was: Bob Dylan, wearing a cream-colored dinner jacket and a hat a little like Jim's, but with a broader brim. The band started playing, and they were a very tight band, which I knew Jim would appreciate. My old Jim anyway, and maybe even Jim as he was now.

As for Bob Dylan—well, he was Bob Dylan. Nobody else is like him, though I also reflected there was no other fan in the entire amphitheater like the one sitting next to me in that wheelchair.

It was late, and normally we'd be in bed asleep by this hour. And the night was cool, even for me. When I asked Jim if he wanted to go home, he said "NO!" in a way that almost sounded angry, but really he was just being firm. My husband wanted to see Bob Dylan. And he wanted to do this with me. And not just for three songs either.

About twenty minutes into the show, Bob Dylan started playing "Tangled Up in Blue," and Jim said "I WANT TO STAND UP."

So I helped him up and he held on to the railing. His eyes were looking wild, but also focused—that look I had been seeing occasionally at this point, as if he were beholding something totally different from the rest of us. He also looked up at the sky a lot, the moon.

Sitting there beside him in the handicapped section with my head on his shoulder, I considered the possibility that Jim might die at this Bob Dylan concert. There would be worse ways to go.

I kept asking if he wanted to go home but he was adamant he did not. So—careful as I always was now—I wrapped myself around him, and not with just my arms, but my whole body—and whispered in his ear from time to time. We stayed that way the whole show. The Rock Medicine nurse, Pam, checked up on us every few minutes and brought me coffee.

I had been worried about how I'd ever get Jim back to the parking garage, but Pam said she and another one of the nurses would help us. The plan was to let me know when it was the second to last song. When Dylan started playing that one, the two nurses lifted Jim and his chair up to the exit ramp and wheeled us through the crowd. Still wrapped in blankets, with his black hat on, Jim stared straight ahead, as if this was some other planet he was visiting, but only temporarily.

We had to go down a very steep hill, which is hard with a wheelchair. If the nurse pushing the wheelchair had lost control, Jim would have crashed right into Bob Dylan's bus—a picture that came to me at this point, in which I imagined Bob Dylan himself in the bus, looking out at us with an air of surprise, though in fact he was still onstage—but this nurse was a very large and strong man, so I knew we were in no danger of that happening.

We wheeled Jim all the way to the parking garage, which was a long way, and the strongest nurse lifted him into the car—the last strains of "Blowin' in the Wind" carrying all the way to our parking spot. For a moment there, I considered whether these good people, the hippie nurses, would think less of us when they saw that our car was a fancy new BMW, but they weren't the type to judge. Jim said nothing through all of this until right at the moment we reached our car. Then he looked up at me and said, in a whisper, "Did you have a good time, baby?"

"The best."

After that, no more words.

THE DRIVE BACK to Hunsaker Canyon took half an hour. I knew it would be very hard when we got home, and it was. I could have called hospice to help us, and they would have come. But I didn't want that. I wanted it to be just the two of us that night.

By this time it was midnight, and I think it probably took me forty-five minutes to get Jim out of the car and into the house, and another forty-five minutes up the stairs to bed.

Then I helped him out of his Bob Dylan jeans and the silver-buckle belt and set his hat on the stair railing. He would not be wearing it again.

But as promised, my husband took me to see Bob Dylan that night. He took me out on the town. He was a man—and always had been—who knew how to show the woman he loved a very good time.

126.

He did not leave the bed again.

At this point he had a way of breathing that made you know he was going to die soon. He no longer ate or took in water and seldom registered the sound of my voice, though I kept talking to him. Singing sometimes.

"Whatever you do," the hospice nurse told me, "don't let him get bedsores." But that was happening now. So every few hours I turned his body over. It was not so difficult to lift him.

One afternoon that last week, a hospice nurse came by—a new one—to help me bathe him, checking his vital signs (vital, but just barely vital) when she suddenly looked up and turned to me.

"Oh my," she said. "I just noticed how handsome your husband is."

In those last weeks we had stopped checking his weight. Who needed to know, when the story was clear: The cancer was eating him up from the inside out, and every day he was thinner than the one before. At 125, and even 120, he had remained an astonishingly handsome man. More so than ever in some ways because every angle of that fine bone structure of his had become so clearly defined.

"You look like Clint Eastwood now," I told him. The new Clint Eastwood, which was to say, the very old one.

Even at ninety pounds, you could see the fineness of Jim's features—a nose that had once inspired a cosmetic surgeon to ask whether she could use it as a model for clients in search of nose jobs—but of course by the time Jim got down to ninety pounds he had the other look too, the look of a man very near death.

Something else had changed in his face, more profound even than the loss of all the pounds and the skin and muscle, and so much harder to witness. His mouth was slack, and his eyes, that always before would have been fixed on me—or turned to the screen of his laptop, checking on what the Republicans were up to now, but turned more often to my face—had gone blank. I had kept talking to Jim—whispering in his ear as the two of us lay in our bed together, telling him things, reading him our poems—but it had been a few days since he showed any sign of taking anything in.

So much of his handsomeness had come from this aspect of Jim too: the intelligence and the kindness forever evident in his face. Also, how funny he was. What a fine, sharp wit he had, and the readiness of his smile when something amused him, as things frequently did. Because it is not just a person's features that make him look as he does, I had learned. It's his spirit too.

Still, he had a beautiful face. Even that day the nurse could see it, though the sunken-in parts of his cheeks had sunk so deep that if he had been lying on his back on the grass in our yard—an impossible image now, but one that came to me incongruously at some point over the long hours I lay there studying his face—or in the hammock maybe, having fallen asleep with his Kindle still in his hands, and if the sky had then suddenly opened and rain poured down, his cheeks would have held water. That's how hollow they had become.

ONE TIME AND one time only, Jim had tried to pull himself up off the pillows. He had opened his eyes wide; they had been mostly shut for days. He wanted, fiercely, to get out of bed. He wanted to get himself to the bathroom. He wanted his glasses. He could no longer tell me this, but I knew what he wanted. He pointed to his eyes, and they were burning into me.

Why was I letting this happen to him? Why didn't I do something? (I, who always came up with one more idea.) I could feel him asking that of me. I was asking it of myself.

HIS OLD FRIEND Leonard came over to sit with him. The two of them had been members of a Bible study group together when they were in their early thirties, both fathers of young children, trying to hang on to a set of doctrines both had come to question, both of them suffering the fact that leaving their religion would mean leaving their marriages, and for both that was overdue.

"Jim always wanted to do the right thing," Leonard said. "It was probably the hardest thing Jim ever did, leaving his children's mother."

In the weeks leading up to these days, Jim had hardly ever wanted friends to come by, but he was past caring about this now. Our friend Margaret came over, and our friend Karen. She sat on the bed. Jim had not taken a sip of water in days, but now he placed his hands around the cup and drew on the straw. "I'm a lucky man," he said, so softly now we had to bend in close to hear. "I have been known."

There was not a whole lot that mattered more. I had been known too. Known and loved.

After that, words left him.

Absent a while, his daughter sent him an e-mail that I read out loud to him, about how much he'd meant to her—and after, when it seemed her words were not getting through, I called her up and then set the phone next to Jim's ear, on speaker, so she could say what she wanted to him. It was no longer possible to know what he was taking in of the world, but the man I loved seemed to have left the room.

BUT EVEN AS his body wasted away, and his mind lost its sharpness, something about Jim had become more substantial. Something about me had changed too. I was a different person than the woman I'd been eighteen months earlier. Grief and pain had been harsh, but they had served as teachers. We had been through a conflagration, the two of us, and I would have given anything to have avoided it, but we'd emerged like two blackened vessels from the forge—our two beating hearts and our trust in each other all that remained.

An odd irony came to me at this moment, when it seemed as if there was almost nothing left of the man I'd loved, almost nothing left of the two of us, as we'd been, or the life we'd made together: It seemed to me, as we approached the moment when everything would be over, finally, that the ordeal of the disease and the treatment— two separate kinds of hell I would wish on no living human—had turned us into two people we might never have become if the disease had spared Jim. Better ones, though only one of us would survive to benefit from this brutal education we'd received.

127.

Every day they told me he would die, and I hoped they were right. I knew he would never want to hang on as he was now. Hard as he'd fought, he would want this to be over.

On one of those days, a social worker came to see me. "I want to tell you a story," he said. It was about a woman he'd worked with once, about Jim's age, dying of cancer. Her brother came to see her—a brother who loved her very much, he told me.

One day the healthy brother had asked this social worker what would happen if he gave his sister more than the prescribed dose of morphine. A lot more, perhaps. She would probably die, the social worker told the man.

And would it be painful?

No.

That night, alone in our bedroom, I took out the morphine. I placed one syringe—his usual dose—between Jim's lips, and slowly released the plunger. Then a second syringe. Then a third.

I lay down on the bed next to Jim with my face against his hair and went to sleep. When I woke in the morning, I put my ear to his chest.

For a few days now he had only taken a few breaths a minute, so shallow it was hard to hear them, and at first I didn't, but his heart was beating. Maybe from all those years he spent as a runner, he had the strongest heart.

I had to call hospice then. I was out of morphine.

"How did this happen?" they asked me. They kept close tabs on how much they'd delivered to me. I should have had two vials left.

I could have told them I'd spilled a bottle of the stuff, but I didn't. "He was just in so much pain," I said. And maybe he was. Impossible at this point to know.

Hospice reported me to the police. The hospice director who told me was apologetic about that, but they had rules about these things, and I couldn't fault them for it. We're not in the business of assisting euthanasia, she told me.

After that, I was no longer allowed to keep morphine in my possession. A hospice nurse brought me each dosage at three-hour intervals, which meant that even in the middle of the night, a nurse would come to our door and climb the stairs to where I lay in the bed beside my husband and give me the syringe.

Then one night a day or two later it seemed important that no one disturb us. I had one vial of morphine left—one that I'd kept separate from the rest of our supply, which was enough to get us through the night without the interruption of a middle-of-the-night delivery. I told the nurse we wouldn't need her until tomorrow. We could be alone in our bed.

128.

Jim died in the middle of a June night four days after his sixty-fourth birthday, nineteen months after receiving the diagnosis of pancreatic cancer, three weeks short of our third wedding anniversary. He died one thousand six hundred and forty-seven days from the one we met. I know this because every first of the month—the first of the month having been the day we first sat down across from each other at that restaurant table in Marin County, California, and began our conversation—we recited the number.

I believe the date Jim died was the sixteenth of the month, but it is also possible that he died on the fifteenth. What I know is that I was lying next to him as I did every night to the end—asleep, but with my hand on the one part of his chest that didn't hurt when I touched him, the part that didn't have drains coming out and scars from surgery. By this point in the ever-downward trajectory of Jim's illness, I was always listening for the sound of the next breath, and for days there at been long spaces between them. Still, I must have drifted off for a few minutes.

It was one in the morning when the feeling awakened me that he had died. A dozen times at least, over those last days, I had placed my head over his heart or my fingers on his wrist or his neck, checking for a pulse, and I would have said at the time, after all we had gone through, that I was hoping to find none—though later the fact that I had ever felt that way would astonish me. *Let him lie motionless in this bed. It will be all right if I never hear his voice again. Just let him keep breathing here next to me, where I can reach out in the night sometimes to stroke his cheek, and his thick, wonderful hair.*

For days I had been saying I wanted this moment to come, or thought I did. But when it came I realized in an instant how mistaken I had been to suppose that his dying would bring any relief.

I stayed there in the bed with him for an hour, probably, though I did not check the time. His pain no longer an issue, I could put my hand on his belly again the way I used to every night in our old days—the days before the diagnosis. Back then we slept naked, and I had made him the promise I would never buy a flannel night-gown, or any nightgown. We were lovers then, and dressed the part.

Within an hour of Jim's death, his handsome, ravaged face had taken on a different look, and not just because his skin was cold now, and the little color that had remained was gone from it. Death happens in an instant, but the life drains out of a person over the minutes and hours that follow. I took this all in as I lay there in the partial dark: felt Jim's skin getting cooler, and then cold, watched his eyes sink deeper into the sockets. His mouth was open, so I closed it.

TUCK. SEVERAL MONTHS had passed since my son Willy had asked Jim and me if we'd take care of his dog while he went out of town for work. Mostly to please me, and to help Willy out, Jim had agreed, though he had never been much of a dog person.

Boston terriers possess the trait of not simply wanting to sleep on the bed with you, but under the covers. Pressed up against your body—all the way down at the end of the bed if possible, curled up around your feet, or maybe around your butt. This was how Tuck slept with us, and though at first Jim had expressed mild shock at the idea of sharing our bed in this particularly intimate way with a snorting, occasionally farting dog, he had come to like Tuck and then to love him.

So when Willy returned from his trip and announced his plan

to come retrieve his dog, I had asked if we could keep him a little longer. As time had passed, and Jim spent more of it in the bed, Tuck's presence there beside him had become a source of comfort, and Willy had agreed to let him stay on.

That's where Tuck was the night Jim died, and after, he had stayed there pressed up against Jim's body and mine. With no more breath coming from my husband, the only breathing I heard then came from my son's dog, and it had the effect of offering a very small measure of comfort.

After an hour or so I got up from the bed and made my way downstairs. Tuck stayed under the covers next to Jim.

I didn't call anybody. It was still the middle of the night.

Later, I knew, people would start coming around and there would be things to do, but at that moment, I wanted to be by myself in our house. Not quite alone yet, as I would be after, because Jim's body remained in our bedroom, even though Jim himself was gone from it.

I stepped out into the night. The moon was high, and it was a good night for stars. So many other nights Jim and I had studied them together. Not simply a lover of science, but a believer in it, Jim could always point out particular constellations and planets. He knew how far away each one was, and how long ago it had been born.

Just a few weeks before, he'd read out loud to me a news report—not from the *New York Times*, which had not covered this event that, for Jim, seemed like one of the biggest news stories of the year—concerning a discovery that one of Jupiter's moons could actually sustain life. Jim followed this kind of thing closely, and updated me on developments as they occurred, even though he had to recognize that, try as I might, I failed to share his level of excitement over them. Few could have.

But perhaps the pleasure Jim took in this most recent discovery was particularly acute for another reason. Maybe the vastness of the universe, and how small we all are in the face of it, how fleeting our presence on the planet that is, itself, so infinitesimally small, offered some small comfort to him as he watched the last days of his own life on it dwindle away. We were all dying anyway, and though he surely could have found no joy in the prospect of the people he loved—like his children, and my children, like me—dying too, maybe it felt less lonely, and the thought of what he was missing less terrible, to be reminded of this.

After I came inside again, I made a pot of coffee. I looked at my watch. Three o'clock. When daylight came I would call the children, but for these few precious hours, I would be the only person who knew that Jim had died. I poured my coffee, same as I had every other morning. Always before, until just four days earlier, I had poured two cups and carried them upstairs, then climbed back into bed with Jim so we could have our coffee together. When so much had been lost of the life we had first pictured for ourselves, this had become one of the last remaining pleasures of our day—so much so that if the coffee hadn't turned out as good as I wanted, I'd pour it down the drain and make a whole new pot. This, at least, should be how we wanted it.

Now there was just my cup, and I set it on the kitchen table and sat myself down in my chair. I opened my laptop then. Brought the mug to my lips and set my fingers on the keyboard. I began to write this story.

Afterword

Here's what happens when you love someone a great deal, and he gets sick, and then he dies.

All those months you spent taking care of him, it was almost as if the two of you were one person. He was the one with cancer, but the pain consumed you both. You were off in the North Atlantic somewhere, stranded on an iceberg, and though it was brutally cold in that place, and every single thing about being there was hard, you were together on your iceberg. There was hardly one thing that took place that you did not share.

Then your iceberg broke in two. You floated off in one direction, he in another. And though the place you ended up is a warmer one, with sailboats passing by, their bright flags fluttering in the breeze, and people waving and calling out to you—sunshine again, and maybe even porpoises circling with their smiling faces—your fellow traveler has disappeared. His iceberg melted away with him on it. New things are happening now that you experience and he does not. (Some wonderful. Some awful. What would Jim have thought about the election of Donald Trump? That would have killed him, I said to a friend, the morning after. If he wasn't already dead.)

Maybe this is what people mean when they say, "Life goes on." This is the good news and the terrible.

It began that summer, this process of drifting out to sea. It doesn't mean you cease loving the person who left. Everything that you had and everything that happened remains with you. Life doesn't stop, is all. Not yet anyway.

★   ★   ★

SOME HOURS AFTER Jim died—after the men who had taken his body were gone—I got up from my chair and began to occupy myself with household chores. I stripped the sheets from our bed and threw away every plastic medicine container. Stuffed that inflatable pillow in the garbage. I did many loads of laundry.

I vacuumed. Before, this had been Jim's job, so it took me a minute to figure out how to turn the machine on. I had never cleaned a house before the way I cleaned ours that day. That night, and every night after, I slept on my side of the bed only.

BACK IN OUR early days, when Jim had first started sleeping over—sleeping over, but not making love; those thirty days when we'd slept on the air mattress under the stars on my Mill Valley deck—he had slowly begun moving a few possessions over to my house: his cameras, of course. His bass. A few CDs, and some books that would never have found their place on my shelves if he hadn't brought them (science fiction, philosophy, law, The Bible).

And clothes. Such fine clothes, with labels from Brooks Brothers and Calvin Klein, ties from Hermès, shoes of the softest leather and a jacket that looked like something Steve McQueen would have worn.

There had been a time when the amount of space I'd reserved for Jim in my bedroom—for his clothes, anyway; the man himself took up more—had been confined to a single box. After we'd moved to Hunsaker Canyon, there was more room for him, of course. More room in every way. We bought an armoire for his suits, and a chest of drawers, and he even annexed part, though hardly half, of the space next to my vast collection of dresses and skirts. But slowly, in a deeper way, my husband moved into a space that had remained unoccupied a very long time, at the core of my heart.

Then he died, and there was no need for his beautiful clothes to remain in our closet anymore, and the armoire could be mine, even, as well as the drawers. All those shoes he owned—some of them ordered online only a month or two earlier—sat on the shelf in their boxes.

I did not want to see his clothes hanging there—empty jackets, shirts without Jim in them. Then there were the T-shirts—the one with the vintage insignia of a motorcycle company from the fifties; the one I'd bought him on our road-trip summer in our Chrysler LeBaron convertible that said PROPERTY OF THE MAINE STATE PRISON (and he had posed for a picture in it, looking the part); another from a show of Ai Weiwei we attended in Toronto on our film-festival trip, with the words EVERYTHING IS ART, EVERYTHING IS POLITICS.

Some of these clothes I boxed up for Jim's younger son, who was his size. A few I gave to friends. I placed a call to Jim's old law school to ask if there might be some scholarship student about to graduate and enter into practice, in need of good suits for court appearances. Someone very trim. Around the size of a Blue Angel fighter pilot.

Some clothes I kept for myself—his blue-and-white-checked flannel shirt, his black jeans, the belt he'd worn to look sharp at the Bob Dylan concert, and the black Patagonia jacket he hardly ever took off by the end, because he was always cold.

I was Jim's size, more or less, though in the last months I'd outweighed him. Time was, I had believed the height and girth of a man might serve as some kind of indication of strength, and look what happened. I had ended up in bed with a ninety-pound man in possession of more fortitude than anyone I ever met.

I did not want to become the keeper of the Museum of Jim, so I cleaned out his office too—the model of the plane his father had worked on back at Hughes Aircraft in the fifties, the biographies of Learned Hand and Benjamin Cardozo, the pictures of Jim with his children when they were small and he was attending Bible study and trying to figure out how God might help him stay in his marriage, the suit his mother sewed for their train trip from Ohio to Los Angeles in 1956, the plaque from 1967 commemorating his having attained the level of Eagle Scout. All these went into the boxes.

But what was I supposed to do with his shotgun, and his other shotgun, and his rifle? (And I found something I hadn't anticipated in the gun closet. There had been a small silver box with a lock on it whose combination remained unknown to me. Finally a neighbor drilled it open. Inside: a Walther PPK, identical to the little handgun Sean Connery carried in the early James Bond movies. Small enough to fit in a pocket, and if there is ever such a thing as a beautiful gun, this was it.)

We had talked through the disposition of Nikon camera lenses and camera bodies, but what was I to do with the negatives and slides from fifty years of documenting the California landscape? And guitar amps, and children's drawings, and Father's Day cards and cigar cases, and eight pairs of glasses in which one of the lenses was only moderately corrective and the other a prescription so extreme it resembled a magnifying glass. What about the cigar cutters, and hand-tied fishing flies and scout badges? What about papers from law school and love letters from Patrice, and his carefully worded eulogy for the father who had beat him up all through his childhood—Jim loved him regardless—and a journal expressing his despair at what leaving his wife might do to his children, and a couple of very angry letters from his older son confirming the worst of his fears?

I kept voice messages I had on my phone—just two, and very

short, my only record of Jim's voice. ("Sweetheart, I'm passing through town. Any groceries to pick up?") I opened his laptop—unsure of the rules here concerning the privacy of a man no longer alive. Suppose he had written something he wouldn't want me to see? There were all those e-mails between him and Patrice. Not my business.

But I clicked on his music library. There were his beloved Mahler symphonies. There was Stevie Ray Vaughan and the New Orleans Klezmer All-Stars. There was every song the Beatles ever recorded.

I thought I was just about finished cleaning out his office when—tucked into the back of a drawer—I came upon a wooden cross. When I found that it occurred to me that as much ground as we'd covered in our not-quite five years together, as many topics as we'd explored over our few thousand miles out on the road (Jim at the wheel; me in the passenger seat with my bare feet on the dash), I had perhaps never known where he had ended up in his lifelong quest for God.

I'd sell the motorcycle. I'd fill a truck with things for Jim's children. I'd bring a suitcase full of size nine-and-a-half shoes to Guatemala, where a pair of good sneakers cost more than a few days' wages. I'd keep the Nikon D-8000M and get Tod to teach me how to use it. I'd drive to the place where Jim was cremated, and kiss his cold cheek one more time before they placed his body in the fire. But I would leave his ashes for his children to scatter, at Point Reyes, perhaps.

THE BOXSTER HAD been in the garage, but one morning a few days later I went out and turned the key in the ignition. Very slowly, because this was the first time I'd sat at the wheel of this car, I backed it out and set off down our driveway. Shifting a manual transmission after all these years proved less difficult than I'd imagined. What threw me was something else: the sound the engine made. It was the sound that had always signaled that Jim was coming home.

A few days after Jim died, Willy drove up from Los Angeles to pick up his dog, and made the crazily extravagant decision to buy us tickets to the final game of the NBA championship, the Warriors against the Cleveland Cavaliers. Though Jim had loved Steph Curry, even he would have agreed that LeBron James deserved the victory that night, and got it. Out in the parking lot after the game, I studied the faces of the devastated Warriors fans, for whom losing the championship appeared to be the worst thing that ever happened. Evidently none of them had loved a person with pancreatic cancer.

A few days after that, just as the sun was coming up, my son brought me to the Oakland airport, where I got on a plane headed for Manchester, New Hampshire. It was July now, my wedding anniversary, and like that day three years earlier, the sky was cloudless. From my seat on the airplane, the sun had come through the window at just the right angle to catch my wedding ring, reflecting little flecks of light that sparkled on the wall of the plane and the armrest and the back of the seat in front of me like stars. When I moved my hand the sparkles moved with me as if something magic were happening here. Wherever my hand went, for that brief moment when the sun hit my ring finger, sparkles encircled me.

Maybe this was why men gave diamonds to women they loved. So there was no chance, ever, that you'd forget them. So they'd come to you at odd moments like this one—well, the giver of this ring came to me all the time and would have regardless—and when they did, you'd be enveloped in stars.

My friend Danny picked me up at the airport that afternoon. It was close to sunset, but he knew where I wanted to go first—to the cottage I'd bought sight unseen that winter. ("Guess what, sweet-heart?" I'd told Jim over dinner that night. "I bought a house on a lake ten miles down the road from where Audrey lives." Never one to question my wilder choices or to suggest that I was capable of anything less than all I aspired to, he'd said, "That's great, baby.")

Later that summer, many things would happen. I would pick blueberries with my daughter and make it to the top of Mt. Monad-nock, the one I had climbed four times with Jim. I would paint the front door of the lake cottage yellow and tear down a wall to let the sun into the kitchen, and drive to Maine one weekend to see Becky at the place where Jim and I had made our annual pilgrimage for corn on the cob and pie, out on the screen porch, watching the sun disappear over the water and listening to her son recite "The Legend of Sam McGee" while we polished off a bottle of zinfandel. (There would be little wine that summer. With illness gone from my life, I found I needed wine less, though sometimes when a friend came by I'd open a bottle.)

I'd attach a picture to the refrigerator from the summer of our wedding three years back, of Jim at the Madison Hut in the White Mountains of New Hampshire at the end of that long hard day we'd tackled Mt. Adams, his green bandana not quite covering that great head of hair, with a smile that suggested there was not one thing in the world he wanted more of life than what was in his grasp at this one perfect moment.

All that summer, I'd sleep in the boathouse, in the bed I'd brought down from the main house. A single bed, but if Jim were here we could have shared it. All that summer—with the exception of that one weekend I'd driven to Maine—I would get up at five thirty every morning. After my swim and my coffee I'd spend my day at the little desk I'd set up in the boathouse, retracing our story. I recognized as I did this that I was reluctant to get to the end—as if, so long as I hadn't reached the last chapter, it might still turn out differently.

Home again in California at the end of the summer, I would start up the Boxster and take the car out on the highway, where, sometime around ten o'clock on a September night, almost five years to the day from when Jim took me for our first drive together—top down, the voice of John Lennon coming to us through those very fine speakers he'd installed—smoke would suddenly surround me in a cloud so thick I could barely see the road in front of me.

I'd pull over then to see flames coming from the exhaust pipe. Firemen would arrive. Then a tow truck.

We had left the Porsche undriven for too long, the mechanic told me later, when he delivered the news that the seals had been broken, the engine destroyed. A replacement would cost more than the car was worth.

"A Boxster is actually just a poor man's Porsche," he told me, but what did he know?

So that fall I'd end up back behind the wheel of my twenty-year-old Honda Civic. Back where I started, I might have said, but I was nowhere close.

Later, I'd sell the motorcycle, and (Jim would have hated this) a repo man would come to take the BMW away. I would turn Jim's office into an art studio and start painting again, as I had not since I was very young. I would host a memorial service at our house—my house now—for which I would bake ten apple pies and print one hundred copies of a book of Jim's photographs—including the one of the bored-looking couple on their cell phones in Valparaíso, and a bristlecone pine tree in the Owens Valley—and a hundred people would come to tell stories about him, and our friend Melissa would sing "The Book of Love" and all the men with whom Jim played music in Storkzilla—fifteen of them, including two horn players, a drummer, a harmonica player, an accordion and many guitars—would gather on the patio where Jim used to smoke his cigar and they would play till almost midnight. I might be partner-less, but I would dance.

I would travel to France on a book tour—also to Budapest, alone this time. I would track down my friend Deborah—the one with whom I once plotted a dinner on one coast or another that we imagined sharing with our two husbands, miraculously cured of pancreatic cancer—all of us raising our glasses for a toast to having beaten the odds. There would be a dinner one day, with fewer places set, and a toast to the two husbands missing from the table.

Three nights after my sixty-third birthday I would gather with a group of writing students on an island in Florida to watch the election. As the returns came in, and we took in the stunning news, and the younger ones began to cry, I'd find myself putting my arms around those younger women, who were twenty-six and thirty-two and thirty-seven. "You wouldn't believe the things a person can survive," I told them—one of the things a person knows when she's sixty-three, that she might not have at thirty.

And one more thing: I'd learn that I was going to be a grandmother.

BUT ALL OF this—the drifting out to sea on my personal iceberg—came later. That July day two and a half weeks after Jim left the planet, when Danny first brought me to the little cottage that I'd bought during the last months of my husband's life, I lifted my suit-case out of the car and set it down on the grass, pausing for a minute to take in the lake before heading inside. I looked out across the water as the last sliver of sun disappeared behind the trees on the other side. Somewhere a child was calling out to her mother. A couple paddled a kayak to no particular destination.

I had been such a person once, a woman in the front of the boat with the man I loved behind me steering our craft. We cut smoothly through the water, matching the strokes of each other's paddles.

I climbed the steps to the porch. The previous owners had taken the rocking chairs but I'd buy another one.

I put the key in the lock. Stepped in the door. Breathed in the smell of an old summer cottage. Through the windows, late afternoon sun streamed in. I could see the water dappling in the places where the trout came up to feed.

"How Jim would have loved this," I said. If he were here with me, he'd light a cigar on the porch and rest his feet on the railing. He'd watch as I walked down to the water, and he would keep his eyes on me until I reached the shore again. My guard dog.

And after, over a good meal, we'd have many things to tell each other. What happens to those things, I asked myself, when there is no longer anyone to tell?

It was just me now—a woman with her laptop, wearing a blue-and-white-checked flannel shirt to keep her warm on chilly nights, looking up at the constellations whose names she tries to remember and sometimes does, though from this hemisphere the Magellanic Cloud was not in evidence.

One solitary woman and one solitary loon. Every night that summer, from where I slept in the boathouse down by the water, I heard his long, mournful cry. Somewhere out there at the other side of the shore maybe, her mate would call out to her. Every morning, just as the sun came up, I'd stand at the water's edge for a moment. Then swim.

ACKNOWLEDGMENTS

So many friends, and strangers who became friends, supported my husband, Jim, and me during the nineteen months of our struggle, as—after—they supported me, alone.

It's not possible to name them all, but I want to single out a few. Rebecca Tuttle Schultze, Bridget Sumser, Karen and Tom Mulvaney, Rona Maynard, Lori Moran, Jenna Termondt, Jim and Bonnie Bell, Jay Holan, Bill Walmsley, Norm and Diana Paulsen, Katharine Schultze and Charles Grant, Kelly Hood, Barbara Floria Orcutt, Daniel Thibeault, Stephen and Garen Tolkin, Dan Geller and Dayna Goldfine, Jenny Rein, Pat Shareck, Helen and Tom Hurley, Kevin Sessums, Diana Hamlet-Cox, Phil Matthews, Susan and Al Guillot, John and Florie Stickney, David Geissinger, Victor and Marie-Helene Yalom, Leonard Nielson, Margaret Tumas, Tom and Kelly Bradley, Leslie and Hrach Krikorian, Beverly Anderson and Woodward Payne, Melissa Warren Vincel, Landon Vincel, Karen Kraut and Jason Adkins, David Schiff, Robert Glazier, Peter Schneider and Jennifer Brehl, Rona Maynard, Laurie Lehman, Pam Loftus and the nurses of Rock Medicine, and the men of Camp Three.

I need to single out a woman whom I have yet to meet. I have quoted extensively here from Deborah Kanter's brave, fierce, terrifyingly honest letters over the course of her own battle to save her husband, three thousand miles to the east of where ours was waged. Gratitude goes in equal measure to Pam Noble, another friend and sister I would never have met if not for our shared experience of loss.

Nobody provided more joyful hours over the course of the past two years than the musician/lawyers (and one chemistry professor) who made up the band known as Storkzilla, and made it possible for my husband to play rock and roll almost to the end of his life: Allan Schuman, Tony David, Jerry Spolter, Garry Spolter, Tucker

Spolter, Rich Saykally, Mike Papanek. Deep gratitude as well goes to Dave Motto for his musical guidance and friendship.

I was humbled by the courage and kindness of the Pancreatic Cancer Men's Breakfast Club—John Snyder, Sean Cooley, Steve Belzer, Jeff Filter, Dave Maclellan, and the one who stands alone now, keeping the fire burning: Dan Baker.

Among physicians, my thanks to the oncology and infectious disease teams at Beth Israel Deaconess Medical Center and Dr. James Moser, UCSF Medical Center, Diablo Valley Oncology, Michael Broffman at Pine Street Clinic, Dr. Brian Wolpin at Dana-Farber, Dr. Ronald Weiss and Asha Gala at Ethos Health. Most particularly, I want to single out Dr. Katie Kelley and Dr. Sarah Doernberg at UCSF, Dr. Joseph Mancias of Beth Israel and Dana-Farber, Dr. Neil Stollman, and the nurses, aides, and counselors at Hospice East Bay. My humble gratitude goes to all the unsung heroes of every hospital where my husband was a patient, and all the other places where he was not a patient too: the men and women of the nursing profession, who make everything else possible.

To my agent, Nicole Tourtelot—who read this manuscript as many times as I did, I think, and offered invaluable counsel—my deepest thanks.

Nancy Miller—a friend when we were sixteen, joyfully rediscovered more than forty-five years later—gave this book nothing less than the most tender attention and care, as have the entire crew at Bloomsbury. I feel huge gratitude that this book came into her hands.

One person, more than any other, remained at my side—though gone from this world—throughout the months of writing this. Jim Barringer. He faced death as he faced life, with nothing less than gallantry and the most steadfast love.

No story I have ever told has mattered to me more than this

one. I send it out into the world with the hope that it will help others who walk some part of the path I have known and those lucky others who have not walked our path, in the hope that knowing of our journey may inspire their own.

A Note on the Author

Joyce Maynard is the author of fifteen books, including the novels *Labor Day* and *To Die For*, both of which became major films, and the *New York Times* bestselling memoir *At Home in the World*—translated into sixteen languages. Maynard has been a reporter and columnist for the *New York Times* and has contributed to NPR, *Vogue*, *O, The Oprah Magazine*, *MORE*, the *New York Times Magazine*, and many other publications. A fellow of the MacDowell Colony and Yaddo, and a frequent contributor to The Moth, she runs workshops in memoir at her home in Oakland, California, and on the shores of Lake Atitlan, Guatemala. www.joycemaynard.com